P9-ARJ-923

Ethics Management for Public Administrators

Building Organizations of Integrity

Donald C. Menzel

M.E.Sharpe
Armonk, New York
London, England

Dedicated to

Kristi Lynn and David Scott—proud am I!

Library of Congress Cataloging-in-Publication Data

Menzel, Donald C.
  Ethics management for public administrators : building organizations of integrity /
by Donald C. Menzel.
      p. cm.
  Includes bibliographical references and index.
  ISBN-13: 978-0-7656-1813-9 (cloth: alk. paper); ISBN-13: 978-0-7656-1814-6 (pbk.: alk. paper)
  ISBN-10: 0-7656-1813-3 (cloth: alk. paper); ISBN-10: 0-7656-1814-1 (pbk.: alk. paper)
  1. Public administration—Moral and ethical aspects. 2. Civil service ethics. I. Title.

JF1525.E8M46 2007
172'.2—dc22   2006015471

Printed in the United States of America

The paper used in this publication meets the minimum requirements of
American National Standard for Information Sciences
Permanence of Paper for Printed Library Materials,
ANSI Z 39.48-1984.

∞

BM (c)   10   9   8   7   6   5   4   3   2   1
BM (p)   10   9   8   7   6   5   4

Contents

Preface and Acknowledgments

I began writing this book about twenty years ago, not literally but figuratively, when I initiated a series of empirical studies to find out what makes individuals in complex public organizations behave in an ethical manner. We have plenty of theories about why people do the wrong thing, sometimes ending up criminals. But we know much less about why people in organizations do the right thing. I am not certain that my search has been fully successful, but I believe it has been sufficiently successful to fill the pages that follow.

This book is about cultivating organizations of integrity. It is written for college and university students contemplating careers in public service, elected and appointed public officials, administrators, and the thousands of career public servants in the United States and abroad. Educators who are responsible for guiding men and women through the labyrinth of professional public administration as a field of study and practice will also find this book useful.

This book is also about issues and controversies facing students and practitioners of public administration who must prepare themselves for brave new ethical futures. After all, the study and practice of public administration in the United States was forged in an age of corruption, patronage government, and, in the words of famed New York City Tammany Hall politician Senator George Washington Plunkitt, "honest graft." Although that age is more than a century past, many issues and controversies remain that will surely form the ethical futures of twenty-first-century public administration. What those futures will look like is difficult to say with confidence. Still, lawmakers, political executives, and career public managers dedicated to building public trust and confidence in U.S. governments must make every effort to sort through important ethics issues that all too frequently become headlines on the front pages of daily newspapers and grist for six o'clock television newscasts.

Acknowledgments

I am indebted to a number of persons who kindly read and critiqued all or part of earlier versions of the manuscript. Professors James Bowman at Florida State University and Jonathan West at the University of Miami provided valuable insight and encouragement very early in this effort. So, too, did Professor Curtis Wood at Northern Illinois University. Others who offered sound advice, information, and encouragement include Professors Terry Cooper at the University of Southern California, Carol Lewis at the University of Connecticut, J. Edwin Benton at the University of South Florida, Rick Green at the University of Utah, H. George Frederickson at the University of Kansas, Frank Anechiarico at Hamilton College, Robert Smith at Clemson University, and Susan Paddock at the University of Wisconsin. Dr. Stuart Gilman at the United Nations Office on Drugs and Crime was also very helpful.

Thanks are extended as well to the many state and local ethics officials who kindly responded to my queries about their programs. These include Amy Calderwood, Ombudsman-Director King County Office of Citizen Complaints-Ombudsman; Christina Prkic of the Miami-Dade County Commission on Ethics and Public Trust; Matthew Conquergood, Assistant to the Ombudsman, King County Office of Citizen Complaints–Ombudsman; Eric Johnson, Director of the Office of Budgeting and Finance at Hillsborough County, Florida; James Spinello, Clark County, Nevada; Joseph M. Stahura, Mayor, City of Whiting, Indiana; John St. Croix, Executive Director, San Francisco Ethics Commission; Mark Davies, Executive Director, New York City Conflicts of Interest Board; Carla Miller, Ethics Officer, City of Jacksonville; Nicole A. Gordon, Executive Director, New York City Campaign Finance Board; Pat Bean, County Administrator, Hillsborough County, Florida; Patrick R. Brannigan, State of New Jersey; Sarah Lang, Director, Department of Human Resources, Tampa, Florida; Steve Berlin, Deputy Director, Board of Ethics, Chicago; Dorthy Eng, Director, Board of Ethics, Chicago; Catherine Clemens, Executive Director, King County Board of Ethics, Seattle, Washington; and Steve Brown, Mayor of Peachtree City, Georgia.

Finally, I wish to thank my wife and best friend, Kay, for her patience, support, and good cheer as the hours and months passed while writing this book. Our moments struggling over the use of the home computer brought forth a new laptop for her and an appreciation of the extent to which we have become techies.

Ethics Management for Public Administrators

1

Ethics Management

"If men were angels, no government would be necessary."
—James Madison, Federalist Papers No. 51

Men and women are not angels, nor are they devils. But it is human nature to be ambitious and self-serving. And, as Alexis de Tocqueville added in his classic nineteenth-century account, Americans "enjoy explaining almost every act of their lives on the principle of self-interest properly understood." The doctrine of enlightened self-interest means that "every American has the sense to sacrifice some of his private interests to save the rest" (Mayer 1969, 527).

More than 200 years later, men and women of ambition continue to seek power and act out their lives, driven by self-interest properly understood. Of course, not all do so, and when self-interest consumes the public interest, much trouble is in store. Those who govern—elected, appointed, and career public officials—are constrained by a myriad of laws and regulations intended to ensure that the public interest is not sacrificed on the alter of self-interest. Still, it is impossible to construct enough laws and rules to check the behavior of human beings, both in and out of government. Thus, self-constraint is thought by many to be the answer to ethical governance. But what are the self-constraints? Where do they come from? How do you know they work? Answers to these questions about human behavior have occupied the attention of philosophers for centuries.

Challenges to Ethical Governance

The vast majority of public servants are conscientious, dedicated, competent, and ethical persons pursuing public service careers with integrity and pride. Yet, as we move into the first decade of a new millennium, the ethical challenges facing those who preside and administer over government organizations are increasingly complex. Among other things, the boundary between those things public and those things private has largely disappeared, leaving in its wake much uncertainty about how to do the right thing in the right way. The age of privatization is upon us and, with it, the increasing inability of citizens, elected officials, and organizational managers to distinguish between public and private organizations, public and private managers, and public and private ethics.

The ethical challenges of privatization are no less daunting than those ushered in by the fast-forward buttons of the Internet, the World Wide Web, electronic mail, satellite TV, and other breathtaking and powerful communication technologies of the Information Age. The future is here; it is now. It is both a virtual "now" and a very real "now." Not only must elected officials and public managers, like their private sector counterparts, understand and harness information technology (IT) within their organizations, they must be able to understand and manage the human-technical-organizational dynamics that IT brings to the workplace. For example, organizational leaders cannot ignore the depersonalization of relationships in the workplace due to the arrival of e-mail. Nor can they ignore the desire of employees to carry out their duties in high-performing organizations with strong ethical cultures.

The knowledge explosion wrought by the electronic age of computers and high-speed space-age communication has truly transformed the world, giving meaning to the global village and citizen in ways unimaginable a mere decade ago. The globalization of economies, communication, education, commerce, and even warfare and peace are redefining the nation-state and presenting innumerable challenges to public officials in the United States and abroad. Public organizations, like private profit-making firms, must add value to their products and services in order to withstand the ever-increasing pressures of worldwide competition. Responsive, high-performing organizations are a necessity, not a luxury. Government agencies are not immune to these pressures, and political executives and career public managers know this. They also know that the forces of globalization can tempt governments to devalue the ethical overhead that is part and parcel of getting things done. Getting things done and staying competitive can be but are not necessarily compatible with high ethical standards.

Building Ethical Organizations

This chapter introduces the important but largely neglected subject of ethics management. The chapter also provides an overview of organizational perspectives that can inform efforts to put into place effective ethics management strategies. There is no magic potion that can be applied to transform public organizations into organizations of integrity. Building an organization of integrity—*workplaces where individuals treat each other with respect, take pride in their work, care about one another, promote accountability,*

and place the public interest over individual and organizational self-interest—
requires substantial time, resources, and commitment, which is no small challenge. Yet it must be met. Most significant, public administrators are on the
front line of this challenge.

> Integrity is often used to describe a person who is of sound moral char-
> acter. When applied to an organization, integrity refers to an environ-
> ment characterized as wholesome and one in which respect for others
> transcends self-serving interests. Building an organization of integrity
> involves cultivating and balancing a range of competencies and virtues
> that improve judgment in making decisions.

Is Ethics Management Possible?

The possibility of ethics management has become a reality only in recent
decades, although interest in ethics in Western culture can be traced to the
Age of Antiquity. The Greek philosopher Aristotle (384–322 B.C.E.) wrote
about moral virtues such as courage, honesty, temperance, and responsibility. Virtue ethics, as this approach became known, has inspired and motivated human beings in vastly different cultures for centuries.

Other philosophers such as the German Immanuel Kant (1724–1804) offer an alternative to virtue ethics. Kantian ethics focuses on duty as exemplified in the famous categorical imperative: "Act only according to that maxim
by which you can at the same time will that it should become a universal
law." An act is accorded moral worth if the motive is principled. Ethical
humans are duty bound to do the right thing.

The Englishman John Stuart Mill (1806–1873) offers yet another view,
asserting that one can know if an act is right or wrong only by its consequences. Thus utilitarian ethics as espoused by Mill calls for acts that result
in desirable ends. The well-known maxim, "Do the greatest good for the
greatest number," continues to undergird the ethics philosophy of many. The
view that moral ends justify immoral means is no more acceptable from a
public ethos utilitarian perspective than is the view that moral means can be
used to justify immoral ends.[1]

These philosophies—virtue ethics, duty-based ethics, or utilitarianism—
rarely serve as pure operating philosophies in day-to-day living. As the well-
known public administration ethicist Terry L. Cooper explains, "We identify,
or assume, certain principles of duty that are important to us and relate those
to the consequences we anticipate by following that duty. The result is that
we almost never act purely on the basis of duty to principle, nor purely by
calculating the consequences."[2]

Given these philosophies, a reasonable question is: "How would we characterize the prevailing ethos of American public administrators?" Do administrators subscribe to one of these views? More than one? None? While it is risky to generalize, the answer is that most public administrators draw on all but are closer to what might be called pragmatic utilitarianism. That is, they are constantly exploring decision alternatives that generate satisfactory outcomes for their (a) elected bosses, (b) employees, and (c) citizens. A public service ethos presupposes that administrators promote the public interest over those of their employees and elected bosses, but doing so is not always so straightforward or clear.

These great philosophers beget an intellectual legacy and presence that remain significant in the twenty-first century. While differing, they share a common bond in identifying and holding the individual responsible for right and wrong behavior. Moral agency—the capacity to make a choice of right and wrong—then is key to understanding ethical choice and behavior. Telling a lie when under physical duress, for example, is an illustration of the lack of moral agency.

Definitions of ethics and morality are provided in exhibit 1.1. While both ethics and morality are concerned with right and wrong, there is a difference. On the one hand, notice that the definition of ethics requires an act, a behavior. It is behavior that matters and, in the end, defines right or wrong. On the other hand, morals can exist independent of behavior. Former president Jimmy Carter's statement during a *Playboy* magazine interview in the 1976 presidential campaign illustrates this point rather well. Candidate Carter said: "I've looked on a lot of women with lust. I've committed adultery in my heart many times. . . ."[3] Jimmy Carter confessed to an immoral act in his mind.

Exhibit 1.1
Definitions of Ethics and Morality

Ethics are values and principles that guide right and wrong behavior. The Golden Rule is an example of an ethical principle that guides behavior. Morals are core beliefs about life, humanity, and nature. Beliefs about going to war, executing criminals (capital punishment), abortion, adultery, and gay life styles are often viewed as moral issues.

Source: author.

An Ethical Blind Spot

The intellectual legacy of the great philosophers has spawned a blind spot in our understanding of ethical behavior. What has been largely overlooked is the *context* in which ethical decisions are made. This blind spot became ever more evident in the twentieth century as the work and play of humans in all walks of life became wholly enmeshed in complex organizations. Social scientists began to study and write about life and morality in the shadow of organization, as Robert B. Denhardt (1981) puts it. Individual morality became dominated by the prevailing ethos of the organization. What is right for the organization is right for the individual. The organizational imperative—do whatever is in the best interests of the organization—requires employees to be obedient to the decisions of superiors, to be technically rational, to be good stewards of other people's property, and to be pragmatic, contend William G. Scott and D. K. Hart (1979, 1989). Above all, "managers must be amoral in order to obtain the most benefits for their organizations" (34).

Empirical studies also began to focus on the organizational context of (un)ethical decision making.[4] For example, studies of whistle blowers have flourished.[5] One study by Lovell (2003, 201) paints a picture of organizational life in which "the fear of impairing one's future career prospects was a significant factor shaping the muteness of many of the managers about their respective ethical dilemmas." Lovell's research points to the suppressing influence that organizational imperatives can have on moral agency. Suppressed whistle blowing, Lovell contends, is an enduring and troubling phenomenon in modern organizations.

Rosemary O'Leary (2006) adds to this literature with a set of provocative cases about career administrators in state and federal agencies who found ways to engage in what she calls the "ethics of dissent." These seasoned public officials found themselves at odds with their political superiors over significant public policy issues. Rather than resign, all worked behind the scenes to correct what they perceived as public programs that did not advance the public interest. Most were successful at this form of guerrilla warfare, as she describes it.

Case studies of ethics stress and decision distress also began to appear.[6] Frederickson and Newman (2001), for example, explored the decision by a high-ranking manager in the U.S. Forest Service to resign her position. She "exited with voice" and, according to the investigators, is a moral exemplar. The episode had to do with Gloria Flora's judgment that, as the supervisor of a national forest in Nevada, she could no longer carry out her stewardship duties in the face of powerful economic and political pressures to exploit protected federal lands from mining, timber production, and livestock grazing. Gloria Flora's more than twenty years of service with the U.S. Forest Service was terminated with less than three years from vestment in the Civil Service retirement system. She paid a high price, emotionally and financially, for her moral courage. Frederickson and Newman then ask, why would she do this? The answer—because she could not compromise her strong belief to do the "right" thing. "She was motivated to act as she did out of a sense of responsibility" (360).

It is often contended that ethics cannot be taught or "managed" in the age of high-tech, performance-driven organizations. Many studies now exist, however, that cast considerable light on what we know and do not know about ethical behavior in complex organizations. There is, of course, still much to know. Nonetheless, a sufficient body of knowledge can be drawn on to build organizations of integrity.

Managers as Ethical Leaders

Before we explore this body of knowledge, however, a question needs to be asked—must managers of public organizations be ethical leaders to have good government? Perhaps, although it might be argued that if good government can be achieved with morally mute managers—managers who do not feel a responsibility to promote ethics or morality in government—then it may be possible to have government that gets the job done efficiently, effectively, and economically. A chilling possibility? Yes. But now consider the question rephrased: If public managers were unethical, would we have good government? Probably not—perhaps definitely not. Conventional wisdom suggests that good government—government that gets the right things done right—cannot be achieved by men and women who lack ethical or moral values or fail to govern or manage on the basis of those values.

Ethics in Government

Government is not in the business of producing ethics, as Dennis F. Thompson reminds us (1985). It is in the business of producing public goods and services such as justice, transportation, air and water quality, consumer and occupational safety, national security, and protection from the misfortunes of age, poverty, or race, to name a few. Thus managers and elected officeholders are charged with providing those collective goods and services deemed desirable but often not provided by private-sector firms.

But why then do so many people, managers included, believe that ethical government is so important? The answer is disarmingly straightforward: Without ethical government, the effective production of public goods and services is not likely. Or, as is so commonly illustrated in the experiences of undemocratic and developing countries, the costs and consequences are so great that whatever goods and services are produced are often not affordable to a vast majority of the population. Moreover, ethical governance is vital to effective and democratic government. *"Ethics may be only instrumental, it may be only a means to an end, but it is a necessary means to an end"* [italics added by author] (Thompson 1992, 255). In other words, well-meaning public managers and policy makers cannot presume that public policies and organizations are achievable in an ethical vacuum. Indeed, such a vacuum is likely to swallow up even the most well-conceived policies, plans, and day-to-day operations of government.

This apparently undeniable law linking ethics, public management, and government has not always been so noteworthy in the United States. Indeed, as Americans fast-forward into the twenty-first century, there is reason to wonder whether such an iron law really exists. Do public managers and elected officeholders understand the vital link between ethics and good government? Does anyone care if they do? Or, have we entered an era of "anything goes" governance so long as somebody else will pay for it?

U.S. Comptroller General David M. Walker (2005) paints an ethically troublesome picture of the U.S. government's "don't pay as you go" mind-set that prevailed in Washington in 2005, and that has enormous implications for future generations. He asserts that the government's liabilities and net obligations as of September 30, 2004, was $43 trillion and rising rapidly, a number that translates into a $150,000 burden for every American and twice this amount for every full-time worker. By 2040 "the federal government could be reduced to doing little more than paying interest on the national debt" if the nation's fiscal policy remains on autopilot (347). This is not an ethical future that anyone wants. "We have a stewardship responsibility to future generations," says Walker. "At the end of the day, we should be able to look our children and grandchildren in the eye and say we did everything we could to pass on an America that is better off and better positioned for the future than when we found it" (351).

Governing Ethically

But can we talk about governing ethically or managing ethics in the same breath or manner in which we do about managing budgets, policies, or people? The answer is a resounding yes! Indeed, the single act of developing and adopting a code of ethics, as James S. Bowman (1981) documented more than twenty years ago, is managing ethics in the workplace. Thus, ethics management is not a new enterprise; it is an old enterprise. What is new is how we think about it. If we think about it as a systematic and consistent effort to promote ethical organizations, as Article IV of the American Society for Public Administration (ASPA) Code of Ethics declares, then there is such a thing as ethics management. Ethics management, however, does not mean "control." *It is not the act of controlling co-workers' behaviors or thinking about ethics in the workplace.* Rather, it is the cumulative actions taken by managers to engender an ethical sensitivity and consciousness that permeates all aspects of getting things done in a public-service agency. It is, in short, the promotion and maintenance of a strong ethics culture in the workplace.

Ethics Management Is Important

Why is ethics management important? This important question has rarely been asked in the past.[7] Why? Because government reformers and scholars focused heavily, if not exclusively, on the core values of efficiency, economy, and effectiveness.[8] Moreover, it was assumed that administrators would be men and women of strong moral character and integrity. Listen to nineteenth-century civil service reformers such as Woodrow Wilson. In his famous essay of 1887, he said that we must clear "the moral atmosphere of official life by establishing the sanctity of public office as a public trust . . . [thereby] opening the way for making it businesslike" (20). "The ideal for us," he argued, "is a civil service cultured and self-sufficient enough to act with sense and vigor . . ." (24). Thus there was little reason to be concerned about the need to add a fourth "e"—ethics—to the holy trilogy of efficiency, economy, and effectiveness. But times change and ethics has become academic talk and office shoptalk. Indeed, it is increasingly common to find public administration graduate programs offering ethics courses and public organizations providing in-house ethics training.

The effort to curb wrongdoing in government is driven by several factors. First, incidents of wrongdoing in the United States and abroad have drawn increasing public and media attention. Corrupt acts at the highest levels of government in local, state, national, and international arenas have not vanished from the earth. Indeed, a persuasive argument can be made that corruption has held steady in developed countries and is rampant in many developing countries. No community or nation is immune. Thus the "why" of ethics management can be tied to stamping out wrongdoing.

Second, at the same time, there is a compelling argument that private- and public-sector managers have come to the recognition that productive, high-performing organizations are value driven. And, most important, they place ethical values high on their list. Insofar as such a link exists between ethics and organizational performance, prudent managers and scholars have focused on understanding the dynamics of the ethical workplace. They have also explored how professional associations armed with ethics codes can help them cultivate an ethical culture.

The Ethics-Performance Linkage

Efforts to probe the ethics-performance linkage in public administration began in the early 1990s. Burke and Black (1990), for example, conducted an exploratory study of organizational ethics and productivity by surveying sixty-nine executives and managers, approximately one-third of whom were from the public and nonprofit sectors. Their findings did not demonstrate a conclusive empirical link between ethics and performance but did motivate Burke and Black to recommend that agencies create "a leadership group focused on identifying ethical concerns and productivity measures" (132). Bruce (1994) also used survey research to study the ethics of municipal clerks. Municipal clerks, she found, are a highly ethical group who feel that city employees are basically ethical and highly productive. She contended that managers and supervisors have a "substantial influence on employee ethics and, by extension, on organizational performance" (251).

Menzel (1992, 1993, 1995) has also probed the ethics-performance link. He surveyed different populations—city and county managers in Florida and Texas and city and county employees in two Florida local governments. One study (1993) included the question: "Do ethical climates of public organizations reinforce or detract from organizational values such as efficiency, effectiveness, excellence, quality, and teamwork?" He hypothesized that as the ethical climate of an organization becomes stronger, organizational performance values such as efficiency, effectiveness, excellence, quality, and teamwork will be strongly supported. The findings led him to accept the hypothesis that an organization's ethical climate has a positive influence on its performance.

Similar results are reported by Berman and West (1997) in their study of the adoption of ethics management strategies. City managers reported that "commitment to workforce effectiveness and the adoption of pay-for-performance policies are associated strongly with ethics management practices." And, "efforts to decrease absenteeism and to adopt a customer-orientation also are significantly associated with ethics management" (26).

Ethics-induced Stress

Other research (Menzel 1996a) has focused on the organizational consequences of ethics-induced stress in the public workplace. Menzel defined ethics-induced stress as a form of cognitive dissonance between an employee's personal ethics and the ethical climate found in the employee's workplace. He asked: Does ethics-induced stress lower employee productivity? Does it result in less job satisfaction? Greater conflict? More employee turnover? Drawing on surveys of city and county managers in Florida and Texas, he found strong statistical associations between managers' high levels of ethics-induced stress and impaired organizational performance. Specifically, as the level of ethics-induced stress increases, job satisfaction decreases, organizational conflict increases, and employee turnover is greater.

Ethics Management in Practice

Public administration practitioners live with ethical and unethical realities day-in and day-out. This places them in the unique position of being able to practice ethics management and, on occasion, to experience the consequences of ethics management. But do they practice ethics management? And, if they do, how do they do it? Gary B. Brumback (1998) offers this advice. There are four key components of ethics management: hiring, performance, training, and auditing. Hire the "right" people, he admonishes. But who knows how to hire the right people? Should some kind of ethics screening be conducted? Yes, Brumback asserts. Hiring authorities should

1. Review background investigation policies and procedures to determine if they are ethical, can be improved, and are used for the right (seductive) jobs.
2. Build the agency's reputation for integrity . . . and then stress that reputation to recruits.
3. Not use surreptitious screening and explain the policy to recruits.
4. Ask new hires to pledge a commitment to ethics in government in the oath of office. (66)

Once hired, Brumback contends that "factoring ethics into the process of managing performance is the best way to ensure that work objectives are achieved in an ethical manner, and that other on-the-job behaviors are ethical" (66). Performance evaluations can and should include an ethics dimension. Assertions that "ethics is not performance" or "ethics is too subjective to be measured" are bogus arguments, he believes.

Ethics management should also emphasize training programs. Employees throughout a public organization are vulnerable to ethics lapses. Thus, a continuous, ongoing ethics training program amplifies the message that ethics matters. "Above all," Brumback (68) asserts, "tell people what the preconditions of unethical behavior are, what the bottom line of ethics is, and what the agency and each individual can do to make ethics a work habit."

Another component in managing ethics in public organizations is an audit. An audit, whether based on a survey of employees or an assessment of occupational vulnerability, should be conducted periodically. Stephen Bonczek (1998), a city manager with hands-on experience in Michigan, Florida, Texas, and Pennsylvania, strongly supports the use of an audit to let employees know the positive as well as the negative effects of their efforts. He also believes that managers should "review with their employees all decisions on ethical issues, asking, What did we do right? What did we not do that we should have done? What should we do in future, similar situations?" (78). He encourages managers to use weekly staff meetings "to review all discussions and decisions for ethical implications" (78). Bonczek fully believes that a strong ethical climate has a positive influence on organizational performance and productivity.

Proactive Ethical Risk Taking

The advice offered by these managers is directed at the "how" of ethics management. Others suggest more. Donald G. Zauderer (1994) adds that integrity includes taking risks to oppose unjust acts (don't just go along); communicate truthfully (do not intentionally deceive others); deal fairly (do not provide others with special advantages or disadvantages because of their affiliations or positions); honor agreements (keep your commitments); accept personal responsibility when things go right or wrong; forgive individuals for mistakes or wrongdoing (don't hold grudges or strive to get even); exhibit humility (avoid unbridled ambition and emphasis of rank and status differences); respect the dignity of individuals by giving earned recognition (don't treat employees as simply vehicles for getting the work done); and celebrate the ability and good fortune of others (suppress envy).

The Council for Excellence in Government (1992–1993) urges every individual in government to recognize that public service is a public trust and that he or she must accept two paramount obligations: (1) to serve the public interest, and (2) to perform with integrity. Furthermore, top leaders in public organizations must advocate and exemplify these core values and obligations. Subordinates' performances, the council asserts, should be evaluated in light of these standards. Leaders should also make every effort to ensure that their organization recruits workers with strong ethical values.

Chris Wye (1994) shares the council's view of the role that top leaders should assume in promoting ethical organizations. "At every level in the organization, but especially at the top," Wye (45) contends, "effective leadership is an essential ingredient for maintaining the highest standards of ethical conduct in an organization." Nonetheless, Wye worries that the present course of action in the United States has been to focus on the "moral minimum," not the "moral maximum." Through the use of and reliance on laws and regulations, certain types of unacceptable behavior have been proscribed that become the default for defining the moral minimum for acceptable behavior. "Shouldn't we," he asks, "spend at least some time encouraging good behavior?"

Managers Speak Out

James S. Bowman's (1977, 1990, 1997 [with Williams]) surveys of public administration practitioners are also suggestive for understanding what ethics management is and how prevalent it is. When he asked managers in 1989 if their agencies had a consistent approach toward dealing with ethical concerns, nearly two-thirds said their organizations did not have a consistent approach. When he asked the same question in 1996, he found that a smaller (58 percent) yet large percentage of respondents replied in the same fashion: "My agency does not have a consistent approach toward dealing with ethical concerns." Do these responses suggest that there is little ethics management in the public sector? Possibly—but not necessarily. Consider the findings reported by Berman, West, and Cava (1994) and Berman and West (1997).

In 1992 Berman and colleagues surveyed more than 1,000 directors of human resource agencies in municipalities with a population over 25,000 in order to find out what ethics management strategies are employed, how they are implemented, and how effective they are. Their results confirmed Bowman's findings about the lack of a consistent approach—if consistent means "formal." A minority of cities surveyed reported using formal ethics management strategies while a majority claimed that their cities relied primarily on leadership-based strategies—an informal strategy. They found four categories of ethics management—two they labeled as formal, one informal, and one a combination of formal-informal.

Formal ethics management strategies involve mandatory employee training, use of ethics as a criterion in the reward structure, and adoption of organizational rules that promote the ethical climate, such as requiring financial disclosure and approval of outside activities.

Informal ethics management strategies involve reliance on role models and positive reinforcement and are behaviorally based (Berman, West, and Cava, 1994, 189).

Code-based and regulatory-based strategies are the two formal strategies used by a large number of cities. Adopting a code of ethics or establishing guidelines for standards of conduct is part of a code-based strategy. Advocates of codes typically presume that codes contribute to a healthy organization and thus a higher-performing organization. Bowman's surveys (1990, 1997 [with Williams]) of practitioner members of the American Society for Public Administration show that the members strongly embrace codes and believe that they have a positive influence on organizational life. Bruce's research (1994) also adds to the believed real-world impact of codes. Her study of members of the International Institute of Municipal Clerks found that clerks "rank a code of conduct as the most powerful way a city can prevent corruption" (29). Using ethics as a criterion in hiring and promotion or requiring approval of outside employment constitutes part of a regulatory-based strategy. Leadership-based strategies, such as demonstrating exemplary moral leadership by senior management, constitute an informal ethics management strategy. Employee-based strategies that incorporate ethics training, protect whistle blowers for valid disclosures, or solicit employees' opinions about ethics constitute a mixed strategy.

Does reliance on an informal strategy, which most cities claim to do, result in ineffective ethics management? Not necessarily. Berman, West, and Cava's research indicates that moral leadership strategies are more effective than regulatory- or code-based strategies in enabling cities to achieve ethics management objectives such as avoiding conflicts of interest, reducing the need for whistle blowers, and fostering fairness in job assignments.

Responses to Ethics Failures[9]

Ethics lapses and failures occur; they are part and parcel of contemporary life. When they happen, what else might be done? At the macro level, codification of acceptable behavior in the form of state law or local ordinance is common practice. Many states and cities, for instance, have opted for ethics laws and regulatory bodies or boards. Megacities like Los Angeles and Chicago, for example, have established ethics commissions to investigate real and alleged cases of wrongdoing. The United States government has also taken action, having established the Office of Government Ethics (OGE) with the Ethics in Government Act of 1978. Now, more than twenty years later, nearly 15,000 full- and part-time ethics officials can be found in the federal executive branch (Gilman and Lewis 1996, 521).

These efforts have not gone unnoticed. Several investigators have attempted to assess what difference ethics laws and commissions make in states and communities. Williams (1996), for example, studied the Florida Commission on Ethics to assess the agency's effectiveness in training officials, conducting ethics audits, investigating complaints, and encouraging an ethical climate. Based on unstructured interviews with commissioners and archival records of the agency, he concluded that the Florida Commission on Ethics was largely ineffective in all four areas. "Unfortunately," Williams (71) says, "the commission apparently serves more effectively as a punitive agent than as an agent of constructive change."

Menzel (1996b) also studied the Florida Commission on Ethics but from a different vantage point—the view from the street. He surveyed persons who had filed ethics complaints (legally referred to as complainants) and public officials (legally referred to as respondents) who were the objects of complaints. He asked three questions:

1. What is the relationship between how an ethics complaint is handled and citizen trust or distrust in government?
2. Do persons who file ethics complaints have a positive or negative experience? Are those experiences satisfactory and therefore build trust and confidence in government? Or are those experiences unsatisfactory and therefore contribute to the erosion of public trust and confidence in government?
3. What are the outcomes of the ethics complaint making?

The study involved mail surveys of 303 complainants (144 responded) and 555 respondents (161 responded) in the time period of 1989–92. He found that complainants were much more likely to say they were dissatisfied with the outcome of the complaint they filed than were respondents who were the object of the complaint.

Furthermore, neither complainants nor respondents differentiate process outcomes from substantive outcomes. How you are treated and how things turn out, regardless of whether you are the person filing a complaint or the person who is the object of the complaint, seem to go hand in hand. Finally, he concluded that "the ethics complaint-making process in Florida may be widening rather than closing the trust deficit."

Trust Building[10]

Closing the trust deficit between the public and government agencies is a legitimate and needed activity and one that ethics managers should embrace.[11] But how to reduce the trust deficit is no small challenge. However, research by Berman (1996) is suggestive. He sought to find out how much trust there is among local government officials and community leaders, what municipal strategies are employed to increase trust levels, and how socioeconomic conditions may influence perceptions of trust in local government. He surveyed city managers and CAOs (Chief Administrative Officers) in all 502 cities with a population of more than 50,000 to obtain their perceptions of trust levels. He found that "community leaders have only moderate levels of trust in local government" but that cities with a council-manager form of government experience a significantly higher level of trust than do cities with the mayor-council form of government (33).

Berman identified three principal trust-building strategies—communication, consultation and collaboration, and minimization of wrongdoing. Communication strategies emphasize providing information about the cities' programs and performance. Consultation/collaboration strategies involve engaging community leaders via partnerships, meetings, panels, and so forth. The minimization of wrongdoing strategies emphasizes the adoption of ethics codes, the provision of ethics training, and so forth. Strategies vary from community to community, and no single one appears to be more effective than the other. However, there is some evidence that "using a range of strategies by local officials increases trust, even though the impact of individual strategies is modest" (34). Socioeconomic conditions, Berman concludes, influence trust levels. Positive conditions in a community such as high economic growth and cooperation among local groups inspire trust in government. "Negative community conditions, such as economic stagnation, low income levels, racial strife and high levels of crime reduce economic and political resources . . . for dealing with community problems," contributing to a distrust of government (34).

A well-functioning democracy cannot survive without citizen trust and confidence in those who govern. Thus, behaviors or acts by officials that diminish citizen trust and confidence are a direct threat to democratic governance. While trust is a renewable resource, "it is much easier to destroy than to renew" (Bellah et al. 1991, p. 4). Many factors can destroy trust in governmental institutions. However, none may destroy trust easier or faster than unethical behavior or blatant corruption by public officials.

> Democracy requires a degree of trust that we often take for granted . . . [but] it is much harder to build trust than to lose it. But that is our problem in the United States: we have begun to lose trust in our institutions . . . the heritage of trust that has been the basis of our stable democracy is eroding (Bellah, Madsen, Sullivan, Swidler, and Tipton 1992, 3).

Several trust-building strategies are pursued by the Miami-Dade Commission on Ethics & Public Trust. For example, the Commission sponsors a Model

Student Ethics Commission Program that "is designed to teach and to engage students in the policies and issues concerning ethics, good governance and accountability in the administration of government. Students review case studies regarding ethical dilemmas, identify solutions to various ethical issues within the local to international arenas and participate in mock public hearings to discuss/debate public policy issues.[12] A second strategy is an ethics education and training program for companies doing business with local government. Free monthly ethics workshops are conducted in the business workplace. The objective is to increase the "company's understanding about best business practices and the ethics rules as they relate to contracting with local government."[13] A third strategy is directed at candidates for municipal office and covers topics such as reporting and filing requirements, the role of the campaign treasurer, and the Ethical Campaign Practices Ordinance.

Organizational Perspectives on Ethics Management

Theories of organization and governance provide different perspectives on the development of effective ethics management strategies. Traditional *bureaucratic theory,* for example, that stresses hierarchy, rules and regulations, standard operating procedures, and work classification fits comfortably with a compliance-oriented ethics management strategy.[14] Know the rules of acceptable/unacceptable behavior and stay out of trouble, this perspective demands. The bad news is that much of what passes for ethics management in government is exactly this—compliance oriented. But, as it is argued throughout the book, this approach is inadequate because it minimizes moral agency.

Transaction-cost theory, which emphasizes decision making under conditions of asymmetrical information exchanges, offers another perspective. Gerald Garvey (1993, 25) describes transaction-cost theory as an effort to reduce "especially the costs of gathering and processing information, as the driving factor in rational human beings' never-ending quest for efficiency." Organizational life is viewed as a series of exchanges within and outside the organization. The principal goal is to minimize transaction costs, that is, strive for greater efficiencies and therefore lower the cost of getting work accomplished. Thus, anything, including (1) information that is inadequate or uneven (some have much more information than others) or (2) corruption or unethical behavior, that raises the cost of work in the organization is undesirable. This view would treat unethical behavior as a cost factor that should be reduced, minimized, or eliminated altogether. Consequently, management must embrace measures that accomplish this goal. Such measures might include "one-shot" ethics inoculations, that is, requiring members of the organization to attend an ethics seminar from time to time, or more long-term investments in training.

One limitation of transaction-cost theory is that it can be very reactive, not proactive. Another limitation is that it may put too much emphasis on an instrumental view of ethics. Thus organizational attention to ethics practices and behaviors are seen as a means to an organizational end—productivity.

Transaction-cost theory, however, draws attention to moral hazards in the workplace. Every occupation contains opportunities that can be corruptible. Police, for example, are always vulnerable to favors and bribes. Planners in public organizations are vulnerable to the influence of developers, including the prospects of post-public employment. Pentagon procurement officers are vulnerable to defense contractors' offers of travel, vacations, and employment.

Organizations can also be viewed as *learning systems* that have the capability to adapt to changes in the environment. One popular theory is advanced by Peter Senge in his best-selling book, *The Fifth Discipline: The Art and Practice of the Learning Organization* (1990). A learning organization, Senge advises, is one " . . . where people continually expand their capacity to create the results they truly desire, where new and expansive patterns of thinking are nurtured, where collective aspiration is set free, and where people are continually learning to see the whole together" (3). The learning organization engages members who work as teams to accomplish organizational objectives and, most important, to learn from one another. This system's view and thinking puts the accent on the whole of the organization, not just the parts. Thus, it offers a long-term view of the organization's well-being that is contrary to the more common emphasis on short-term performance.

A learning theory approach is attractive from an ethics management perspective for several reasons. First, specific steps taken to promote ethical behavior are not treated as one-shot efforts. For example, ethics training, although directed at specific members of the organization, is presumed beneficial because those who have received the training will influence others. Stated differently, the learning process extends beyond the individuals who are trained. Second, the long-term emphasis of a learning organization would buffer attempts to cut back on, say, ethics training when organizational resources are threatened. Training activities are commonly reduced when organizational budgets are challenged. Despite these positive features of the learning organization, fashioning an effective ethics management strategy is quite challenging. As Mark K. Smith (2001) points out, "while he [Senge] introduces all sorts of broader appreciations and attends to values—his theory is not fully set in a political or moral framework . . . his approach largely operates at the level of organizational interests."

Recent trends in *governance by networks* provide yet another perspective that can be taken toward building organizations of integrity. Stephen Goldsmith and William D. Eggers (2004, 7) point out that "in the twentieth century, hierarchical government bureaucracy was the predominant organizational model used to deliver public services and fulfill public policy goals . . . but its influence is steadily waning." Rather, governments are relying ever more frequently on networks to deliver public goods and services. The growth of third-party government "is transforming the public sector from a service provider to a service facilitator" (10). Outsourcing, contracting, privatization, and the commercialization of public-private partnerships are, as they put it, "the new shape of government." Networked government promises greater speed, flexibility, and responsiveness in meeting the needs and demands of the public. The implications for ethical governance and the development of effective ethics management strategies are difficult to predict with confidence. However, the blurring of public-private-non-governmental boundaries, as the networked model posits, calls for the development of creative ethics management strategies.

Organizational Cultures

Another significant organizational perspective derives from research on *organizational cultures.* This perspective has a long and respectable heritage dating to Chester Barnard's (1938) famous observations about informal organizations—that is, what happens in organizations is impersonal and not reflected by the organizational chart. In the same era, Mary Parker Follet (1924) wrote at length about the importance of group relationships in organizations, noting that authority in organizations derives from relationships among members of the organization.

Interest in culture as a conceptual lens for viewing organizational behavior languished for decades after Barnard and Follet drew attention to it. In the early 1980s, however, with the publication of popular books such as *In Search of Excellence* (1982) by Thomas J. Peters and Robert H. Waterman and *Theory Z: How American Business Can Meet the Japanese Challenge* (1981) by William G. Ouchi, there was a renewal of interest in culture as a determining influence in organizations. Values, these scholars argue, must be understood, cultivated, and drawn on to build high-performing organizations.[15]

Viewing organizational life though the values embedded in the culture has much to offer in building organizations of integrity. The ethical culture of the organization then becomes an important subset of values that constitute the overall organizational culture. Managers who have a good grasp of the organization's culture understand the importance of ethical values and practices in contributing to the effectiveness of the organization and are likely to devote time and energy to building and sustaining an organization of integrity. A culture perspective, therefore, is among the more promising organizational perspectives to consider when devising a successful ethics management strategy.

Building an Ethical Culture[16]

But how can managers build ethics and integrity into the organizational culture of their agencies? The quick answer is not easily! Creating and sustaining an ethical workplace takes many hands and much time. It is not that public organizations are staffed with unethical workers but that over the years many fall prey to a series of false assumptions about the role and place of ethics in agencies. So, the administrator who wants to build ethics into the organizational culture must first dismiss the following false assumptions.

Ethical Values Are Personal and Are Not Expressed within the Organization

Part of the mythology of working in the public sector is that employees should not act on their values and beliefs because to do so would undermine their ability to be fair and impartial. In other words, it is okay to have personal values and ethics but do not bring them to the workplace! This approach will breed ethical complacency and eventually contribute to ethical lapses within an organization.

Ethical People Always Act Ethically Regardless of What Goes on in the Organization

To assume that ethical people will not experience ethical lapses is a false assumption. Recruiting ethical people is certainly an important first step, but it is not sufficient to ensure that ethical government will result. Employees with sound ethical intentions still need support or reinforcement in the workplace.

Ethics Discussions in Public Organizations Contribute Little, if Anything, to Productivity, Morale, or Problem Solving

This is another false assumption. Many managers may believe that it is nice to talk about ethics in the workplace but that such talk matters little when it comes to getting the job done. Indeed, time devoted to ethics discussions or formal training might be viewed as a major distraction from time that could be devoted to providing services in a more cost-effective fashion. Growing empirical evidence shows a significant correlation between the presence of a strong ethical climate and the emphasis the organization places on values such as efficiency, effectiveness, quality, excellence, and teamwork.

It is important for managers to develop strategies that encourage dialogue on issues with ethical implications and to provide an approach to establishing an ethical workplace. The creation of a shared value system based on principles requires meaningful and serous dialogue through an inclusive, not an exclusive, process. The involvement of employees in training and development seminars that allow for questions and confrontations will give individuals the confidence needed to take action, resolve problems, and raise productivity.

Ethics Cannot Be Learned, Taught, or Even Discussed in any Meaningful Way

There is a widespread belief that ethics are acquired as a youngster, and therefore, any effort to teach or learn about ethics as an adult is fruitless. A corollary is that one can learn ethics only through the crucible of personal experiences. These views reduce ethics to whatever values and life experiences workers bring to the workplace and are hardly reassuring to managers who wish to build ethics into their organizational culture.

Neither ethical persons nor workplaces are entirely products of past experiences, whether personal or organizational in nature. This "naturalist" view of how an ethical sense is acquired or transmitted must be rejected. Rather, ethical behavior must be viewed as learned behavior that can be relearned and modified, if needed.

> Ethical behavior is learned behavior, and managers can build organizational processes and strategies that contribute to this learning effort. Initiatives such as placing ethics stories in newsletters and training, for example, might not transform unethical employees into good organizational citizens, but they can facilitate decisions that reflect organizational values and purpose. When training is successful, employees become aware of choices and have the knowledge and resources to choose and carry out the right choices.

Creating and Distributing a Written Ethics Policy Eliminates any Further Responsibility of the Organization or its Leaders

False! While it is important to have guidelines and to provide these to employees, this action alone will fall short of guiding behavior and can do little to change it, when such change is needed. Building ethics into the organizational culture is not a one-shot event. It is a continuous happening that finds expression in many ways. A written statement of principles is an important beginning point and no organization should be without one. Equally valuable, however, are the moral cues sent out by the top management. Managers who do not "walk the ethical talk" will soon experience a credibility gap that employees will see as hypocrisy—"do as I say, not as I do."

Appearing to Do Wrong and Actually Doing Wrong Are Different Matters

Factually true but "so what?" when it comes to building ethics into the organizational culture. The belief that a person's ethics should be judged not by appearance but by facts does not reflect the power of perception. Appearing to do wrong when we actually have done nothing wrong may have the same negative impact as doing wrong. The appearance of impropriety erodes employee and public trust in public agencies and weakens the principles of accountability. It may, for example, be legal for a manager to invest in a business that does business with her agency, but she will have difficulty convincing a skeptical public and workforce that she is not using her position for personal gain. The appearance of impropriety is inescapable, regardless of the reality. Appearances matter!

Practical Wisdom

Beyond dismissing these false assumptions, administrators should rely on both formal and informal ethics management strategies to strengthen their agencies' ethical environment. Managers do not need to run through a daily checklist to achieve an ethical workplace. No algorithm or methodically correct manner will cultivate an ethical organizational culture. Still, the literature reviewed here suggests that managers should take a systemic and comprehensive approach. Evidence collected to date, although limited, points to the need to incorporate a wide range of ethical practices into the total fabric of an agency. Doing so is likely to have a lasting imprint on ethical life in the organization. Moreover, managers are likely to enjoy the benefits of a sustained ethical workplace by encouraging employees to participate in professional associations, finding creative ways for ethical behavior to be rewarded, establishing an ethics conscience within their organizations, adopting a code of ethics or statement of principles, providing for ethics training or dialogue, and "walking the talk."

Organizations of integrity are places where human beings carry out their daily duties with pride and respect for others. This view is especially embraced by practitioners whose viewpoints were examined in this chapter. Character, integrity, accountability, moral competency, and exemplary behavior are words that one finds threaded throughout the practitioner literature. These core values are exemplified in practice by the U.S. General Accountability Office. If you come to Washington, Comptroller General David M. Walker says, you can see three core values over the entrance to GAO's headquarters—accountability, integrity, and reliability.

Ethical governance is not an oxymoron. Ethical workplaces can be found in many federal agencies, states, cities, counties, and special districts. Yet, no one size fits all. But how do government leaders and professional managers know which size to pick? Perhaps the advice that President John F. Kennedy offered is a helpful starting point: the ultimate answer to ethical problems in government is honest people in a good ethical environment. Honest people can certainly contribute to an ethical workplace but more is needed—a strong ethical environment. The components of a good environment include exemplary ethical leadership, a community that cares about its least advantaged citizens, and a management profession that values integrity and demands high standards of performance.

But how does one create a strong ethical environment? Certainly not from the manager's book shelf, as helpful as that might be. Rather, it is built and maintained the same way a new home is built—stick by stick, nail by nail, day by day. Ethical organizations require the same kind of care, competence, and attentiveness to build and maintain. There is no magic elixir to ingest or wand to be waved that produces ethical governance. And without a strong infusion of ethical leadership and management in organizations, it is not likely that we will find good government. Federal, state, and local government officials and appointed public managers can—indeed must—do all within their power and imagination to build ethical organizations.

Key Themes

Five key themes are threaded throughout the pages that follow. First, scandal is the most common trigger for bringing about ethics reform. Nearly every instance recounted in this book about a city, county, state, or national government adopting an ethics ordinance or law or code to foster integrity in governance was preceded by a scandal. And more often than not, the scandal involved elected officials, not appointed administrators. Public managers, nonetheless, often become "guilty by association" and become the target of bureaucratic reform while political reform is left untouched. Ethical governance must encompass both political and bureaucratic spheres of action.

Second, ethics issues and efforts to deal with them are not limited to the American experience. As chapter 6 on ethics management internationally illustrates, these matters are ubiquitous. Moreover, it is clear that efforts to manage ethics internationally cannot be reduced to a "one size fits all" boilerplate. Creative solutions are needed that allow for cultural differences while at the same time not treating ethics as something that depends on the situation.

A third theme is that building organizations of integrity is not a one-shot affair. Rather, it is an ongoing process in much the spirit that it's the journey, not the destination that matters. Still, the destination is very important, even if never reached. Earlier in this book I described the destination as "workplaces where individuals treat each other with respect, take pride in their work, care about one another, promote accountability, and place the public interest over individual and organizational self-interest." This is the idea and ideal of an organization of integrity. Have you worked in such an organization? Probably not. Would you like to work in one? Does this question even need to be asked?

A fourth theme is that a compliance approach to building an organization of integrity is not sufficient. Indeed, in its most pernicious form it can lead to the lowest common denominator that if it's legal, it's ethical. This low road approach will never lead to an ethical workplace. Rather, the workplace becomes one in which rule evasion and dodging go hand in hand with a "gotcha" mentality. The high road of aspirational ethics must be taken. Members of the organization must always ask themselves, "What is the right thing to do?" Rules and regulations may help answer this question, but they will never be sufficient. Each person must strive to ensure that his or her ethical compass is working correctly. Having a floundering ethical compass is the surest way to get lost in the quagmire of today's complex organizations.

The fifth and final theme is that there is no checklist for building organizations of integrity. The tools described in chapter 3—exemplary leadership, training, codes, ethics audits, and human resources management—are powerful tools when joined together in a systematic, comprehensive manner. Each tool must be used by ethics managers in a skillful manner, perhaps similar to that of an orchestra conductor who must be able to produce harmonious music from diverse musicians and instruments. No tool is the single best tool to transform the sour notes of unethical behavior into the reassuring culture of an organization of integrity.

The why, what, and how of ethics management have been discussed in this chapter. It should be apparent that there is no magic formula for achieving the ethical workplace. Still, there are ways and means to strengthen an organization's ethical culture, and it seems rather foolish not to employ those means to build organizations of integrity.

Plan of the Book

This book takes a public management perspective toward cultivating organizations of integrity. This perspective presumes a pro-active posture toward governing rather than a passive, caretaker posture. Administrators and their elected bosses are not content to simply "let things happen" but seek out best management practices and knowledge to make the wheels of governance turn more smoothly.

But do we know enough about cultivating ethical cultures in organizations to draw on for this purpose? Without question. There has been considerable research on this subject over the past two decades that can be tapped to provide direction and suggestions. Among other things, the accumulated scholarship provides ideas and recommendations for resolving ethics and values conflicts, managing ethics-induced stress, fostering strong ethical climates, preventing ethics failures, and even changing organizational cultures to make them more integrity friendly and responsive to the needs of employees and the community of which they are an integral part.

In this chapter, you were provided with an introduction to ethics management. Chapter 2 follows with a discussion of the U.S. constitutional and administrative environments in which public officials carry out their duties and grapple with the challenge of building organizations of integrity. Chapter 3 describes and assesses the tools available to elected and appointed officials who are committed to building ethical organizations. Among others, these include ethics training, audits, codes, and oaths. Chapter 4, "Ethics Management in American Cities and Counties," explores this largely unmapped terrain. Three cities—Tampa, Chicago, New York City—and three counties—King County, Washington; Salt Lake County, Utah; and Cook County, Illinois—are examined in some detail. In addition, the ethics management in two consolidated governments—Unified Government of Wyandotte County and Kansas City, Kansas; and Jacksonville-Duval County, Florida—is described.

Chapter 5 canvasses legislative and administrative measures taken by the U.S. Congress, American presidents, the judiciary, and the fifty states to foster ethical governance. This chapter also assesses state ethics laws, commissions, and boards, with three states—Florida, Illinois, and New York—singled out for closer examination.

Chapter 6 examines the international world of ethics management with particular attention focused on Europe and Asia. The final chapter, chapter 7, outlines the challenges confronting citizens and public officials committed to ethical governance. These include the meshing of boundaries brought about by the privatization movement, the enormous challenges of Information Age technology, globalization, and professional ethics education.

Accompanying each chapter are two ethics management skill-building exercises that enable the reader on his or her own or as a member of a small group to engage in "hands-on" active learning. The exercises cover a wide range of issues and settings. Some are presented in a city or county setting; others are presented in a state, national, or international context. All are designed to stimulate the reader to think about the day-to-day world of ethics management and to challenge the reader to explore the intricacies and complexities of the subject matter.

Ethics Management Skill Building

Practicum 1.1. A Late Night Surprise!

Dennis, the city manager of a financially strapped municipality, is working uncharacteristically late at night. The offices are empty and quiet. As he is leaving, he notices a sliver of light coming from the door of the new budget director, Susan. He decides to stop in and praise her for her excellent report in which she discovered errors that will save the city millions of dollars, projecting for the first time in many years a budget surplus. As he approaches her office he can see through the few inches the door is open that she is in a passionate embrace with Gary, the assistant city manager. The city's employment policy forbids dating between employees, threatening dismissal to those who do.

The city's code of ethics requires him to enforce this policy, yet at the same time he does not want to lose either or both of his valuable employees. It would be difficult if not impossible to bring in someone else with their experience and credentials for the amount of money the city is able to pay.

Questions

1. What should Dennis do? Should he report Susan and Steve, in accordance with policy? Is it his ethical duty to do so?
2. Should he overlook the situation believing the city will be best served in the long run? Is this a pragmatic utilitarian approach?
3. Should he speak to each of them and threaten to tell his elected bosses if they don't end the relationship? Would this cause other employees to pay more attention to the city's code of ethics?
4. Does Dennis have any right to interfere in a personal affair between two consenting adults?
5. Is this a management problem? An ethics problem? Both?
6. Can ethics problems be separated from management problems? Why or why not?

Practicum 1.2. Moral Management?

Assume that you are the top elected official of a county constitutional office, such as the clerk or property appraiser. As part of your campaign to get elected, you promise that you will demand that employees of the organization not behave in a manner that jeopardizes the credibility and integrity of the office. A week after you take office you learn that several employees who are married but not to each other are engaging in intimate behavior that offends your sense of morality and is causing disruption in the agency.

The agency's written policy is quite clear. It states:

> Agency personnel, whether married or single, shall not develop an association with another member whom they know or should have known is married to another person. Married members also shall not develop an association with agency members who are single. Excluded from this are members who are separated and residing apart from their spouse, or those who have legally filed for divorce. For the purpose of this policy, "association" means residing with, dating, or entering into any intimate relationship with.

Questions

1. What do you do? Do you turn your head and hope the situation disappears? Is this solution in the best interest of the organization?
2. Are you obligated to enforce the agency's written policy?
3. Do you call the employees to your office and have a conversation about adultery?
4. Do you consider revising the agency's written standard of conduct?
5. What changes would you make in the existing policy?

Notes

1. An excellent discussion of philosophical perspectives in administrative ethics is contained in Part II of Terry L. Cooper, Ed., *Handbook of Administrative Ethics,* 2nd ed., New York: Marcel Dekker, Inc., 2001. This discussion covers virtue ethics as well as deontological and teleological approaches to administrative ethics.

2. E-mail message to the author, February 27, 2006.

3. www.playboy.com/worldofplayboy/interviews/. Accessed February 27, 2006.

4. The first serious attempt to bring empirical research to bear on administrative ethics took place in 1991 at Park City, Utah, when H. George Frederickson organized a conference for this purpose. The conference papers were published in *Ethics and Public Administration,* Ed., H. George Frederickson, Armonk, New York: M.E. Sharpe, 1993.

5. See Brewer and Coleman Selden 1998; Folks 2000; Perry 1993; Glazer and Glazer 1989; Jos 1989; Miceli and Near 1985.

6. This discussion relies heavily on Menzel (2005a).

7. This discussion relies heavily on Menzel and Carson (1999) and Menzel (2001b).

8. See Richard J. Stillman II, *Preface to Public Administration: A Search for Themes and Direction,* 2nd ed., Burke, VA: Chatelaine Press, 1999, for an excellent overview of the evolution of public administration practice in the United States.

9. This discussion relies in part on Menzel (2001b).

10. This discussion relies on Menzel (2001b).

11. A thorough discussion of trust building is presented by David G. Carnevale's *Trustworthy Government: Leadership and Management Strategies for Building Trust and High Performance,* San Francisco: Jossey-Bass, 1995.

12. www.miamidade.gov/ethics/training.asp. Accessed June 21, 2006.

13. www.co.miami-dade.fl.us/ethics/beam.asp. Accessed June 21, 2006.

14. Max Weber is widely recognized as the intellectual father of modern bureaucracy. Weber identified six key characteristics of bureaucracy: (1) official duties are fixed by rules, laws, or administrative regulations; (2) offices are arranged hierarchical with a clearly ordered system of super- and subordinate relationships; (3) management is based on written documents; (4) management is selected and promoted via the merit principle; (5) the official is a full-time employee; and (6) management follows general rules that are stable and can be learned. *From Max Weber: Essays in Sociology,* New York: Oxford University Press, 1958, translated and edited by H.H. Gerth and C.W. Mills.

15. For an excellent overview of issues and research on organizational cultures from a sociobehavioral perspective, see Benjamin Schneider, Ed., *Organizational Climate and Culture,* San Francisco: Jossey-Bass, 1990.

16. This discussion relies on Menzel (2001b).

2

Constitutional and Administrative Environments

"Where a man assumes a public trust,
he should consider himself a public property."
—Thomas Jefferson

The Founding Fathers believed that democratic governance requires leaders with impeccable moral and ethical credentials. Those who occupied office, whether appointed or elected, were expected to demonstrate the highest degree of integrity and conduct themselves in honorable ways. A democratic government—one that is open and accessible to popular will and thought—could be achieved only by morally committed men and women. As Louis C. Gawthrop (1998) notes in *Public Service and Democracy,* the fifty-five men who gathered in Philadelphia to draft the Constitution for a new republic wove a garment threaded with ethical values and moral virtues. Those values "constituted an indivisible presence in all of the practical and pragmatic decisions made concerning the structure and functions of the new government" (38).

A cursory examination of the historical record—the Constitution and the Federalist Papers—to identify the framers' expectations of the qualifications one must possess to hold office suggests that, beyond age and residency requirements, members of Congress (especially the Senate) should have "stability of character" and be "truly respectable." A morally imbued constitution required nothing less than morally imbued officials to ensure that a true democracy would prosper. Still, the framers were somewhat schizophrenic as they recognized a darker side of the human spirit—ambition, greed, and revenge. In Federalist Paper #6, Alexander Hamilton asserts that in creating a government of the people we must not forget that "men are ambitious, vindictive and rapacious." James Madison (Federalist Paper #51) shared that view, arguing that "ambition must be made to counteract ambition." Checks and balances, the separation of powers among the three branches of government, and the division of power between the national government and the states (federalism) were put forward as the structural means to "counteract ambition." And, as Madison so eloquently proclaimed, "In framing a government which is to be administered by men over men, the great difficulty lies in this: you must first enable the government to control the governed; and in the next place oblige it to control itself" (Federalist Paper #51).

This chapter examines this history and its implication for ethical governance. Particular interest is focused on the evolution of government ethics in the United States over the past two hundred years.

Government of, by, and for the People

The framers' contradictory views of human nature and the need for government conducted by upright persons was not without some tarnish in the early decades of the new republic. Washington's secretary of war Henry Knox found himself deeply in debt as a result of an extravagant lifestyle and gambling debts incurred by his wife (Gilman 1995b). In 1791, in an effort to cope with his debts, he engaged in land speculation in Maine that resulted in lawsuits challenging the transactions. Friends came to his legal rescue, and he later rewarded them with recommendations for public office (63). Embezzlement was also a problem in the early republic. "A pointed example," Gilman (1995b, 64) notes, "is the embezzlement case of Dr. Tobias Watkins, a close friend of President John Quincy Adams (1824–1828) and a high-ranking officer in his administration." Dr. Watkins was later tried and imprisoned by the Jackson administration.

These transgressions, however, paled alongside the rampant patronage bestowed on political followers when Andrew Jackson (1828–1836) occupied the White House. Jacksonian Democracy, as historians dubbed it, meant that the common man could lay claim to any job in the federal government. And, perhaps most important, the credentials for this claim were neither the possession of moral character nor workplace competency; rather, they were rooted in political and personal connections. Thus the "spoils system," whereby those who won political office and rewarded their friends and supporters, came to the fore.

Patronage politics was to dominate much of American government—city, state, and national—for the next fifty years. Even during the Civil War, President Lincoln spent much of his time receiving and responding to federal job seekers. The war itself bred numerous accounts of corruption ranging from exorbitant sums of money changing hands in the purchase of rifles to the meat contained in food rations for soldiers. Nonetheless, as Gilman (1995, 65) succinctly notes, widespread corruption resulted in "America's development of a legal foundation for ethical behavior." The first set of conflict-of-interest statutes were drafted in the postwar years under the Grant administration in an attempt to stop federal officials from "participating in negotiations that might bring financial benefits to the employee either directly or indirectly" (Roberts 1988, 12).

Still, government by "incompetent," "immoral," and "unethical" officials approached epidemic proportions by the end of the nineteenth century. Courthouses and state capitals became breeding grounds for the corrupt and ambitious. In New York City, for example, the Boss Tweed gang and a string of Tammany Hall political successors handed out jobs and dollars with impunity. Among the more famous personalities was New York state senator and ward boss George Washington Plunkitt, son of Irish-American immigrants who entered politics to amass and lose a fortune in his lifetime (1842–1924). Plunkitt's ethics—or more appropriately, lack of ethics—eventually became the anathema of good government reformers.

> "This civil service law is the biggest fraud of the age. It is the curse of the nation. There can't be no patriotism while it lasts. How are you goin' to interest our young men in their country if you have no offices to give them when they work for their party?"
>
> —Senator George Washington Plunkitt

Despite the lively condition of big city political machines and patronage government in the second half of the nineteenth century, reform was launched with the passage of the Pendleton Act of 1883 (also known as the Civil Service Act). This new law aimed to inject "merit" and "political neutrality" into the operations of the national government and presumably lead to a modern civil service imbued with an ethical impulse. Joining the reformers, then Princeton professor Woodrow Wilson (1887) called for "a civil service cultured and self-sufficient enough to act with sense and vigor. . . ." His clarion call included a separation of politics from administration, contending that "administration lies outside the proper sphere of politics." The result of civil service reform, Wilson argued, is "but a moral preparation for what is to follow. It is clearing the moral atmosphere of official life by establishing the sanctity of public office as a public trust. . . ."

Administration, Science, and Ethics

Wilson's plea to remove the running of government from the "hurry and strife" of politics in order to have effective and moral government required two additional considerations: (1) that the field of administration be viewed as a "field of business," and (2) that efforts be undertaken to build a "science of administration." These pronouncements, when taken together, provide the first embryonic definition of public management and, as the industrial age roared into the twentieth century, found an intellectual home with the emergence of the "Scientific Management" movement founded by Frederick Taylor.

Taylor, an engineer who believed that America suffered enormously from inefficiencies in the factory and government, advocated "one best way" to accomplish work and introduced tools such as time-and-motion studies to find the one best way. The application of scientific management principles in industry and government, Taylor argued, would lift America out of its wasteful and unproductive habits to the benefit of all. His siren call resonated well with good government reformers and the movement to create an impartial, merit-based civil service. Inefficiency, after all, was closely identified with corruption and other misdeeds so prevalent in America's cities and states. Moreover, in creating a "neutral" cadre of public servants to carry out the work of government, the proper emphasis would be placed on work processes, not on personal or political friendships.

Scientific Management—an approach to management that emphasizes the application of "scientific" knowledge to work processes. Frederick W. Taylor (1856–1915), an engineer and the father of scientific management, published *The Principles of Scientific Management* in 1909.

A science of administration and Taylorism, as the Scientific Management school became known, became the dominant paradigm in the evolution of public management and administration. The ethic associated with this paradigm was utilitarianism (or instrumentalism—getting the job done right benefits the greatest number), and it found overt expression in the evolution of the city management profession. Staunton, Virginia, appointed the first person ever with the title of city manager in 1908. The manager was expected to be competent and politically neutral and to know how to get the city's streets repaired and sewer and water lines working properly. This separation of management from politics was exactly what Wilson had in mind, and the fact that the prevailing ethic was utilitarian was not especially concerning to anyone. Indeed, utilitarianism fit very well with a work ethos. It also fit well with the evolution of the City Managers' Association, which was established in 1914, although it should be noted that the Association recognized early on that it was important for its members to live by a strict code of ethics.

Morally Mute Public Management

Although these efforts to turn administration into a scientific practice began to waiver with the onset of World War II, they still stirred the imaginations of managers and organizational theorists well into the 1960s. Science, progress, and modern management, inextricably inter-woven, had become dogma by the late 1930s (Stillman 1991). The war effort—its scale, planning, and execution—brought a new reality and thinking. The politics-administration dichotomy floundered under the reality of policy makers who administered wartime programs and administrators who were heavily involved in policy making. Planning, coordinating, and executing programs and policies were not driven by scientific principles but by the necessity to get the job done quickly, efficiently, and effectively. And, with the advent of the destructive potential of nuclear weapons, many began to question whether progress needed to be redefined.

The war years contributed to a proactive management style and led to the "golden years" of working in the federal government in the 1940s and 1950s. Gone was some of the intellectual baggage, especially the identity of managers as "neutrally competent" problem solvers. Neutrality, as epitomized through local, state, and federal civil service, had grown larger than the Wilsonian legacy of removing partisanship from government work. In conjunction with the ethic of utilitarianism and Weberian norms of impartiality and hierarchy, neutrality meant either that public servants had no claim to values (personal, social, political), especially insofar as they might enter into the carrying out of one's official duties, or at best, as a professional, one could make an argument for a preferred course of action but must fall into line once a policy decision is made by organizational or political superiors. The end result of these influences was the emergence of amoral management—organizations led by perhaps moral men and women who refused to voice their beliefs.

Indeed, as managers and organizations became more morally and ethically sterile, a movement was launched to do something about it. In the late 1960s, at the height of civil unrest and diminishing confidence in the ability of the United States to become a Great Society, a group of young academics gathered in upstate New York at a retreat called Minnowbrook and put forth a call for a "New" Public Administration. A "New" Public Administration would be one in which administrators and managers accepted responsibility for promoting social justice and equity. This value-infused movement was seen by many as an antidote to the perilous plight of the morally mute manager.

What was new about the New Public Administration? Namely that administrators could and should become proactive in promoting the welfare of those less advantaged in the society. The Old Public Administration required administrators to be obedient and passive purveyors of the wishes and demands of their elected superiors.

For a variety of reasons, the "New" Public Administration did not have as great an impact as some had hoped. But, as Terry L. Cooper asserts (2001, 12), " . . . when one surveys the history of administrative ethics during the last hundred years it seems clear that this movement made an important contribution to the emergence of a field of study focused on ethics in public administration . . . [especially] around a commonly shared ethical concept— social equity." Nonetheless, its proactive posture made many managers and public officials question whether it was a proper role for nonelected officials to be so presumptuous in defining the public interest. After all, is that not the responsibility of legitimately elected officeholders?

No Road, Low Road, or High Road Ethics?

There's a saying that "if you don't know where you're going, then any road will get you there!" These words of wisdom may have some relevance to the role and place of ethics in public management during the past several decades. The tumultuous 1960s came to a close with a quest to make managers more relevant morally and ethically, but then there was Watergate—and the aftermath. The secret White House tapes not only revealed a president who conspired with others to cover up a politically motivated break-in of the Democratic Headquarters at the Watergate Hotel, they revealed a president whose moral compass seemed ajar, if not altogether spinning aimlessly in the breeze. President Nixon's resignation in 1974 spawned a wave of legislative initiatives in Washington and the states to prevent wrongdoing in government and punish those who choose to break the law. State after state enacted ethics laws and established ethics boards or commissions, with some given substantial powers to investigate alleged cases of wrongdoing by officials. At the federal level, Congress moved with dispatch to enact the Ethics in Government Act of 1978, a law that, among other things, created the U.S. Office of Government Ethics and the controversial Independent Counsel whose broad investigatory powers were put on display in Kenneth Starr's investigation of President Clinton's financial and personal affairs.

These efforts to legislate the ethical behavior of local, state, and federal officials, including high-ranking appointed managers and often frontline members of the government workforce, have produced dubious results. There is precious little empirical evidence that ethics laws, ordinances, or boards have given us good government. Indeed, there is even the suggestion that this legislation allows officials to employ the lowest common denominator in deciding right and wrong behavior. That is, by stating in law what are punishable offenses, lawmakers have given elected and appointed office-holders the opportunity to define ethics as "behaviors and practices that do not break the law." Stated in the vernacular, "if it's not illegal, its okay!" This approach has been appropriately labeled by John Rohr, a noted ethics scholar, as the "low road" to ethics. The low road features compliance and adherence to formal rules. "Ethical behavior," Rohr (1989,63) asserts, "is reduced to staying out of trouble" and results in "meticulous attention to trivial questions."

But is the low road the only road? It is certainly arguable that it is the "best" road. In fact, many scholars believe it is even a poor substitute for "no road." What then might be a more agreeable or desirable alternative? The "high" road to ethics behavior for public managers, Lewis and Gilman argue in *The Ethics Challenge in Public Service* (2005), is the path of integrity. "Relying on moral character, this route counts on ethical managers individually to reflect, decide, and act" (16). This approach blends accepting responsibility for one's behavior with honorable intentions and personal integrity, that is, adherence to morals and principles. But to whose morals and principles should one adhere? Herein lie the challenge and difficulty of the high road.

The legislative flurry to enact laws in the 1970s is regarded by some as an important step forward. However, insofar as this step fosters the low road of compliance to ethical behavior, it may actually be a tiny step at best. To be sure, scholars are not advocating a blanket repeal of ethics laws and ordinances. Rather, they are calling for an awakening, perhaps a reawakening, of what might be referred to as the "moral sense" that inheres in every single human being. A tall order? To be sure. Indeed, one that is fraught with real-world challenges that were amply illustrated in the decade of the eighties.

The thrashing around to find an ethical road for public managers and elected officeholders to follow improved and worsened with the "me" generation of the 1980s. Scandals on Wall Street, in the U.S. Department of Housing and Urban Development (HUD), and in the White House with the Iran-Contra affair sent ethical compasses spinning wildly. Why would inside traders such as Ivan Boesky on Wall Street use their knowledge to skim off thousands and thousands of dollars? Why would the leader (Samuel Pierce) of a federal agency (U.S. Department of Housing and Urban Development) sell out to the highest bidders? And, why would an American president, Ronald Reagan, who was so well liked, lie to the American public about selling arms to an unfriendly Iranian regime to raise money for an insurgency in another part of the world thousands of miles away?

The answer to the first set of questions is greed, with some overtones of Plunkitt ethics—"I saw my opportunity . . ." The Wall Street and HUD scandals clearly involved men and women of ambition and avarice. Some believe that these incidents were merely symptomatic of the 1980s "me" generation. Neither government officials nor private-sector managers and CEOs seemed immune to the question, "what's in it for me?"

> The Iran-Contra controversy in the mid-1980s involved the secret illegal sale of arms to Iran to raise money that the Reagan administration used to support the Contra rebels in Nicaragua, who were trying to overthrow the socialist-led Sandinista government. At the same time, U.S. officials believed that the arms deal would move Iranian leaders to use their influence to win the release of the American hostages in Lebanon.

Lying, as in the Iran-Contra affair, was equally troublesome and symptomatic of a moral malaise that was gaining ground in America. This particular scandal was especially disturbing because the chain of command from the president through his top security advisors, and eventually Oliver L. North, seemed to be an unbroken lie bound together by patriotism, duty, and blind loyalty. As Lieutenant Colonel North explained to Congress, "Lying does not come easily to me. But we all had to weigh in the balance the difference between lies and lives" (U.S. Senate 1987). That President Reagan actually lied is arguable, however, given the congressional testimony of Admiral John M. Poindexter, the president's national security advisor. Poindexter testifying before a joint Senate and House hearing in July 1987 said: "I made a very deliberate decision not to ask the president [about whether arms should be sold to Iran to raise money for the Nicaraguan Contras to fight the socialist-controlled Nicaraguan government] so that I could insulate him from the decision and provide some future deniability." In other words, Poindexter deliberately withheld information from Reagan about the money-for-arms transactions that Congress had specifically legislated against. Lying? No. Evasiveness? Yes. Poindexter provided the president with plausible deniability that, in effect, undermined the constitutional responsibility of the highest elected official of the nation.

> Plausible deniability is the act of withholding information from a superior so that he or she will be able to speak in a truthful manner about an issue. Admirable Poindexter provided President Reagan with plausible deniability by withholding information about the sale of illegal arms to Iran to raise funds in support of the Contra guerrillas.

The ethical angst of the 1980s spilled into the world of public management as well—so much so that a number of countermeasures were initiated. One was the promulgation in 1984 of a Code of Ethics by the American Society for Public Administration (ASPA). ASPA was established in 1939 by men and women of the New Deal generation to promote professional values and ethical behavior in public service. Yet it took more than forty years to build a consensus needed to adopt a code. Another countermeasure was the recognition by many schools of public affairs and administration that it was time to place ethics courses in their curricula. By the end of the 1980s, forty schools had added an ethics course to their graduate program of study (Menzel 1997). A related initiative was taken by the National Schools of Public Affairs and Administration (NASPAA) in 1989 when a new curriculum standard on ethics was promulgated. Schools seeking accreditation, NASPAA asserted, must demonstrate that their programs have the capacity and means to "enhance the student's values, knowledge, and skills to act ethically."

Scholarship on administrative ethics also expanded significantly in the 1980s as evidenced by the number of ethics books and journal articles appearing in print.[1] Additionally, the International City/County Management Association published an influential volume, *Ethical Insight, Ethical Action* (Keller 1988), and the *Public Administration Review* published insightful articles.[2]

These collective efforts by individuals and professional associations constituted a major push to ensure that men and women who entered public service could contribute to ethical government as well as to competent government. Whether these results have been achieved remains an important but mostly unanswered question. In fact, the pluralistic nature of these initiatives in combination with the rethinking of administration and management in the 1990s may have diffused the presumed desirable outcomes.

Administration as Management

The discussion thus far has assumed that public administration and public management are essentially the same—getting the job done in an efficient, effective, and economical manner. Therefore, it might be presumed that any discussion of ethics is relevant to either. During the past several decades, however, the meaning of managing and administering public programs and organizations has sufficiently changed to make it necessary to rethink what it means to be a public manager or administrator and to reassess the ethical implications associated with each role.

But what are the changes? Where did they come from? The most important change was the enlargement of management and the diminishment of administration as operating concepts and practices in public affairs. One might go so far as to say that public administration in its most traditional fiduciary sense has been pushed aside in favor of a public management defined as business management. Entrepreneurialism, get me results, just do it, pay for performance, contracting out, competition, satisfy the customer, outsource the work, and more is the language and siren call of managerialism. Echoes of Woodrow Wilson's assertion that administration is a field of business administration? Perhaps.

Another important change was the erosion of the meaning of *public* in public service. Where has the *public* gone in public administration? When institutions of higher education began to recognize the importance of educating men and women for public service careers, the line between governmental and non-governmental employment was fairly clear. Thus the rise of MPA (master's of public administration) degree-granting programs responded to the need to supply city, state, and national governments with talented and capable administrators. The degree, however, was supposed to convey more than competency on its holder. It was presumed that an MPA degree recipient understood why competent administration was essential in a democracy and why he or she, in bringing competence to administration, was also serving the public interest. Normative commitments to promoting democratic governance and the public interest explain precisely why graduate degrees in public administration are rarely named MGAs—master's in government administration.

Nonetheless, times change, and over the past thirty years it has been increasingly difficult to separate public-sector from private-sector employment—not to mention the enormous growth of third-party-sector employment (nonprofits, special districts, and quasi-public agencies). The result, some believe, has been an unwitting redefinition of the MPA degree to emphasize competency only. H. George Frederickson in *The Spirit of Public Administration* (1997) argues that this approach is wrongheaded and potentially dangerous. A democracy, he contends, requires a democratic administration, that is, one in which managers and workers are competent and morally committed to serving the public. Redefining administration as management poses some risks and is also concerning with regard to "managerial" ethics, especially the utilitarian views describe next.

As noted, the 1980s witnessed a renewal of interest in public-sector ethics issues and problems. This decade also witnessed the steady blurring of private/public-sector lines, unending bashing of bureaucrats and bureaucracy by the media and Republican presidents (remember, it was Ronald Reagan who quipped "Washington is not the solution to our problems: It is the problem), and a steadily growing belief in the application of private-sector management tools to public-sector management problems (Quality Circles, Total Quality Management, Team Building, and so on). Thus, when management consultant David Osborne and former city manager Ted Gaebler published *Reinventing Government* (1992), the stage was set for even more dramatic change in our thinking about administration and management. The "Reinvention" movement, as it is often called, was galvanized when the Clinton administration assumed office. In October 1993, the Clinton administration released the *National Performance Review,* a document that embodied the spirit and soul of reinventing government per Osborne and Gaebler, by promising to turn the federal government into a government that "works better and costs less."

Quality Circles and Total Quality Management are management techniques that were first applied in private profit-making firms to improve product quality and sales. Quality circles were popular in Japan in the early 1960s and later used in the United States. They involved small work groups who met regularly in the factory or business to discuss problems and solutions. Total Quality Management (TQM) emerged in the 1980s as an organization-wide approach to improve the quality of products and services. TQM is widely employed by private firms, government agencies, and nonprofit organizations.

The "New Public Management" calls for managers to steer organizations— not row them; empower citizens and coach workers through teamwork and participation; thrive on and promote competition; reject rule-driven organizations in favor of mission-driven organizations; seek results not outcomes; put customers first; foster enterprising and market-oriented government; and embrace community-owned government. New Public Managers (NPMs) are also likely to find the privatization of public goods and services an attractive alternative and adopt new management tools such as benchmarking, strategic planning, reengineering, and Total Quality Management as the situation warrants. This new way of thinking about management casts public managers into the forefront of getting the job done in an economical and cost-effective fashion. The era of the administrator who responds to citizen requests and demands rather than meeting the customers' needs, fixes problems when they arise rather than preventing them before they become uncomfortable, and promotes the public interest per the New Public Administration or some other value set is passé.

But what are the implications of the New Public Management for ethical behavior and practices? Advocates are not encouraging NPMs to break the law or engage in unethical management practices. Rather, they are mostly silent about the place of ethics or morality in public management. This silence has not gone unnoticed and has caused some observers to worry a great deal about what might be ahead. Larry Terry (1993, 393–394), an outspoken opponent of New Public Management, believes that NPMs go too far in embracing entrepreneurial values such as "autonomy, a personal vision of the future, secrecy, risk-taking, domination, coercion, and a disrespect for tradition." H. George Frederickson (1997, 22) also worries that NPMs' acceptance of utilitarianism, much as in years past when the tenets of science were believed well suited to public administration, will reduce the public interest to the "sum of atomistic individuals." A public interest so defined is, essentially, no public interest, only competing interests. Furthermore, Frederickson cautions against the downside of turning citizens into customers, which may result in a collective escape from responsibility and diminish civil discourse as individuals and groups vie against one another to extract promises and favors from government. He is equally concerned about the effect of the reinvention movement and privatization on public affairs.

> Government . . . is being reinvented to put together public-private partnerships, "empower" citizens with choices, and so on. In sum, it is now fashionable to de-governmentalize on the promise of saving money and improving services. If previously governmental functions are shifted to the private sector or are shared, it is a safe bet that corruption will increase. It is no small irony that government is moving in the direction of privatization at the same time that there is a rising concern for governmental ethics (171).

Louis W. Gawthrop (1999) has spoken about the risks of debureacratizing government and treating public service as merely work. In *Public Service & Democracy* (1998, 17) Gawthrop is unrelenting:

> We are faced with a new reality in which the citizen has been reinvented into the customer; interest groups—broadly defined to include private-sector contractors, suppliers, and so on—have been re-designated stakeholders, and, most significantly, public servants have been recast in the mold of entrepreneurs. In the process of reconfiguring public bureaucracies, however, little attention is being given to how this new reality conforms to the ethical-moral values and virtues that are deeply embedded in our democratic system.

This new reality represents a break from the old but no less reassuring reality of the administrator as a detached, dispassionate rational provider of objective information and advice to elected bosses. Good men and women with good intentions who allow themselves to be seduced by a sense of duty as competent purveyors of neutral information became neither moral nor immoral actors. Rather, they became amoral and, in this capacity, can contribute little to ethical or democratic governance. Notions of faith, hope, and love, Gawthrop contends, are not "generally recognized as significant components of public administration in America today. Instead, it is the logic of utility that still provides the basic rationale for the classical management tenets of efficiency and control" (87).

Despite the enormous influence of the old and new management realities, Gawthrop is an optimist, not a pessimist, about public service, ethics, and democracy. A moral impulse, he contends, must suffuse bureaucracy and democracy if the common good, as promised by a democratic society, is to be achieved. But from where could and should a moral impulse radiate? From the public? Elected officeholders? Administrators? Gawthrop places his confidence in administrators if, and only if, they can break out of "the habits of the self-serving good which allow public servants to pursue a procedural, quasi-ethical life" (139). In other words, an ethical life rooted in procedural correctness—avoiding conflicts of interest, disclosing financial information relevant to one's office holding, and conducting public affairs in the sunshine—is, in Gawthrop's view, a hollow ethical life at best. At worst, a procedural, quasi-ethical life produces a "government of persons without fault, operating in a society without judgment, through the ministrations of a Constitution without a purpose" (139).

Ethics is morality in action, he believes. It is, therefore, a mistake to separate morality and ethics, as is often done. Ethics defined only as compliance —"tell me what is right; what is wrong; what is legal; what is not permissible" —is also unacceptable. It is imperative that public administrators and managers understand that ethics is morality in action and that there is a moral dimension of democracy.

One other issue that might be amplified considerably by NPMs is the challenge of managerial discretion. As John Rohr notes, this is an enduring issue in public affairs that remains an unsolved problem. Put as a question, "how can a democratic regime justify substantial political power in the hands of people who are exempt by law from the discipline of the ballot box?" (Rohr 1998,6). He has dared to "solve" this unsolved problem in his book *To Run a Constitution* (1986). The oath of office, Rohr asserts, legitimates a degree of professional autonomy for the public manager and "can keep this autonomy within acceptable bounds" (69). The oath of office, he reminds the reader, is more than a mere promise; it is a morally binding commitment to uphold the Constitution. As such, it is a "statement of professional independence rather than subservience" (72). The oath guides autonomy and deters public managers from becoming maximizing bureaucrats.

A maximizing bureaucrat is an appointed public official whose single-minded goal is to expand his agency's authority, resources, and power.

As appealing as Rohr's solution might appear, it is not without problems. For example, not all managers take an oath of office. Those in the U.S. federal government do so, but this is not the case with all state or local managers. Then there are those who manage nonprofit or quasi-government corporations. These managers might not take an oath as well. Finally, there is the bleak reality that those who do take an oath of office might still not grasp or understand Rohr's contention that an oath places self-imposed limits on the exercise of discretion.

An Unfinished Portrait

Ethics in American public administration has a long, evolutionary history. The portrait sketched here remains unfinished in light of the changes and challenges in managing twenty-first-century public organizations. These changes are in no small measure exacerbated by the forces of privatization, globalization, computerization, and the rapidly moving world of information technology.

The threat of the resurrection of the morally mute manager is real and must be taken seriously. The New Public Management movement has yet to define itself ethically or morally. Or, in the worse case, it has redefined itself as a pernicious brand of moral muteness that reduces citizens to customers and public service professionals to businesspeople whose major task is to make citizen-customers satisfied with what they want and receive from government. This pathway, as Gawthrop reminds us, is certainly not a pathway to the common good. It even raises the question of whether such an approach can avoid the worse pitfalls of unethical behavior and practices in government.

Moral courage is the willpower to do the right thing with the knowledge that it will cause pain for another person or members of one's organization.

Public managers who do *not* understand why the word *public* cannot be removed from their job descriptions or cannot grasp why managerial/ethical competency are essential to effective governance should ply their trade in less demanding occupations. "No web of statute or regulation," as President John F. Kennedy put it, "can hope to deal with the myriad possible challenges to a man's integrity or his devotion to the public interest" (Lewis

1991, 14). And, as U.S. Comptroller David M. Walker adds, "we need more leaders with three key attributes: courage, integrity, and innovation . . . we need leaders who have the integrity to lead by example and to practice what they preach" (2005).

Even more is needed to build and sustain organizations of integrity. We turn next to an examination and assessment of the tools that public administrators can use to transform their organizations into high-performance agencies that embrace ethical governance.

The Evolution of Government Ethics in the United States

1792–1828: Character and Integrity in Governance

George Washington set the moral tone of the new government by insisting that public officeholders be men of integrity and high moral character. He served as an exemplar of the values he exalted and appointed men to the federal bureaucracy who were reputed to be persons of character as well as competence (Henry 1995, 240). Not all appointees, however, were persons of character.

1828–1870: Age of Patronage Governance

The election of the Tennessee populist Andrew Jackson in 1828 ushered in patronage politics and the spoils system. Government jobs were handed out freely to friends and political supporters. Corruption reached alarming levels as time passed and political machines in New York, Philadelphia, and Chicago put down deep roots among immigrants needing help.

The first code of public ethics for the U.S. government was developed by Postmaster General Amos Kendall in 1829.

1870–1900: Anti-patronage Movement

In 1883, the Congress passed the Civil Service Act (also known as the Pendleton Act), which called for a federal civil service system based on competence and merit in appointments and advancement. Federal administrators were to conduct themselves in a politically neutral manner. The law followed the assassination of President James A. Garfield in 1881 by a disappointed office seeker.

In 1887, then Princeton professor Woodrow Wilson penned the famous essay "The Study of Administration," which was a clarion call for the separation of politics and administration. Civil servants were expected to carry out their duties in an efficient and ethical fashion.

(continued)

1900–1930: Zeal for Government Integrity

Demands to end corruption and advance good government resulted in a zeal to reform the entire political system, not just the bureaucracy. Progressive reformers advocated removing partisanship from officeholding, especially at the municipal level; staggering election cycles so that local elections are not held in the same year as state or federal elections; eliminating ward-based districts and replacing them with at-large districts; establishing independent commissions and authorities; ending patronage appointments.

Theodore Roosevelt waged a vigorous campaign to end patronage appointments as a U.S. Civil Service Commissioner (1889–1895). He led efforts to investigate fraud and political abuse in government and expose corrupt government officials. As president, he championed the expansion of competitive civil service, which was increased from 110,000 to 235,000, approximately 63.9 percent of the whole executive civil service. And for the first time, the merit system surpasses the spoils system in numbers of jobs in the executive service.[3]

The early twentieth century also witnessed the adoption of new local government models such as the Council-Manager Plan, which recognized the growing need for professional public management. New professional associations sprang up with the founding of the International City Managers Association in 1914. Thirty-two local governments in the United States and Canada became charter members as the ICMA became the front line in the battle for good government. A decade later (1924) the ICMA adopted the first public service code of ethics for local government administrators.

In 1914, the Society for the Promotion of Training for the Public Service was established, "a forerunner of the American Society for Public Administration, which was established in 1939" (Henry 1995, 23).

University of Chicago professor Leonard D. White published the first textbook *Introduction to the Study of Public Administration* in 1926, creating a benchmark for public administration as a professional field of study and practice.

Scientific Management, as enunciated by its inventor Frederick Winslow Taylor, demanded greater planning, specialization, standardization, and "one best way" to accomplish the work of the organization. As a moral code, Taylor claimed that Scientific Management "aids the worker in general intellectual and moral development" (Fry 1989, 63). But the reality is quite different. Attention to moral self and ethical behavior gives way to moral muteness and amoralism.

(continued)

1930–1960: Administration as Science

These decades of strife, war, and recovery ushered in new views, attitudes, and realities of government and governance. Government was widely viewed as a positive instrument for social and economic advancement. "Can do" administrators armed with the science of administration occupied senior posts in government and became social engineers. Many brought to their work a philosophical view of ethics that is pragmatic and utilitarian.

States began to focus on ethics issues in this period. In 1954, New York became the first state to adopt an ethics law after a series of scandals involving the bribery of public officials by organized crime.

1960s: Rise and Demise of "Can Do" Government

The 1960s witnessed the "can do" government of the Great Society launched under President Lyndon B. Johnson and, by decade's end, the steady diminishment of public trust and confidence in government as an instrument to advance social justice and improve the average American's quality of life. Social upheaval, spawned by disillusionment with the Vietnam War and the inability of the federal government to resolve difficult social problems, pushed administrators into a defensive and ethically challenging corner. By decade's end, growing concern with the irrelevance of public administrators motivated a call for a "New Public Administration." Administrators were challenged to reconnect themselves ethically and morally and commit themselves to placing social equity at the forefront of the public interest. Most failed to respond.

The first government-wide executive order on standards of conduct affecting all executive branch employees was promulgated on May 8, 1965.[4]

1970s: Ethical Breakdown

The foiled break-in of the Democratic National Headquarters in 1972 at the Watergate Hotel in Washington, D.C., by Republican operatives produces a cover-up that shocked the nation and forced President Richard M. Nixon from office in 1974. A year earlier, Vice President Spiro T. Agnew was charged with accepting bribes and falsifying income tax returns. He entered a plea of "no contest" to the income tax falsification charges and was forced to resign. He was fined $10,000 and placed on probation for three years.

In 1978, the Congress enacted the Ethics in Government Act to prevent future Watergates. Many states followed the lead of the Congress and enacted ethics statutes before the decade's end.

(continued)

1980–1990: Into the Ethical Wilderness

Despite the flurry of legislation to discourage unethical behavior at all levels of government, problems continued in both the private and public sectors. Wall Street scandals involving insider trading brought attention to the "me" generation and eroded public trust in America's financial institutions. Scandals rocked the federal government and reached the highest office of the land with the Iran-Contra affair during the Reagan administration.

The American Society for Public Administration unveiled its first public service code of ethics in 1984 with a decided emphasis on the public interest. Law making to regulate and investigate charges of unethical practices in states and communities continued with many laws adding provisions dealing with gifts, outside employment, and post-employment.

Congress passed the Ethics Reform Act of 1989, placing greater restrictions on federal employees in the solicitation and acceptance of gifts, outside earned income from professional services, and financial reporting.

President George H. W. Bush issued E.O. 12674 in 1989, outlining "Principles of Ethical Conduct for Government Officers and Employees." For the first time, as many as 250,000 federal employees received annual training on the laws and regulations (Gilman 2005, 73).

The legal-punishment trend toward outlawing corruption and cracking down on unethical behavior intensified, but not all viewed this as a positive development. Frank Anechiarico and James B. Jacobs describe the decade as dominated by a panoptic vision, one in which public employees were regarded as similar to "probationers in the criminal justice system" (1994, 468).

1990s: Benign Neglect and Reawakening

Governmental ethics and reform moved to the sidelines in the early 1990s as the first Gulf War occupied the attention of both the public and President George H.W. Bush. Bill Clinton was elected president in 1992, and the "reinvention" of the federal government got underway in 1993 with much sound and fury. Vice President Al Gore, in charge of the "reinventing" of the federal government, issued a report in October that outlined a government that works better and costs less. The Gore report called for reforming the federal bureaucracy, not political institutions. The Gore report did not mention the need for ethical governance. Benevolent neglect of government ethics prevailed.

In 1998, the Clinton-Lewinsky scandal ensnarled all within its reach, especially President Clinton. The White House is lambasted by critics for moral indignities that eventually placed the president on the path to impeachment. The country recoiled at the tawdry details publicized during the Senate im-

(continued)

peachment trial in 1999 as questions were raised about the president's behavior, including lying under oath.

2000: Restoring Ethical Governance?

George W. Bush was elected in 2000 with the campaign promise to restore "integrity in the White House." He put the country on the road toward a moral America. The White House pushed for restrictions on stem cell research and abortion. Ten months later, a wartime president emerged with an agenda that challenged the moral fiber of the nation. By 2005, accusations of White House deception, misinformation, secrecy, domestic spying, torture, and leaking classified information abounded.

In October 2005, President Bush ordered ethics training for all Executive Office personnel.

Ethics Management Skill Building

Practicum 2.1. When the Chief Asks You to Lie

Chuck is the captain of one of the city's fire stations. The fire station is in serious need of repairs—a critical portion of the station has settled, causing it to become unusable. A tropical storm has blown across the city causing heavy damage and flooding. The area in and around the city has been declared a disaster area, and both state and federal disaster officials are assessing damage for emergency relief. The fire chief has advised federal/state officials that the damage to the station was caused by the storm. Prior to relief officials arriving to assess the damage at the station, the fire chief calls Chuck to advise him of their impending arrival and tells Chuck to inform the relief officials that the damage is a result of the storm.

While not stated, annual evaluations are due next month, and the chief is known to use the evaluations to reward loyalty and punish those who do not follow his wishes. Due to a previous illness in the family, Chuck is dependent on his annual evaluation to keep up with inflation.

Questions

1. Should Chuck lie for the chief? If Chuck turns his head and does what the chief wants, is he culpable of moral muteness? Or is he being unethical?
2. Should Chuck complain to the chief that he is being put in a position that he cannot agree with?

3. Should Chuck pass the lie onto another staff member by asking him or her to deceive the assessment team?
4. What ethics management strategy would you employ to prevent situations like this from occurring?

Practicum 2.2. Moral Courage

Imagine you are an inspector in the Village Engineering Department and have the responsibility to inspect the sidewalks of residents whose streets are being resurfaced. The village policy is clear—residents who live on streets that are partially resurfaced must pay up to $1,000 per home for their sidewalks to be replaced. But, residents on streets that are fully resurfaced are not required to pay. Your job is to determine how much a resident who lives on a partially resurfaced street must pay to replace the sidewalk. The technical criteria to determine the cost difference between a full resurface and a partial resurface are murky. Moreover, as the inspector, you have found it frustrating to try to explain the system to residents who are impacted. Moreover, it is your strong belief that the required fee is too great of a burden, particularly for a large percentage of the residents who are retired. After years of expressing your frustrations to the director of the engineering department and having them ignored, you decide to take the matter directly to the mayor.

The engineering director does not find your conversation with the mayor amusing. Indeed, he becomes quite angry with you for going around him to the mayor and having his policy decision questioned. He instructs you to proceed with collecting money from residents and lobbies the mayor to support the current policy. You continue collecting checks and contracts from residents but decide not to cash them or process the contracts because you feel the mayor will rule in your favor. And, you are right. The mayor concludes the system is unfair, and resident contributions are eliminated for all sidewalk replacement projects.

On hearing the mayor's decision, you return the unprocessed checks and destroy the contracts. The director, not having budgeted for the change, instructs you to continue with the old policy for the upcoming construction season and to initiate the new policy the following year. Concerned about losing your job, you lie and say that you had not collected any money. You feel it would be impossible to collect the money for the upcoming project year as the change in policy had already been announced in the local press.

In the meantime, the director investigates and finds that the money had indeed been collected and subsequently returned. In his opinion, this action was contrary to a direct order. You admit lying but claim that you had merely followed the wishes of the elected officials. The director gives you a pink slip, thus terminating your employment with the village. You decide to appeal the decision to the assistant administrator.

Questions

1. Imagine you are the assistant administrator. What should you do?
2. Was the director right to fire the employee for her behavior? Was the director acting out of his anger at having his decision overturned?
3. Did the inspector exhibit moral courage? Did she act in the best interest of the community?
4. Is it ethical to disobey an order when you feel it is the right decision? Should the inspector be disciplined?

Notes

The discussion in this chapter draws in part from Menzel (2001a).

1. See Burke (1986), Cooper (1982, 1984, 1987), Denhardt (1988; 1989), Gawthrop (1984), and Rohr (1989).

2. See Cooper (1987), Hart (1984), Frederickson and Hart (1985), and Thompson (1985).

3. www.opm.gov/about_opm/tr/. Accessed February 28, 2006.

4. www.usoge.gov/pages/laws_regs_fedreg_stats/lrfs_files/exeorders/eO11222.html. Accessed February 28, 2006.

3

Tools for Ethics Managers

Management is doing things right; leadership is doing the right things.
—Peter F. Drucker

What are the tools available to public managers to build and sustain organizations that promote ethical behaviors and practices? How well do they work? Are some more effective than others? These are the critical questions addressed in this chapter. Ethics management tools range from soft, even symbolic measures to more concrete measures such as ethics audits and training. No single one will suffice to build an organization of integrity. Rather, effective ethics management requires a comprehensive approach with top-down and bottom-up commitments. The first tool, a soft but ever so vital tool, is exemplary leadership.

Exemplary Leadership

Managers like to say that you must "walk the talk"—that you cannot lead a modern-day organization simply by issuing rules, policies, and standard operating procedures. Effective leaders must demonstrate through their behavior that they believe what they say. Those who pronounce that their supervisors and street-level workers must adhere to the highest ethical standards in the conduct of their work must themselves adhere to those same standards. Leaders must be exemplars in their personal and professional lives. Easier said than done? Certainly, but it is essential. Much the same can be said about peer leadership. Middle-managers or even the cop on the beat must demonstrate day in and day out his commitment to ethical behavior. Failure to do so can result only in organizations without integrity.

Fast-forward to 2005 Hillsborough County, Florida, home of the pro football team, the Tampa Bay Buccaneers. The county has a long and checkered history of wrongdoing among elected county commissioners with three of the five commissioners convicted in the mid-1980s of bribery, kickbacks, and extortion. And, more recently, newly elected commissioners have found themselves awash in free tickets to lounge in lush sky boxes during Buccaneer games. One commissioner explained that it was necessary to accept tickets because he couldn't otherwise afford to attend all the community events at which people would like to see him.

This form of unethical, but not illegal, leadership can have a ripple effect on the entire 9,718-member county workforce. Consider the twenty-six-year-old after-school program leader for the Hillsborough County Parks and Recreation Department who was arrested for accepting a $150 bribe by an undercover officer. The bribe was offered in exchange for the young man's willingness to falsify the records showing that the undercover officer had performed community service hours at a county facility (Graham 2005). It cannot be unequivocally asserted that the commissioners' behavior motivated this young man to accept a bribe. But it is not too much of a stretch to suggest that the example set at the top of the organization does have an influence on the ethical culture of the county workforce.

Elected officeholders can also serve as exemplars, although it is sometimes challenging to find an example. But it is not so challenging in the case of Mayor Steve Brown, Peachtree City, Georgia, population 31,580. Brown ran successfully for office on a platform of bringing ethical government to his community, yet was soon embarrassingly sitting before the Peachtree City Ethics Board accused of violating the city's ethics code. What happened? He found himself in a situation in which he needed to get his daughter to summer camp and, at the same time, negotiate an agreement for a local option sales tax. His assistant volunteered to help and drove his daughter to camp—on city time! The city manager advised the mayor that he may have committed an ethics violation. Forty-five minutes later, Brown realized that the city manager could be correct so, embarrassed by this ethical lapse, he took out his pen and filed an ethics complaint against himself. After subsequent deliberation by the Ethics Board, it was determined that no formal reprimand was necessary but that Brown should reimburse the city for the assistant's time away from the office. Mayor Brown readily complied and reimbursed the city $8.94 (Brown 2005).

Some high-level managers exercise ethical leadership by helping a subordinate understand that he (the subordinate) had a lapse in ethical judgment. Here is an example:

> We had an incident whereby a manager hung some of her colleagues out to dry by blaming them for a problem and thereby deflecting her responsibility for a mistake. In counseling with her, I used the GFOA Code of Ethics to explain why her conduct violated a provision in the professional code. She recognized the problem, and there has been no recurrence of unethical behavior (Berman and West 2003, 36).

How Does One Become an Ethical Leader?

So exemplary leadership really matters, doesn't it? But what more do we know about the leadership-ethics link? How does one become an ethical leader? An ethical follower? Is one simply born more or less ethical? James Q. Wilson (1993) argued more than a decade ago in his book *The Moral Sense* that all humans are born with a moral sense, an innate quality that enables us to understand and act on the difference between right and wrong. He points to how children at the very earliest age know when they are being treated fairly or unfairly. Still, even if we accept this view, we are not likely to believe that each of us has an ethical autopilot that will prevent us from straying onto the path of wrong behavior. So, there must be more.

Maybe the more has to do with how we were raised. What did we learn from our mother, father, sisters, brothers, friends? Fairness is certainly one of those ethical values that we probably learned about. It's also likely that we were told to treat others the way you would like to be treated—the Golden Rule. We may even have had a mother or a father tell us about the importance of human dignity, although maybe not in those exact words. Treat others as an end, not as a means—each of us is worthy—timeless advice from eighteenth-century philosopher Immanuel Kant. Perhaps you were given a list of virtues—honesty, courage, benevolence, bravery, patience, respect, trustworthiness, loyalty, to name a few—and told to follow your heart. And, if practiced often enough, these virtues would become so fully instilled in your being that you would no longer face the dilemmas posed by right and wrong choices. Your "habits of the heart" would have taken over your life so completely that you begin to become a virtuous person, a lofty goal that, however worthy, is never attained. Pursuing a life of integrity is just that.

Beware of the Utilitarian Trap

These are noble possibilities, but do they make sense in the rough and tumble world of the twenty-first century? Men and women of ambition are thrown into the lion's den of "getting ahead" no matter what. How then is one to make sense of right and wrong? Enter the utilitarian. The admonishment to serve the public interest gets translated into making decisions that benefit the most people. As the top executive of a public agency, you might conclude that recommending an across-the-board pay raise to employees is better than a recommendation to raise the pay of a smaller number of employees on the basis of performance. The organization as a whole, you might rationalize, would perform worse if there are a large number of dissatisfied employees and only a small number of satisfied employees.

Ethics managers must not sacrifice the right thing to do by trying to satisfy too many people. This utilitarian trap is hazardous. So too is the prospect of justifying an unsavory or unethical means to achieve a highly desirable result. The ends do not justify the means of getting something done, no matter how attractive the goal may be. This utilitarian trap is Machiavellian.

Niccolò Machiavelli was a sixteenth-century Italian who wrote *The Prince* (1513), a slim volume that advised rulers how to gain power and keep it by whatever means worked best. The term Machiavellian is used to describe a person who is cunning and ruthless in the pursuit of power.

A utilitarian approach, of course, is attractive because one can calculate, however roughly, possible desirable outcomes. Thus the right thing to do becomes an exercise in smart, and maybe lucky, calculations. But where does the administrator learn to do this? Maybe it is in the common sense of life to make such calculations. Or, maybe it is in the educational experience one receives. Public executives typically hold master's degrees in business, public administration, or public policy. And, educational institutions that award these degrees are often committed to teaching students how "to act ethically," to borrow the phrase in the standards promulgated by the National Schools of Public Affairs and Administration. Accredited business schools are equally vociferous in this regard, although not everyone feels that such standards make a dime's worth of difference. One business school graduate put it this way: "We had classes on ethical behavior. But if you are a rotten person going into B-school, you will probably still be a rotten person when you came out" (Bellomo 2005).

The manipulative, calculative act of projecting right and wrong outcomes might well grate on one, and it might be incorrect to charge public administration educators with teaching ethics as an exercise in calculation. Yet, many educators believe that one can learn how to engage in a reasoning process that will more likely than not yield a "right" behavior or decision. Terry Cooper, a well-known ethics scholar, is the best-known proponent of what he calls moral reasoning. And, if the popularity of his fifth-edition book *The Responsible Administrator* (2006) is any indication, he is certainly not alone. At the risk of oversimplifying his argument, Cooper contends that learning how to resolve an ethical choice, one involving right versus wrong—and sometimes, right versus right—one must develop the skill of moral imagination: have the ability to produce a "movie in our minds" that takes into account the dynamics of the environment in which a choice must be made.

Ethics Training

Ethics training was a cottage industry a short while ago. No longer: It is now a big-time enterprise in both the private and public sectors. Scarcely a large American corporation does not conduct some form of ethics training. And governments at all levels in the United States are spending ever more taxpayers' dollars for ethics training.

Ethics training is typically different from ethics education in the approaches taken and the emphasis given to laws, rules, and regulations. Normative ethics theories such as utilitarianism, principle or duty-based ethics, and virtue theory are unlikely to be touched upon in ethics training. Even the concept of "moral reasoning" is unlikely to be addressed in a direct fashion, although some training employs moral reasoning exercises.

Compliance Training

One model dominates ethics training in American governments at the federal, state, and local levels—the compliance model. It is designed to regulate employees' conduct. As Carol Lewis (1991, 9) notes, this model is "a largely prescriptive, coercive, punitive, and even threatening route . . . to spur obedience to minimum standards and legal prohibitions." The model emphasizes training in what the law says, what the rules mean, and what one needs to do to stay out of trouble. An alternative model is the integrity model. This model, April Hejka-Ekins (2001, 83) contends, attempts "to create an awareness of a public service ethos, ethical standards and values, plus a process of moral reasoning to inspire exemplary actions or ethical conduct. The emphasis is on the promotion of moral character with self-responsibility and moral autonomy as essential components."

Law is the touchstone of public organizations. Thus, it is not surprising that the compliance model is so prominent. Nor is it surprising that the ethical comfort level for public officials involves understanding the law and following it. Still, there is much to be said for adopting the integrity model. Perhaps a more realistic expectation would be to encourage governments to combine the two models into what Lewis calls the "fusion" model. Other ethics experts who recommend a fusion approach are Grosenick (1995) and Truelson (1991). Truelson further argues that the fusion model should blend with the organizational culture. That is, ethics training would both influence and be influenced by the organizational culture, thus fostering a genuine and deep-seated culture of organizational integrity.

Effectiveness of Ethics Training

The steady growth in ethics training at all levels of government in the United States is prima facie evidence that it is believed effective in discouraging unethical behavior and encouraging ethical behavior. Definitive evidence, however, is difficult to find. There are few systematic studies of the effectiveness of ethics training in either the public or private sectors. The local government experience strongly suggests that training is effective. Among the fifty states, however, it is a much more problematic story due to the heavy emphasis placed on a compliance approach to ethics training and/or an inoculation approach, as exemplified in the state of Illinois's ethics management initiative.

> Inoculation training is a one-size-fits-all effort to test large numbers of employees about their knowledge of ethics laws and regulations. This approach reinforces a legalistic interpretation of ethics—that is, what you need to know to stay out of trouble.

One recent study of business professionals strongly supports the view that ethics training makes a difference. Valentine and Fleischman (2004, 381) report "significant statistical support for the notion that business persons employed in organizations that have formalized ethics training programs have more positive perceptions of their companies' ethical context than do individuals employed in organizations that do not." They further note that employees in business organizations that have a stronger ethical context are more satisfied with their work than employees in organizations with a weak ethical context.

The results of the U.S. Office of Government Ethics (OGE) Executive Branch Employee Ethics Survey 2000 also confirm the value of ethics training. Employees, especially supervisors, who receive more regular training than other employees (1) have a positive perception of the ethical culture of their agencies, and (2) perceive a lower incidence of unethical behavior. Ethics training is an important factor in building a strong ethical culture in federal agencies.

We turn next to a more detailed look at the scope and type of training and make some judgments regarding the effectiveness of ethics training as a management tool, keeping in mind that the compliance model dominates ethics training.

City and County Experiences

Should formal or informal ethics management strategies be adopted? What is the best strategy to adopt? No one size fits all. Rather, managers need to adopt ethics management strategies—formal or informal—that seem to fit their organization. Although, if Berman, West, and Cava's findings (1994) are proven valid over time, comprehensive strategies may be most effective.

The cliché that "too much is not enough" may be an apt characterization of the size and scope of ethics strategies needed in the public sector. At the same time, there may be two larger, perhaps overlooked issues: (1) the failure of managers to understand that ethics management is attainable, and (2) the political willingness of managers to exercise the leadership to put ethics management strategies into place.

To learn more, West and Berman (2004, 189–206) conducted a follow-up study in 2002 of all 554 U.S. cities with populations over 50,000. City managers and administrators from 195 cities responded. How much ethics training is taking place? A great deal, with two of every three cities reporting that they do training. New employees are the target of most training in six of ten cities while four of ten cities reported that managers are also trained. A smaller number of cities said that ethics training is mandatory.

Subject Matter and Methods

Most municipal training focuses on the city's ethics code and/or the state's ethics law. This information typically includes (1) knowing what a conflict of interest is, (2) what "having financial interests" means in a day-to-day, practical sense, (3) the meaning of personal honesty, (4) how to address ethics complaints, and (5) due process. However, some cities go beyond these topics to include subjects such as deciding if something is unethical, coping with an ethical dilemma, evaluating ethical choices, and understanding the importance of transparency.

Live instruction, as opposed to computer-simulated or Web-based instruction, is the most common method employed by ethics trainers. This method includes the use of hypothetical scenarios, realistic case materials, role playing, and lecturing. Web-based or other electronic means for delivering ethics instruction is used in fewer than 10 of every 100 cities.

Strategies

The ethics management strategies span sixteen elements, ranging from exemplary moral leadership by senior management to the use of an ethics hotline. Among all but one of these elements (requiring approval of outside activities), cities are doing more than ever to discourage unethical behavior and encourage ethical behavior.

The most notable changes the researchers reported between 1992 and 2002 were in adopting a standard of conduct (up 27 percent), monitoring adherence to a code of ethics (up 26.5 percent), and requiring familiarity with the city's code of ethics (up 24.5 percent). Also noteworthy is the fact that more cities were using ethics as a criterion in hiring and promotion and mandating ethics training for all employees. And, more cities were making counselors available for assistance in dealing with ethical issues.

These data suggest that cities are moving aggressively to put into place a wide array of ethics management elements. But what is the evidence that these elements, in part or in whole, are making a difference? West and Berman address this question by examining the correlates between the sixteen elements of ethics management and three important organizational variables—organizational culture, labor-management relations, and employee productivity. Cities that offer ethics training report that they experience improvements in their organizational culture, better labor-management relations, and higher employee productivity. West and Berman also find positive correlations between leadership strategies and improvements in the organizational culture, better labor-management relations, and higher employee productivity. Code-based strategies, those that stress adopting a code and monitoring adherence to it, are much less likely to be correlated with these three organizational variables.

Ethics Training in State Government

Ethics training in the states lags behind the federal and local government ethics training initiatives. Indeed, many states provide no ethics training while others offer very limited training. New Jersey, which has provided some online ethics training in years past, initiated a much more ambitious ethics training program in 2005 for all state employees in the executive branch. Among other things, the training includes mandatory annual briefings on ethics and standards of conduct for all employees.[1] Texas offers an online slideshow presentation to familiarize employees with state ethics laws.

New York State does not mandate ethics training but does offer a Web-based training course that was brought online in late 2003. The course covers the fundamentals of the state's ethics laws. More than 900 people took the course in 2004. "Those who complete the course successfully can print out a certificate. At least two agencies have used the course as the basis for their own on-line training programs," according to Walter C. Ayres, Director of Communications, New York State Ethics Commission.[2] The commission staff also provided fifty-five personalized training sessions in 2004 that were attended by 2,027 employees.

State ethics training, where it does exist, is heavily compliance oriented. And, in some instances, the training consists of little more than a superficial effort to inoculate the workforce against errant behavior. Illinois and California are examples. The State of Illinois, one of the newest entrants into the ethics training field, has put into place Web-based training aimed at all state employees, including state college and university faculty and staff. All were trained in 2004 and by law must be retrained annually. The online ethics training program installed in 2004 has resulted in the training of 115,000 state employees. While it may be premature to judge the effectiveness of this "inoculation" style training, it is unlikely to do more than increase awareness of the "do's" and "don'ts" in the state's ethics law.

Web-based ethics training is growing in popularity because it is relatively inexpensive compared to live instruction. However, there is little evidence to date of its effectiveness.

California employs a similar approach. State officials must complete ethics training every two years. Online training consists of interactive and noninteractive modules that cover conflicts of interest, gift limitations, misuse of public funds, bans on honoraria, post-government employment, and more. The goal, according to the California Office of the Attorney General, is not to make a state official an expert in ethics. Rather, it is to expose officials to ethics laws and their application in order to alert one to potential conflict-of-interest situations.[3] The interactive module is a full Web-based audio and visual program that requires as much as two hours to complete. Upon completion with a sign-off by one's agency, the participant is issued a certificate of completion, which the participant signs. The certificate is retained by the agency and is available for disclosure to the public.

In 2002, Florida designed a free online training course to reach approximately 10,000 public officials in the state. Other public officials and employees can register for the course with a private provider for $15 a person. In 2004, 244 individuals registered for the course with 188 completing the training by the end of the year. One-third of those registered were members of the Florida Bar. A total of 854 public officers and employees have completed the course since its inception (Florida Commission on Ethics 2004). These statistics indicate that Florida has a long way to go with this privatization effort to inform and educate its constituencies about ethics laws and rules.

Other outreach efforts by the Florida Commission on Ethics are occasional conferences that focus on the standards of conduct and financial disclosure requirements of the Code of Ethics and invited presentations made by Commission staff members. In 2004, for example, a conference held in Tampa was attended by more than 200 public officers and employees (2004).

The Federal Experience: How to Stay Out of Trouble

The U.S. Office of Government Ethics (OGE) is the primary provider of ethics training and education materials for agencies and departments located in the executive branch. The OGE Web site (www.usoge.gov/home.html) contains an impressive collection of training materials that the Education Division, a unit with seven specialists, has developed. The materials are provided in a variety of formats such as instructor-led, Web-based, and video and cover a variety of topics to enable agency ethics officials to meet their training needs. One of the more recent training video is "Get Advice or Pay the Price," a seven-minute video. It focuses on an employee who tried to do the right thing but ended up violating ethics rules. "The video challenges employees to recognize some warning signs of unethical behavior and reminds them to seek ethics advice if they need help sorting through a situation" (U.S. Office of Government Ethics 2005). Examples of the computer- and Web-based training materials are modules dealing with the "misuse of position," "gifts between employees," and "gifts from outside sources." Other government sites containing computer- and Web-based ethics training are identified as well. These include the Departments of Agriculture, Defense, Interior, Justice, and Treasury and the National Institutes of Health.

The OGE conducts an annual conference for federal employees with ethics responsibilities that is attended by 1,000 persons. The agency also offers numerous workshops and seminars throughout the year, both in Washington, D.C., and in other parts of the country. A four-day workshop was offered in Washington in February 2005, and a three-day workshop was offered in Atlanta in September 2004. The Washington workshop covered topics such as conflicting financial interests, gifts, travel, post-employment, misuse of one's position, managing an ethics program, and training tips.

The 13th Annual Conference that was held in New York City in 2004 dealt with a number of topics over several days—confidential financial disclosure, issues in contracting out services, legal ethics, travel involving frequent-flyer benefits and premium-class accommodations, participation in professional associations, the Hatch Act and political activities of federal employees, book contracts and writing as an outside activity, how supervisors can encourage ethical behavior in the workplace, and rules on job hunting and seeking post-government employment. As these topics indicate, the annual conference is designed to assist federal employees sort through important hands-on issues.

OGE Ethics Survey

In 1999, OGE engaged a management consulting company to conduct a mail-based ethics study called the Executive Branch Employee Ethics Survey 2000.

The study sought to assess (1) the effectiveness of the executive branch ethics program, and (2) the ethical culture from the employees' perspective (Final Report, 1). More than 7,000 employees in twenty-two executive branch departments and agencies were selected randomly to receive the survey. Some 2,704 employees, or 37 percent, responded. Among the key findings were that employees have strong awareness of the ethics program, ethics officials (each agency has a Designated Ethics Officer) are helpful, and the ethics program is successful and effective in reaching executive branch employees with substantial responsibilities (30). An important related finding was that supervisors find OGE training to be more useful in their jobs than do non-supervisory employees. An explanation for this finding is that supervisors are more likely to encounter ethically challenging situations than are rank-and-file workers. Ethics training, in short, makes a difference.

The executive branch of the federal government has certainly launched a major effort since the OGE was established in 1978 to raise the ethical bar and encourage federal employees to do the right thing. Still, ethical lapses occur, as evidenced by the U.S. Air Force–Boeing air tanker scandal. This scandal involved a high-level senior civil servant, Darlene Druyun, the chief acquisition official with the Air Force, who collaborated with high-ranking Boeing executives to secure jobs for her daughter, her son-in-law, and herself in exchange for an Air Force contract to lease tankers from Boeing for a whopping $23 billion! The scandal broke in 2003 and landed Druyun nine months of jail time for violating conflict-of-interest laws. Boeing's chief financial officer, Michael M. Sears, pleaded guilty to a conflict-of-interest charge for negotiating with Druyun over a Boeing job before she retired in 2002. At that time, Druyun was responsible for overseeing Pentagon contracts with Boeing. Sears was sentenced to four months in a federal prison.

This single instance does not condemn the federal government's entire ethics education and training initiatives, but it does cast some doubt on its effectiveness among the highest levels of civil servants, especially in the field of contract management.

Codes

Elected and appointed public officials typically express a very positive attitude toward codes of ethics. The conventional wisdom is that codes have a positive influence in governance, especially in deterring unethical acts by ethically motivated public servants. That is, unethical officials are likely to be unethical regardless of whether a code exists, but those who want to be ethical find a code helpful in guiding their behavior. Of course, the motivation for adopting a code is often a series of unethical behaviors or scandal.

What are ethics codes for? First, codes increase the probability that people will behave in certain ways. Second, they focus public servants on actions that result in doing the right things for the right reasons. Third, codes do not take away one's own moral autonomy or absolve the public servant from the obligation to reason. Fourth, codes of ethics help provide the pride of belonging to a group or a profession. (Gilman 2005, 8–9)

Professional Association Codes

Professional codes can be very helpful to public managers. Most professional organizations such as the International City/County Management Association (ICMA), the American Society for Public Administration (ASPA), American Public Works Association (APWA), International Personnel Management Association (IPMA), and the Government Finance Officers Association (GFOA) have ethics codes. Two professional codes that receive considerable attention are the ASPA Code and the ICMA Code. The ASPA Code emphasizes aspirational values such as obey the law and serve the public (see exhibit 3.1). The ICMA Code, which has provided guidance for practicing city and county managers for more than eight decades, is a mix of aspirational values and practical wisdom. That is, while it admonishes managers to "be dedicated to the highest ideals of honor and integrity . . ." to merit the respect of elected officials, employees, and the public, the code and accompanying guidelines offer specific directives about appropriate and inappropriate behavior. For example, it is inappropriate behavior for a member to endorse commercial products. Guidelines for Tenet 12 state that:

> Members should not endorse commercial products or services by agreeing to use their photograph, endorsement, or quotation in paid or other commercial advertisements, whether or not for compensation.

Managers who violate the code can be reprimanded and even expelled from ICMA. An expulsion is a serious matter as it can sideline a promising career.

But how do managers use a code? Some exhort members of the organization to adhere to a professional code by encouraging them to join associations such as ASPA or ICMA or GFOA or IPMA. Others demonstrate through their own behavior that they walk the talk. Still others even go so far as to require subordinates to endorse their code publicly. For example, here is what one city manager claims:

> I require managers to sign their professional codes and to hang them on their office wall, and I list the values that are most important to me on a plaque on my wall, as well (Berman and West 2003, 36).

**Exhibit 3.1
ASPA Code of Ethics**

I. Serve the Public Interest

Serve the public, beyond serving oneself. ASPA members are committed to:

1. Exercise discretionary authority to promote the public interest.
2. Oppose all forms of discrimination and harassment, and promote affirmative action.
3. Recognize and support the public's right to know the public's business.
4. Involve citizens in policy decision-making.
5. Exercise compassion, benevolence, fairness and optimism.
6. Respond to the public in ways that are complete, clear, and easy to understand.
7. Assist citizens in their dealings with government.
8. Be prepared to make decisions that may not be popular.

II. Respect the Constitution and the Law

Respect, support, and study government constitutions and laws that define responsibilities of public agencies, employees, and all citizens. ASPA members are committed to:

1. Understand and apply legislation and regulations relevant to their professional role.
2. Work to improve and change laws and policies that are counterproductive or obsolete.
3. Eliminate unlawful discrimination.
4. Prevent all forms of mismanagement of public funds by establishing and maintaining strong fiscal and management controls, and by supporting audits and investigative activities.
5. Respect and protect privileged information.
6. Encourage and facilitate legitimate dissent activities in government and protect the whistleblowing rights of public employees.
7. Promote constitutional principles of equality, fairness, representativeness, responsiveness, and due process in protecting citizens' rights.

(continued)

Exhibit 3.1 *(continued)*

III. Demonstrate Personal Integrity

Demonstrate the highest standards in all activities to inspire public confidence and trust in public service. ASPA members are committed to:

1. Maintain truthfulness and honesty and to not compromise them for advancement, honor, or personal gain.
2. Ensure that others receive credit for their work and contributions.
3. Zealously guard against conflict of interest or its appearance: for example, nepotism, improper outside employment, misuse of public resources, or the acceptance of gifts.
4. Respect superiors, subordinates, colleagues, and the public.
5. Take responsibility for their own errors.
6. Conduct official acts without partisanship.

IV. Promote Ethical Organizations

Strengthen organizational capabilities to apply ethics, efficiency, and effectiveness in serving the public. ASPA members are committed to:

1. Enhance organizational capacity for open communication, creativity, and dedication.
2. Subordinate institutional loyalties to the public good.
3. Establish procedures that promote ethical behavior and hold individuals and organizations accountable for their conduct.
4. Provide organization members with an administrative means for dissent, assurance of due process, and safeguards against reprisal.
5. Promote merit principles that protect against arbitrary and capricious actions.
6. Promote organizational accountability through appropriate controls and procedures.
7. Encourage organizations to adopt, distribute, and periodically review a code of ethics as a living document.

(continued)

Exhibit 3.1 *(continued)*

V. Strive for Professional Excellence

Strengthen individual capabilities and encourage the professional development of others. ASPA members are committed to:

1. Provide support and encouragement to upgrade competence.
2. Accept as a personal duty the responsibility to keep up to date on emerging issues and potential problems.
3. Encourage others, throughout their careers, to participate in professional activities and associations.
4. Allocate time to meet with students and provide a bridge between classroom studies and the realities of public service.

Source: American Society for Public Administration.

Requiring members of the organization to sign and display a code does not always produce desirable results. Consider an example from the private sector—the Boeing Corporation. Boeing suffered a string of corporate scandals in the early 2000s that motivated the company to require its top managers and 150,000 employees to sign a code of ethical conduct. CEO Harry C. Stonecipher, who was charged with the responsibility of restoring Boeing's reputation, also signed the code. Alas, he was forced to resign a mere fifteen months after taking the wheel because of a tryst with a female executive officer. The board of directors concluded that while a personal consensual affair is a private matter, Stonecipher's extramarital affair had become a management and public relations issue. The non-executive chairman of the board said that Stonecipher had violated Boeing's code but that having an affair was not a violation of the policy. Boeing's Code of Conduct does not address the question of whether an affair between two employees is a violation. However, the code does state that "Employees will not engage in conduct or activity that may raise questions as to the company's honesty, impartiality, reputation or otherwise cause embarrassment to the company." The code further states that integrity must underlie all company relationships, including those with and among employees.

Local Government Codes of Ethics

Codes of ethics are often written into state statutes or local ordinances but not always. Pinellas County, Florida, for example, adopted a "Statement of

---

Exhibit 3.2
Pinellas County Statement of Ethics

We, the employees of Pinellas County, as providers of public service; and, in order to inspire confidence and trust, are committed to the highest standards of personal integrity, honesty and competence.

To This End We Will:

- Provide open and accessible government, giving courteous, responsive service to all citizens equally.
- Accept only authorized compensation for the performance of our duties and respectfully decline any offers of gifts or gratuities from those with whom we do business.
- Disclose or report any actual or perceived conflicts of interest.
- Comply with all laws and regulations applicable to the County and impartially apply them to everyone.
- Neither apply nor accept improper influences, favoritism and personal bias.
- Use County funds and resources efficiently, including materials, equipment and our time.
- Respect and protect the privileged information to which we have access in the course of our duties, never using it to stir controversy, to harm others or for private gain.

Source: www.co.pinellas.fl.us/persnl/handbook/ethics.htm.

Ethics" (see exhibit 3.2). The Statement was preferred because it emphasizes the aspirational values of right behavior rather than the "follow the rules or else" mentality that many law-derived codes espouse.

Across Tampa Bay from Pinellas County another large, urban county, Hillsborough County, adopted a more detailed statement of ethics in 2005.[4] The ethics statement contains five key elements, as can be seen in exhibit 3.3, along with seventeen subelements. Notice how much more detailed the Hillsborough statement is, with the emphasis placed on the individual as illustrated by the "I will" statements. Which code do you feel will work the best? The brief aspirational code of Pinellas County or the more detailed code of Hillsborough County?

Some agencies draft codes specific to their mission and work. Most local government agencies do not have stand-alone codes. The typical rationale is that employees are covered by the state's ethics laws, so it is not necessary to have a

Exhibit 3.3
Hillsborough County: Statement of Ethics

As a Hillsborough County employee:

In order to fulfill my role as a public servant I will adhere to legal, professional and trade rules and standards. I will demonstrate and be dedicated to the highest ideals of honor and integrity in all public and personal relationships to merit the respect, trust and confidence of government officials, other public officials, employees, and the public.

1. Responsibility
   a. I will be sensitive and responsive to the rights of the public and their changing needs.
   b. I will strive to provide the highest quality of performance and service.
   c. I will exercise prudence and integrity in the management of funds in my custody and in all financial transactions.
2. Employee development
   a. I will devote my time, skills and energies to achieving excellence in my job and my department both independently and in cooperation with other professionals.
   b. I will abide by approved practices and recommended standards for my line of work.
3. Professional Integrity—Information
   a. I will not knowingly sign, make any oral or written statement or report which contains any misstatement or which omits any material fact.
   b. I will respect and protect privileged information as I respect the right of citizens to access public records and public meetings.
   c. I will be sensitive and responsive to inquiries from public officials, the public and the media, within the framework of Hillsborough County policy
4. Personal Integrity—Relationships
   a. I will strive to exhibit respect and trust in the affairs and interests of Hillsborough County government.
   b. I will not knowingly be a party to, condone or conceal any illegal or improper activity.

(continued)

Exhibit 3.3 *(continued)*

    c. I will respect the rights, responsibilities and integrity of fellow employees and customers with whom I work and associate.

    d. I will manage all matters of supervision within the scope of my authority so that fairness and impartiality govern my decisions.

    e. I will promote equal employment opportunities, and shall oppose any discrimination, harassment or other unfair practices.

5. Conflict of Interest

    a. I will perform my duties without favor.

    b. I will refrain from engaging in any outside matters of financial or personal interest incompatible with the impartial and objective performance of my duties.

    c. I will not, directly or indirectly, seek or accept personal gain which would influence, or appear to influence, the conduct of my official duties.

    d. I will not use public property or resources for personal or political gain.

Source: www.hillsboroughcounty.org/administrator/resources/publications/statementOfEthics.pdf.

local code. Those agencies that do draft a local code often cite the process of drafting the code as important as the final product itself. Of course, if a code is not viewed as a living document, it may become little more than a nicely framed ornament that adorns office walls and glitters in the agency's literature.

> *Question:* I am being considered for a job with the State of Connecticut. Am I required to sign an ethics statement?
>
> *Answer:* All state employees and officials are required to abide by a Code of Ethics. Before accepting employment with the State, applicants will be given a summary of the State Code of Ethics and the hiring agency's ethics statement. Each new employee must sign a statement acknowledging receipt of such documents and agree to comply with the requirements of the state ethics laws.

Code Implementation

But how can a code be more than words on a piece of paper? Administrators, especially at the highest organizational level, must demonstrate their commitment to the values and principles contained in the code. One approach toward doing this is for top managers to conduct special sessions on the code, including sessions for newly hired employees. A study of employees in one high-tech organization found that sessions delivered on the ethical code of conduct by high-ranking executives had an enduring impact on employees (Adam and Rachman-Moore 2004). Such sessions can "leave an unforgettable impression about the importance assigned to ethics in the work place" (2004, 239).

Codes should be regarded as living documents that are integrated into the fabric of the organizational culture. Ethics managers who take pride in their professional code of ethics by displaying it in the work environment are taking an important step in cultivating an ethical culture.

Why Codes Succeed or Fail

Stuart C. Gilman (2005) has written extensively on this subject. Here are his explanations for why some codes succeed and others fail. Successful codes must have clear behavior objectives. The behaviors you want to encourage and discourage should be spelled out. Successful codes must fit with the mission of the agency. A tax collection agency, for example, must be respectful but firm. "They must demand honesty from not only public servants but from the public as well" (61). Codes that are successful must have pragmatic goals; codes that promise too much are not likely to succeed. Codes that promise to end corruption are promising too much— nothing will end corruption, Gilman asserts. Finally, successful codes must be supported by feedback. "Aggregate data such as the number of administrative actions taken or successful prosecutions not only helps administrators understand the effect of their program, but it also provides insights as to changes or necessary resource reallocations that might be necessary" (63).

Most codes fail because they raise unrealistic expectations or they try to control too much. Codes that require excessive reporting and tracking can produce cynicism within the organization and among the public. The pursuit of absolute integrity can be a fool's pursuit if the result is organizational ineffectiveness. A shift in political leadership can also bring a working code to its knees. "It is not uncommon for new political leaders to either de-emphasize ethics programs or to criticize them as being ineffective (65). Finally, codes can fail if there is no notion of a professional public service or if they simply get old. Changes in technology, the legal structure, or the organizational culture that occur over time require a continuous examination of the code of ethics.

Oaths

Oaths signed by employees are also used to encourage ethical behavior and can be considered a key element in an integrity or fusion model. Oaths are challenging to adopt because they are difficult to frame in a manner that public officials find agreeable. Public service oaths such as those shown in exhibit 3.4 are widely used in the federal government and some states and local governments have developed their own version of an oath. Consider the oath noted in chapter 4 for the Unified Government of Wyandotte County and Kansas City, Kansas. It requires elected and appointed officials, including employees on the front lines of service delivery, to swear (signature) that they will support the U.S. Constitution and the State of Kansas' Constitution and abide by the provisions of the Code of Ethics of the Unified Government.

A similar local government oath was adopted in Salt Lake County, Utah, in 2004. In response to several scandals, county reformers put into place the oath shown in exhibit 3.5 (see page 72). Notice that the oath applies to all persons employed by the county, including elected and non-elected officials. Notice also that all officials and employees are required only to "read and review" the oath—nothing more.

Some scholars believe that oaths have lost much of their value in the modern age. Stephen L. Carter (1997, 108), for example, claims that "In the cynicism of our age, nobody assumes that simply because an individual swears by God to tell the truth that the person is telling the truth . . . An oath . . . is seen as a silly little formality, like the stamping of a passport." It might be recalled that President Clinton was impeached largely on the basis of lying under oath. Other scholars take a different view. Stuart C. Gilman (2006) puts it this way:

> I take a slightly less cynical view of oaths and their impact. I have been in a position to really watch them work, and work the way they are supposed to. To suggest this occurs all of the time would be silly. But I have watched the mighty fall, most notably Mr. Edwin Meese III, former U.S. Attorney General in the Reagan Administration, and Mr. John Sununu, former White House Chief of Staff under President George H.W. Bush, because of ethics violations. Each was ultimately allowed to resign because the violations were tied to their oath of office.

Oaths, especially those tied to a code of ethics, are uncommon in state and local governance. John A. Rohr, a highly respected ethicist, would take strong objection to this oversight. He contends it is the oath of office that defines

Exhibit 3.4
Public Service Oaths

U.S. Presidential Oath of Office

I do solemnly swear (or affirm) that I will faithfully execute the office of President of the United States, and will to the best of my ability, preserve, protect, and defend the Constitution of the United States. — Article II, Section 1, U.S. Constitution.

U.S. Senator Oath of Office

I do solemnly swear (or affirm) that I will support and defend the Constitution of the United States against all enemies, foreign and domestic; that I will bear true faith and allegiance to the same; that I take this obligation freely, without any mental reservation or purpose of evasion; and that I will well and faithfully discharge the duties of the office on which I am about to enter: So help me God.

Source: www.senate.gov/artandhistory/history/common/briefing/Oath_Office.htm. Accessed July 4, 2006.

The Athenian Oath

The Athenian Oath was recited by the citizens of Athens, Greece, over 2,000 years ago. It is frequently referenced by civic leaders in modern times as a timeless code of civic responsibility.

We will never bring disgrace on this our City by an act of dishonesty or cowardice. We will fight for the ideals and Sacred Things of the City both alone and with many. We will revere and obey the City's laws, and will do our best to incite a like reverence and respect in those above us who are prone to annul them or set them at naught. We will strive increasingly to quicken the public's sense of civic duty. Thus in all these ways we will transmit this City, not only not less, but greater and more beautiful than it was transmitted to us.

Source: www.nlc.org/about_cities/cities_101/146.cfm. Accessed July 4, 2006.

Exhibit 3.5
Salt Lake County, Utah, Oath

All county elected officials, appointed officers, deputies and employees, in the employment of Salt Lake County, before commencing the duties of their respective offices, shall read and review the following *ethics* statement:

Employees of Salt Lake County support, obey and defend the Constitution of the United States, the Constitution of the State of Utah, the laws of the State of Utah, and the ordinances of Salt Lake County, to the best of their abilities and will always strive to meet the highest ethical standards implicit in their employment and in the furtherance of the best public interest.

Source: Salt Lake County Ord. 1543 § 1 (part), 2004. Also available on line at ordlink.com/codes/saltlkco/.

---

the public servant as a professional. In his classic *To Run a Constitution* (1986, 192), Rohr asserts

> The oath to uphold the Constitution can then be seen not simply as a pledge to obey but also as an initiation into a community of disciplined discourse, aimed at discovering, renewing, adapting, and applying the fundamental principles that support our public order. The task is to see the oath more as an act of civility than submission.

The point here is that oaths provide officials with the legitimacy and empowerment to carry out their duties in a transcendent manner that is both ethically and morally sound. This approach contrasts significantly with the "follow the rules" approach that many codes become when transformed into lawlike documents.

Ethics Audits

A proactive tool for building organizations of integrity is the ethics audit. Although not widely employed, an ethics audit can serve as a very useful tool. An ethics audit can be described as an "appraisal activity, the purpose being to determine if changes need to be made in the climate, environment, codes, and the enforcement of ethics policies" (Wiley 1995). An ethics audit is not an accounting or financial management audit. By way of example, the New York State comptroller recently completed an audit of the accounting

---

Exhibit 3.6
Oath of Office for Employment in the U.S. Postal Service

Before entering upon their duties and before receiving any salary, all officers and employees of the Postal Service shall take and subscribe the following oath or affirmation:

"I, _____, do solemnly swear (or affirm) that I will support and defend the Constitution of the United States against all enemies, foreign and domestic; that I will bear true faith and allegiance to the same; that I take this obligation freely, without any mental reservation or purpose of evasion; and that I will well and faithfully discharge the duties of the office on which I am about to enter."

Source: www.access.gpo.gov/uscode/title39/partii_chapter10_.html. Accessed June 30, 2006.

---

and expenditures of a Long Island school district and found that the former district superintendent and the assistant superintendent for business had for eight years plundered the district's treasury of $11.2 million (Lambert 2005). This affluent school district had a stellar record in graduating students who went on to top universities. Perhaps this is the reason why the school board, the treasurer, and the external accounting firm hired by the school district failed to exercise adequate oversight. Failed oversight is in itself unethical.

But why are audits uncommon? There are several reasons. First, it can be threatening if presented as an effort to root out wrongdoing. And, when done for the first time, it raises anxiety levels and questions about why it is needed anyway. After all, don't most public employees believe they are ethical and work in an ethical organization? Perhaps. Second, to be done in a satisfactory manner, the audit should be comprehensive in the information solicited and coverage of members of the organization. It can be challenging in the time and effort required, which, in turn, places a demand on the agency's budget. Third, employees and managers might not be convinced of the confidentiality of the audit, especially in states with strong sunshine laws. These are often the reasons for not carrying out an audit. But these "don't do it" reasons should be weighed carefully in light of the organizational pay-offs of increased productivity, greater worker satisfaction, lower turnover rates of personnel, and the building of public trust and confidence in the agency.

There are other important reasons to conduct an ethics audit. An audit can identify gaps in policies and procedures, including gaps in the need to increase awareness of areas of potential ethical risk (McAuliffe 2002). Another plus for conducting an audit occurs if the agency contracts with a university to conduct the audit. An internally, agency-conducted audit is automatically suspect and unlikely to be viewed as trustworthy by employees. Moreover, a university-conducted audit benefits agency officials through "ethical conversations, opportunity for critical reflection, and the support that could be offered to staff with no professional qualifications" (4).

An ethics audit might also include an assessment of occupational risk or vulnerability. That is, some organizational work is inherently vulnerable to unethical abuse if not criminal wrongdoing. For example, occupational work that involves the handling and processing of financial matters, purchasing and contracting, conducting inspections, and enforcing rules and regulations are high risk, especially for workers whose ethical compass is ajar in the first place. A systematic assessment of the ethical risk factor of work is a necessary first step in putting into place appropriate accountability and transparency mechanisms. It is also a valuable step in identifying ethical training priorities.

Exhibit 3.7
An Ethics Audit in Austin, Texas

In 2000, the City Auditor's Office used survey data collected annually by the city's Human Resources Department to assess the ethical climates of the city's departments (Waring 2004). Here's what the audit discovered. Statistically significant correlations were found between a department's ethical climate and

1. Costs and number of successful damage claims against the city—a strong ethical climate resulted in fewer and less costly damage claims.
2. The number of complaints filed by the public—a strong ethical climate resulted in fewer complaints.
3. Lost time due to injuries—a strong ethical climate correlated with fewer departmental injuries thus less time lost.
4. The amount of sick leave taken—a strong ethical climate resulted in employees who worked in less stressful environments and thus taking time less time off for sickness.

Source: Waring 2004.

Local Government Ethics Audits

To illustrate further what an ethics audit is and the benefits that may accrue, consider the audits conducted in a city and a county in Florida. The city had a population of 67,000 and a council-manager form of government. The county, with a population of 850,000 and a commission-administrator form of government, was on the Florida Gulf Coast. Both governments have a history of stability with appointed city/county managers who typically serve for many years.

Methodology

Questionnaires were sent to randomly selected samples of employees from each government. The surveys were mailed in-house with a postage-paid envelope that identified the university as the recipient. Two hundred sixty-five (N = 265) city employees returned usable questionnaires for a response rate of 53 percent. Four hundred sixty-five county employees (N = 465) returned usable questionnaires for a response rate of 62 percent.

Both samples were drawn from alphabetized payroll lists using a fixed interval selection method. All participants were informed that their participation was voluntary and all responses would be treated confidentially. Cover letters from the city manager, the chief personnel officer of the county, and the principal investigator (a faculty member at a local university) explained the purpose of the study and assured anonymity. To provide additional anonymity, participants were not identified by sex, race, or work unit.

All major organizational subunits (police, fire, and so on) in the city participated in the study. The county study population included all employees under the county administrator's jurisdiction, the supervisor of elections, the Property Appraiser's Office, and the clerk of the circuit courts. Employees under the appointing authority of the sheriff did not participate.

Each respondent was asked to provide information about the ethical climate of his or her organization. This approach assumed that the respondent could perform as a reasonably objective observer. This type of measurement does not focus on whether the respondent believes he or she behaves ethically nor does it emphasize whether the respondent sees the ethical climate as good or bad (Victor and Cullen 1988). The questionnaire elicited *descriptions* of, rather than feelings toward, the ethical climate (see exhibit 3.8).

Results

Statistical analysis indicated that a strong ethical climate is associated with the values of efficiency, effectiveness, quality, excellence, and teamwork.

Exhibit 3.8
Ethics Climate Survey Items

1. It is not unusual for member of my department to accept small gifts for performing their duties.
2. Some members of my department use their position for private gain.
3. Members of my department have misused their position to influence the hiring of their relatives and friends.
4. My supervisor encourages employees to act in an ethical manner.
5. Managers in my department have high ethical standards.
6. The people in my department demonstrate high standards of personal integrity.
7. There are serious ethical problems in my department.
8. Members of my department sometimes leak information that benefits persons who do business with the city.
9. My superiors set a good example of ethical behavior.

Source: Menzel (1993, 197).

Indeed, the city results showed that the ethical climate was the single most-important influence on organizational performance. Stated differently, organizational efficiency, effectiveness, quality, excellence, and teamwork are strongly reinforced by a strong ethical climate. These findings challenge the conventional wisdom that ethics and high performance are incompatible.

Also challenged is the conventional wisdom that bureaucratic environments, with their emphasis on hierarchy and rule following, are incompatible with a strong commitment to organizational ethics. Indeed, the study's results support the opposite view, that is, procedural emphases in combination with other variables in the workplace reinforce an ethical workplace. Although limited to two local governments in a single state, the results are provocative in light of the attention given to the "evils" of hierarchy. Could it be that the defining if not essential characteristics of ethical public organizations are order, authority, and rules? Or, is it conceivable that hierarchy and rule following merely reinforce the prevailing ethical climate, regardless of how strong or weak it may be?

U.S. Office of Government Ethics Audit

The U.S. Office of Government Ethics (OGE) conducted an audit in 2000—*Executive Branch Employee Ethics Survey 2000.* The audit was an ambitious effort by OGE to determine how well the federal program was working. Was it making a difference? A rigorous sampling methodology along with a sophisticated statistical analysis were employed to identify respondents and assess their responses. Overall the audit found three important things. First, ethics training encourages employees to take a positive view of ethics in their agency. Second, unethical behavior is perceived by employees as infrequent. And third, "supervisors play a critical role in promoting and maintaining an ethical culture" (7). How OGE has used these findings, however, is not clear. Nor has the agency conducted a follow-up survey.

United Nations Integrity Survey

The United Nations contracted with a management consultant to conduct an integrity survey in 2004 of all U.N. staff and leaders in the Secretariat—a population of 18,035. A total of 6,086 (33 percent) returned the questionnaire. The purpose of the survey was "to measure both attitudes and perceptions about integrity among U.N. staff" (United Nations 2004, 5). What did the results show? As the final report notes,

> Staff care most about what they see others doing and saying. Organizational integrity is about: eliminating discrepancies in what leaders and supervisors say and do; living the U.N.'s vision, mission and values while limiting political and cultural influences; doing the right things even when it's inconvenient, uncomfortable or without precedent; demonstrating the value of integrity by rewarding those who do while disciplining those who do not.

The findings indicate that staffers are very satisfied with their work and committed to the organization's goals but that many are reluctant to become whistle blowers or report misconduct. "Staff members feel unprotected from reprisals for reporting violations of the codes of conduct." Not surprisingly, staff personnel are uncomfortable about approaching their managers with ethical concerns, and many do not feel that their supervisors and colleagues regularly discuss ethical issues that arise in the workplace.

In November 2005, United Nations Secretary-General Kofi Annan used the audit findings to put forward a proposal to the General Assembly to establish an Ethics Office. The proposal was favorably received and the office became a reality on January 1, 2006. The primary objective of the Ethics Office is "to assist the Secretary-General in ensuring that all staff members observe and perform their functions in consistency with the highest standards of integrity . . . through:

- fostering a culture of ethics, transparency and accountability;
- developing and disseminating standards for appropriate professional conduct;
- providing leadership, management and oversight of the United Nations ethics infrastructure (United Nations General Assembly 2005, A/60/568).

The United Nations ethics audit, although meritorious, illustrates some limitations of an audit. For example, the U.N. Director of Elections, Carina Perelli, was dismissed from her post in December 2005 as a result of accusations of sexual harassment and abuse of authority. A management review, not an ethics audit, of her office conducted earlier in the year "faulted her for an abusive style of leadership and favoritism and said she had created an atmosphere where 'sexual innuendo is part of the "fabric" of the division'" (Hoge 2005). Ms. Perelli was unceremoniously escorted from the U.N. Headquarters in New York and told "she would no longer be permitted to enter the building unless she had a scheduled appointment to discuss her appeal" (A23).

When Serious Wrongdoing Turns Up

An ethics auditor may discover serious incidents of wrongdoing. This is more likely to occur when interviews rather than mail surveys are employed to collect information about the ethics climate. If these incidents are of sufficient scale and severity to be potentially criminal in nature, such as that in the Long Island school district, what are the auditors to do? The answer is straightforward—they must report their suspicions and findings to the appropriate legal authorities. The line between criminal acts and unethical acts is not, however, always so bright. Auditors must be convinced that an unethical act has a very high probability of being unlawful. Reporting an egregiously unethical behavior that is unlikely to be illegal will bring an ethics audit to a swift and unsatisfactory conclusion.

Although objectivity is at a premium in conducting an audit, administrators "must recognize that an assessment of this nature involves considerable subjective judgment" (Reamer 2000, 364). Nonetheless, an ethics audit, whether done by a third party such as a consultant or university, is a valuable tool in fostering integrity in the workplace.

Human Resources Management

Personnel decisions—hiring, evaluating, promoting, firing—are essential features of all organizations. Should the ethical behavior of an employee be considered in these decisions? Should only "honest" people be hired? Promoted? Hiring and promoting honest people is no easy task. How does an agency know if a person is honest? Should a lie-detector test be used? Or an integrity test? Or a fitness of character test? And, even if we could determine if a person is honest or of high moral character, can we presume that these qualities will persist over the years of employment? Not necessarily, given what we know about the moral challenges facing individuals in complex, modern organizations of the twenty-first century.

Stephen J. Bonczek, a city manager with many years' experience in Michigan, Florida, Texas, and Pennsylvania, is a strong advocate of raising the ethical awareness of employees through hiring, evaluation, and promotion. He is equally adamant about installing an ethical consciousness in the organization through the use of codes, audits, committees, and weekly staff meetings. "It is advantageous, "he claims, "to use weekly staff meetings to review all discussions and decisions for ethical implications. When a potential problem is identified, a staff member can be assigned to clarify the issue and develop a strategy for resolving it at the next meeting" (Bonczek 1998, 78).

Hiring Practices

Screening of a job applicant for her ethical judgment is, of course, challenging. One approach that can be taken during the interview is to ask the candidate to respond to hypothetical situations. Here are several examples. Mary Jane Hirt, the former city manager of two Pittsburgh communities, recommends this scenario: "You are the assistant manager in a community and have just been informed by a council member that council intended to fire the town manager at the next public meeting. The council member asked whether you are interested in being considered for the manager's position. What is your response? Do you warn the manager that s/he is about to be fired?" (2003).

Ann Hess with the City of Boston asks a specific question during the interview process by posing a hypothetical situation. "When I interview staff for the City Council (one staff; fourteen bosses), I try to gauge an applicant's understanding of the need to be confidential while respecting divergent interests across bosses" (2003). She presents the candidate with this scenario:

> You as a Central Staff member are asked to compile some research for one councilor. Another councilor comes to you with a request for information on the same issue, but the councilor has a different position on the issue. Part I: How do you comply with each person's request? Part II: The first councilor comes back to you and asks who else is working on the issue and what else have you produced for them. What do you say?
>
> I usually give the applicant five minutes to draft some informal comments and responses and then we talk about it. I look for how they come to

the decision—while no specific right answer, better candidates will discuss wanting to know level of confidentiality in advance, providing both sides of the story to both councilors with focus on the particular position they are advocating, the inability to disclose who else they are doing research for and how they present that fact to the requesting councilor with respect and understanding.

Scenarios like these can be helpful in screening job applicants, but more probing may be needed as well. To query applicants about their personal lives—have you ever stolen anything, lied, cheated—can be a tricky matter. Of course, there is also the possibility of prying too deeply into one's private affairs when taking this approach. Considerable care and caution needs to be exercised.

Annual Evaluations

Putting an ethics component into human resources management is a daunting task but one that many managers believe should be done. While challenging to incorporate an ethics criterion into evaluation, it would not be difficult to require employees to complete an ethics education or training course before being promoted. Mayor Steve Brown of Peachtree City, Georgia, urges local governments to "create a study course on ethics that has to be completed in order to be eligible for promotion."[5] The U.S. Department of Defense Acquisition Workforce requires ethics training annually but does not mandate this as a condition for promotion. "To be a DoD Program Manager or Contracting Officer," Keith McAllister (2005) notes, "one must be certified to an appropriate level. Certification as a Program Manager includes a series of formal classes (continuous learning credit) . . . [T]he DoD spends significant public resources annually. It is imperative that those resources be used in a manner consistent with public expectations and trust—hence the embedded ethics training."

One approach that could be taken to incorporate an ethics component in an employee's annual evaluation is to place a checkbox on the evaluation form. The checkbox could read: "Employee treats others with respect and dignity." As simplistic as this solution might be, it would certainly make every employee sensitive to the fact that he or she will be held ethically accountable once a year. And, if multiplied over hundreds or perhaps thousands of employees, what a difference it could make.

Ethics Counselors

Another tool for ethics management is the ethics counselor. An example is a clinical psychologist working as a federal employee in a Department of Veterans Affairs Medical Center. She is chairperson of the hospital ethics committee and is the Employee Assistance Program coordinator as well. Her committee members function as consultants when people confront dilemmas and wish to discuss them. These issues come to her as an EAP counselor as well when someone is attempting to resolve an ethical issue between a superior and a subordinate; for example, they may come to her to discuss it and seek advice. There is also a VA-wide national Center for Ethics in Health Care that provides formal and informal consultation. If she has a thorny issue come up in the Hospital Ethics Advisory Committee and wishes to get an outside perspective, she can call the National Center to get ethics advice.

The Department of Veterans Affairs Medical Center also has a monthly hotline teleconference where issues are discussed (for example, the Pope's declaration on patients in a persistent vegetative state, or whether gifts or meals provided by vendors can be accepted by service providers). Most of these issues deal with clinical or organizational ethics, and the consultants represent a variety of disciplines, including medicine, nursing, social work, psychology, law, and chaplaincy (West 2005).

Human resources management can be drawn on to promote ethics and integrity in governance. This discussion has demonstrated the many possibilities that lend themselves to this task. The failure by officials to include human resources management in their ethics management arsenal will limit the ability of any city, county, state, or federal agency to build an organization of integrity.

Are Some Tools More Effective Than Others?

Public administrators must use all tools available to them to put into place a comprehensive and integrated program. Still, it is reasonable to ask whether some tools are more effective than others. One study of a private-sector organization provides help in answering this question. Adam and Rachman-Moore (2004) examined several methods used to implement a code of conduct. Among others, they assessed three tools discussed in this chapter—managerial leadership, the means of enforcement, and ethics training. What did they find? First, they found that training was more important than either managerial leadership or the means of enforcement. Second, the surprise finding was that the means of enforcement, that is, signing an oath, performance evaluations, and so forth, were the least important in influencing employees "to behave in accordance with organizational ethical rules." This is contrary to the "common view that organizational enforcement mechanisms are of prime importance as control mechanisms and are considered to effectively impact on the conduct of employees" (238).

As this chapter has shown, many tools are available to cultivate an ethical culture in public organizations. However, no single tool is the single most effective. Ethics managers must use all tools at their disposal.

Ethics Management Skill Building

Practicum 3.1. An Ethics Audit for Your Agency?

You have decided that an ethics audit for your agency is needed. There have been no serious incidents of unethical behavior, but you are not sure that agency personnel are paying enough attention to ethical issues. And, there is some evidence that most of your middle-level managers are complacent about promoting proper behavior. Ethics issues are never discussed during staff meetings. It just seems as if ethics doesn't matter that much to most managers. An ethics audit, you believe, will get people in touch with their own ethics and will have a positive influence on the agency's culture of "getting the job done."

Now, you say to yourself, where am I going to find an ethics auditor? And, what do I really want an auditor to do? You know that an ethics audit can't be done on the cheap, so the first task is to estimate the costs of conducting an audit, but you can't do this in-house because you do not have staff who are sufficiently familiar with an audit to properly estimate the cost. An RFP (Request for Proposal) will get the job done, you muse.

You decide to ask the director of the Human Resources Division to develop the RFP. As you are talking with him, he asks: "How should I state the objective of the RFP?" What exactly is it that we want an ethics auditor to do? Do we want the auditor to investigate the (un)ethical behavior of all employees? Some employees, say, frontline workers, and not others? Is there a time line when we want the work completed? Is there a limit on how much we should budget given that our agency employees 500 people?

Questions

1. How would you reply to the director of the Human Resources Division?
2. What should be the key components of an RFP?
3. What guidance should you provide the auditor about releasing the results of the audit?

Practicum 3.2. Ethics Training for the Trainer

Your urban county government has nearly 10,000 employees who are responsible for streets, sewers, water, solid waste pickup and disposal, and an array of social services such as dealing with homeless people and curbing drug abuse. As the head of the county's Division of Training, it is your job to provide a range of training exercises that fits the needs of a diverse workforce. Some training, for example, helps frontline employees deal with angry people.

Other training involves following proper procedures when a citizen complains about an employee or a public service.

The county administrator who recently attended an ethics program conducted by her professional association returned with a great deal of enthusiasm for establishing a comprehensive ethics training program for all 10,000 county employees. Recognizing that the training division does not have trainers with this expertise but knowing that you do have a strong background in this area, she asks you to put into place a "train the trainer" initiative.

You immediately call your staff of six trainers together to discuss the situation. The staff is somewhat uncertain and uneasy about taking on this responsibility. In fact, one of your trainers pipes up and says, "Adults can't be taught ethics. People learn ethics from their mother or father or church or wherever. It's a waste of county time and money to take this on. You should go back to the county administrator and respectfully tell her to forget it."

Questions

1. How would you respond to your staff member? Would you tell him he's totally off base—that acquiring ethics is a lifelong endeavor?
2. If you and the staff agree with the trainer who spoke up, how would you approach the county administrator? Would you say that the training staff feels strongly that a county-wide ethics training program will not be successful? Or, would you tell her that the training staff does not feel that they can teach adults ethics but will go through the motions anyway?
3. Would you say to the administrator that we can teach compliance with ethics ordinances and state law but nothing more? How would you defend this assertion?

Notes

Some material in this chapter is drawn from Menzel 2005b.

1. For more information about New Jersey, see www.state.nj.us/sos2005/ethics.html. Accessed December 29, 2005.

2. E-mail communication.

3. See www.ag.ca.gov/ethics/accessible/essentials.htm. Accessed June 23, 2006.

4. See www.hillsboroughcounty.org/administrator/resources/publications/statementOfEthics.pdf. Accessed December 30, 2005.

5. See www.gmanet.com. Accessed June 23, 2006.

4

Ethics Management in American Cities and Counties

"I think we're probably just too comfortable out here to do our civic duty."
—Neil Morgan, former columnist for the *San Diego Union-Tribune*, commenting on corruption in San Diego, 2005

American cities and counties are known historically for their lack of ethics and integrity in carrying out the people's business. Courthouse gangs and city hall bosses once ruled a vast number of cities and counties by handing out jobs, contracts, and other favors to friends and political cronies. Senator George Washington Plunkitt of New York City's Tammany Hall fame once proudly proclaimed, "I seen my opportunities and took 'em!" Indeed he did, becoming a millionaire in his lifetime as a power broker. Corrupt local officials still roam the corridors, although not as freely as in the past. Monmouth County (New Jersey) is a prime example. Eleven officials, including three mayors, were arrested in early 2005 on federal corruption or money laundering charges as a result of an FBI sting (Smothers 2005). San Diego has also had its share of troubles. In 2005 two councilmen were convicted on extortion, wire fraud, and conspiracy charges. They were charged with accepting money from a strip club owner and his lobbyist in exchange for efforts to repeal a ban on touching between dancers and patrons (Gustafson 2006). Six former members of San Diego's pension board stand charged with conflict of interest for their roles in underfunding the pension system. Financial irregularities and other problems prompted then mayor Dick Murphy to resign in mid-2005 after only seven months into his second term.

Still, times change, and so do cities and counties. Both are increasingly adopting the tools and practices needed for ethical governance. In San Diego, for example, newly elected mayor Jerry Sanders moved promptly to establish an Office of Ethics and Integrity to work alongside the city's five-year-old Ethics Commission. The new office enforces standards of conduct and provides ethics training for the city's 11,400 employees who work in departments under the mayor. Other cities and counties have launched similar initiatives.

Cities and Counties in the American Federal System

Cities and counties are legal artifacts of the states. Their power and authority are set by the state. Counties do not exist in every state; Rhode Island and Connecticut do not have counties. In forty-eight states, however, America's 3,034 counties occupy an unusual niche in the American federal system. They are a hybrid government, with both state and local government characteristics. They have responsibility for many state functions such as maintaining vital records on births and deaths, marriage and divorce, property transactions, taxation, and so forth. At the same time, counties, especially the more urban counties, provide numerous services such as public safety, emergency medical services, solid waste collection and disposal, road repair, parks and recreation, and more.

Many county governments are highly fragmented with independently elected "row" (also referred to as constitutional) officers such as sheriff, tax collector, property appraiser, clerk, and others sharing power. Even more fragmentation can be found in highly urbanized counties that have many municipalities. Cook County, Illinois, for example, has 133 municipalities including the City of Chicago; the most densely populated county in Florida, Pinellas County, has twenty-four municipalities. Further south, Miami-Dade County has thirty-four cities.

More than two dozen counties are consolidated with a city government, such as Jacksonville-Duval County; Honolulu, Hawaii; Indianapolis-Marion County; and New Orleans-Orleans County. Thus the challenges of coordinating and managing cities and counties are as huge as the challenges to building and sustaining organizations of integrity.

Ethics Management and Local Governance[1]

Ethics management among local governments is even more varied than that found at the state and national levels. Among America's 84,000 local governments, some large cities and counties have impressive ethics management programs. King County (Seattle, Washington), Miami-Dade (Florida), Anne Arundel (Annapolis, Maryland), and Cook County (Chicago, Illinois) have local ethics commissions armed with substantial investigatory powers. Among cities, Los Angeles has one of the most comprehensive programs in the country. Jacksonville also has a proactive program with an ethics code that touts "aspirational goals for the conduct of city employees."

Other cities—for example, New York City—have ethics codes and agencies to enforce them, although they are less comprehensive because the primary emphasis is placed on managing financial conflicts of interest. Some cities, such as St. Petersburg, Florida (population 248,232), do not have a separate ethics commission but have an ethics investigatory process. Under these circumstances when a violation is alleged, city council members put on their hats as members of an ethics commission to investigate the allegations and render a ruling. Unlike many cities, St. Petersburg has an "appearance standard" in its Code of Ethics for City Employees.

> An appearance standard is a very high standard because it requires an employee to behave in a way that a reasonable person would not perceive the employee's behavior as unethical. In other words, an appearance of unethical behavior is as unwelcomed as an actual occurrence of unethical behavior.

Agency rules that define acceptable behaviors of employees are commonplace among local governments. In Kansas City, Missouri, for example, the *Ethics Handbook* issued to all employees asserts that it is unacceptable behavior to spend several hours a week on city time to download Internet information on a relative's medical condition.[2] In California, many local governments place restrictions on employees receiving gifts. In San Diego, for instance, employees "shall not accept gifts, gratuities, or favors of any kind which might reasonably be interpreted as an attempt to influence their actions with respect to city business."[3] In the Town of Los Gatos, administrative regulations are even more restrictive.[4] For example, one rule states that "no employee shall accept money or other consideration or favor from anyone other than the town for any reason" (Simmons, Roland, and Kelly-DeWitt 1998).

Smaller municipalities are even less likely to devote resources to ethics and integrity in governance. And, some experts contend that this is a significant deficiency. Mark Davis, executive director of the New York City Conflicts of Interest Board, asserts that contrary to what people think, " . . . small municipalities are most in need of ethics boards, because in small municipalities conflicts of interest are absolutely unavoidable" (1999, 408).

Not all small communities, however, are without ethics management initiatives. Whiting, Indiana, a community of 5,137 located twenty minutes from Chicago, is an example. In 2004 the city adopted an ethics ordinance that applies to all officials, elected and appointed, and the workforce of 150 employees.[5] It proudly proclaims that city officials shall conduct the government "with loyalty, integrity and impartiality." To achieve this lofty goal, the ordinance set forth rules for financial disclosure, the acceptance of gifts, electoral activities, and the use of city property. The ordinance also established a three-member Ethics Commission consisting of the mayor, the chair or president of the board or commission of the alleged non-compliant person or the head of a city department if the complaint is filed against an employee, and the Ethics Officer. The Ethics Officer, who is also the city's water superintendent, was appointed by the Board of Public Works and Safety and charged with the responsibility of overseeing investigations into alleged wrongdoing (Stahura 2005).

Among the 19,000 special districts in the United States, few have launched ethics management initiatives. One notable exception is the Los Angeles County Metropolitan Transportation Authority. The authority has an impressive program directed by a chief ethics officer and six colleagues in a separate Ethics Department and a budget of $800,000. The ethics staff "educates and advises employees, board members, contractors and the public about ethics rules and maintains the records concerning lobbyist reports and employee statements of economic interest disclosures" (COGEL 2004). The Authority has issued three ethics codes—an eleven-page code for the thirteen-member board of directors, a six-page code for contractors, and a ten-page code for the Authority's 10,000 employees.[6]

The New York City Transit Authority also has issued a code of ethics that "established a 'zero-tolerance policy' toward employees who receive gifts from companies and individuals conducting business with the authority" (Chan 2005). Additionally, it has published a Vendors Code of Ethics that prohibits vendors from giving gifts or contingent fees to authority employees, spells out negotiating rules for a vendor who might want to hire an authority employee, limits the ability of former employees to appear before the Transit Authority, and obligates vendors to report any solicitation of gifts by transit employees.[7] The authority adopted the code after a string of ethical lapses involving fourteen high-level managers who were charged by the New York Ethics Commission with accepting gifts from companies and individuals who do business with the authority. The commission also charged the president, Lawrence G. Reuter, with accepting improper gifts. He admitted that he had accepted $633 in gifts from companies that do business with the authority and reached a settlement with the commission to pay a fine of $1,200 (Chan 2005).

As can be seen in exhibit 4.1, some city/county ethics agencies operate with few employees and few resources (for example, Denver Board of Ethics) while others (such as Los Angeles, New York, and San Francisco) have a number of employees and a respectable budget. And, while most agencies

Exhibit 4.1

Selected Cities with Ethics Management Programs

	Operating size		Jurisdiction over . . .		
	Budget	# Employees	Elected officials	Appointed officials	Employees
Atlanta	$193,000	2	Yes	Yes	Yes
Buffalo	n/a	n/a	No	Yes	Yes
Champaign, IL	n/r	n/r	No	Yes	No
Chicago	$604,000	9	Yes	Yes	Yes
Denver	$89,000	1	Yes	Yes	Yes
Honolulu	$158,000	2.5	Yes	Yes	Yes
Jacksonville, FL	$75,000	1	Yes	Yes	Yes
Los Angeles	$2.1 mil	24	Yes	Yes	Yes
New York City	$1.5 mil	19	Yes	Yes	Yes
Oakland	$220,000	2	No	Yes	Yes
San Diego	$398,000	6	Yes	Yes	Yes*
San Francisco	$1.7 mil	8	Yes	Yes	Yes
Seattle	$450,000	6	Yes	No	Yes
Tampa	$0	0	Yes	Yes	Yes

Source: COGEL (2004) and agency Web sites.

*The Mayor's Office of Ethics and Integrity has jurisdiction over all employees that work in departments under the mayor. The Ethics Commission has jurisdiction over the elected officials and unclassified city managers. See www.sandiego.gov/ethics/about/differ.shtml.

n/r = not reported in COGE; n/a = not available.

have jurisdiction over elected officials, some do not. Programmatic responsibilities are more consistent across units (see exhibit 4.2). Nearly all provide advisory opinions and provide some type of ethics training. Most are authorized to investigate alleged ethics violations at their own initiative (see exhibit 4.3, page 90). It is difficult, however, to assess the variance in activity levels as shown in the number of advisory opinions issued and investigations conducted. While some agencies appear to be quite active, others are less so. The differences could be a result of the variation in local ordinances, resources, personnel orientation, or culture of the community.

Filing and Investigating a Complaint

The filing of an ethics complaint is a serious matter. The filing of a malicious complaint can be tempting for a citizen who wishes to "get even" with a public official or for a person who wishes to seek a political advantage. Consequently, cities and counties are careful about investigating a complaint unless there is persuasive evidence that a violation has occurred. The handling of a complaint passes through a series of steps and stages.

Exhibit 4.2

Selected Counties with Ethics Management Programs

	Operating size		Jurisdiction over . . .		
	Budget	# Employees	Elected officials	Appointed officials	Employees
Miami-Dade County	$1.65 mil	14 plus 2 contractors	Yes	Yes	Yes
Maui County, HI	n/r	n/r	No	No	Yes
Cook County, IL	$100,000	2	Yes	Yes	Yes
Anne Arundel County, MD	$143,200	2 part-time	Yes	Yes	Yes
Montgomery County, MD	$190,000	2	Yes	Yes	Yes
New York	$1.5 mil	19	Yes	Yes	Yes
King County, WA	$142,551	1	Yes	Yes	No
King County Office of Citizen Complaints, WA	$750,000	9	n/r	Yes	Yes

Source: COGEL (2004) and agency Web sites.
n/r = not reported in COGEL.

The process conducted in Miami-Dade County is fairly typical across the country (see exhibit 4.4, page 91). First, a written, notarized complaint must be filed by a citizen. Second, the commission staff then examines the complaint to assist the commission in determining if is "legally sufficient"—that is, relevant to the city's ethics ordinance. A complaint such as "city council member Jones interferes with the work of the city manager" would not be legally sufficient. Third, if the complaint is found to be legally sufficient, then the commission must rule on whether there is "probable cause." That is, is there sufficient reason and evidence to believe that a violation has occurred? If the commission finds there is no probable cause, then the complaint is dismissed. However, if a finding of probable cause is rendered, then a public hearing is scheduled before the Ethics Commission. Evidence and arguments presented at the public hearing are the basis for the commission ruling on either a finding of a violation or a finding of no violation.

Ethics management in three cities—Tampa, Chicago, and New York City—

Exhibit 4.3

Advisory Opinions, Investigations, and Training in Selected Cities and Counties

	Advisory opinions		Investigations		Training required
	Authority to issue	# per year	Authority on own initiative	# per year	
Los Angeles Ethics Commission	Yes	n/r	Yes	150	Yes
Oakland Public Ethics Commission	Yes	1–2	Yes	30–40	Yes
San Diego Ethics Commission	Yes	4	No	38	Yes
San Francisco Ethics Commission	Yes	n/r	Yes	38	Yes
Denver Board of Ethics	Yes	50	15	Yes	No
Jacksonville, Fl	Yes	n/r	Yes	n/r	Yes
Tampa	Yes	n/r	Yes	n/r	Yes
Miami-Dade Commission on Ethics & Public Trust	Yes	215	Yes	80 in 2004	Yes
Atlanta Board of Ethics	Yes	8	Yes	0	No
Honolulu Ethics Commission	Yes	5–10	Yes	20–30	Yes
Maui County Board of Ethics	Yes	10	5	n/a	No
Chicago Board of Ethics	Yes	30	Yes	25	Yes
Champaign, IL	Yes	20	No	n/a	No
Cook County Board of Ethics, IL	Yes	5	Yes	3	Yes
Anne Arundel County Ethics Commission, MD	Yes	38 in 2003	Yes	5–15	n/r
Montgomery County Ethics Commission, MD	Yes	10	Yes	4	n/r
Buffalo Board of Ethics	Yes	0	Yes	1–2	n/r
New York City Conflicts of Interest Board	Yes	535	Yes	62	n/r
Seattle Ethics & Elections Commission	Yes	30	Yes	75	n/r
King County Board of Ethics, WA	Yes	n/a	Yes	n/r	Yes
King County Office of Citizen Complaints, WA	n/a	n/a	Yes	10–20	n/r

Source: COGEL (2004) and agency Web sites.

n/r = not reported in COGEL (2004); n/a = not available.

Exhibit 4.4 **Citizen Complaint Process in Miami-Dade County**

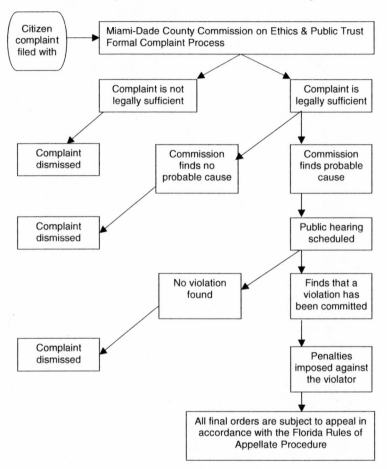

are examined in the next section. Then, programs in three counties are described—King County, Washington; Salt Lake County, Utah; and Cook County, Illinois. This discussion is followed by an examination of programs in two consolidated governments—the Unified Government of Wyandotte County and Kansas City, Kansas, and Jacksonville-Duval County in Florida. These cities and counties were chosen because of their geographical diversity, innovation, and variation in ethics management styles and practices.

Tampa, Florida

Nearly every municipality that has begun to put into place sound ethics management practices has faced difficulty along the way, and most have acted because of a scandal. The City of Tampa, Florida, is among the newcomers to scandal-driven ethics reform. The scandal that triggered ethics reform in Tampa began in 2001, with a romantic relationship between the city housing chief, Steven LaBrake, and his top aide, Lynne McCarter, who had moved rapidly through city ranks. The housing chief and his aide built a 4,200–square-foot home for a bargain-basement price of $105,000. Adding more suspicion to the situation, the builder had received more than $1 million in housing contracts through the city's housing department.

Along the way, the city under then mayor Dick Greco began an investigation of LaBrake's handling of his office, and in October 2001, placed LaBrake on a ninety-day paid administrative leave pending the resolution of criminal charges. The following month the Florida Ethics Commission reported that LaBrake did not violate state ethics laws. Later in the same month, however, the Ethics Commission repudiated the report saying that the information submitted by the city and Mayor Greco was unreliable.

A year later, the LaBrakes and several others were indicted on fraud and corruption charges. The accusations eventually landed LaBrake and McCarter in court in 2004, where the builder confessed to bribing the city housing chief. The LaBrakes (now married) were tried in 2003 and found guilty of more than twenty-five counts of conspiracy, wire fraud, and accepting bribes and gratuities. LaBrake was sentenced to five years in a federal penitentiary and McCarter three years and five months. The developer was handed a five-year probationary sentence.

"What strikes me about the LaBrakes' situation is that they were part of the culture that permeates Tampa government, where you do me a favor and I'll do you a favor, even though it violates the public trust."

—U.S. District Judge Richard A Lazzara who sentenced the LaBrakes
(Testerman 2005)

Tampa's Ethics Code

In 2003, the city council began to deliberate on the wisdom of an ethics code that would guide the behavior of its 4,800 employees. The same year, a new mayor who is a strong advocate of integrity in city governance was elected. The city promulgated its first ever code of ethics in November 2003. Not surprisingly, the code includes a prohibition on "fraternization." That is, no employee or officer shall appoint, employ, advance, nor recommend or advocate the appointment, employment, or advancement to any position "any individual with whom they have a close personal relationship."[8] Enforcing this prohibition is another matter and will most likely be resolved at some future date in a court of law.

Ethics Commission

The Code of Ethics also created a five-member Ethics Commission comprising faculty members from two local universities, two citizens appointed by the chief judge of the Thirteenth Judicial Circuit, and one member (who has held elective office at the local level) appointed by the mayor. One university appointee is a faculty member who is knowledgeable in legal ethics while the other appointee is a faculty member who is knowledgeable in ethics more broadly defined. Ethic Commissioners are appointed for staggered four-year terms and are precluded from partisan political activity or being employed by the city.

The commission is empowered to "review, interpret, render advisory opinions and letters of instruction and enforce" the code. Advisory opinions must be requested in writing, and the facts may be real or hypothetical. If an advisory opinion is rendered, it is binding on the conduct of the person who sought the opinion. A written, sworn complaint by a citizen submitted to the city Ethics Officer initiates the enforcement process. The complaint is then delivered to the commission for a preliminary investigation. If the commission finds "probable cause" that the code has been violated, it must notify in writing the complainant and the alleged violator. A public hearing may or may not be called, depending on the circumstances. If the commission finds that a violation has occurred, it then recommends to the appropriate body—agency head, city council, mayor—that "appropriate action for correction or rectification of that conduct" be taken. The commission has no enforcement power, that is, it cannot impose a disciplinary action on a code violator. Disciplinary measures can range from a verbal admonishment to censure, suspension, or removal from office.

Code Implementation

The city's new code and its implementation, however, includes much more. The Department of Human Resources is designated as the Ethics Office, and the HR director is the city's designated city officer. The Ethics Office is charged with overseeing the code's implementation. The Ethics Officer is assigned the task of developing education and training programs for city officers and employees. Moreover, the Ethics Officer is expected to "serve as the liaison between the ethics commission and the officers and employees of the city."[9] Each city department has an ethics liaison who assists the Ethics Officer in the formulation of ethics-awareness training sessions, conferences, and seminars.

Ethics education and training are required of every elected official who must attend an ethics-in-government program within ninety days of taking office. Newly appointed employees must participate in an ethics training program within six months of their first day of employment. The code also mandates that current employees be trained as soon as practicable. There is no requirement that elected officers or employees attend an ethics-in-government program on a continuing basis. Nor are there whistle-blowing provisions in the code to protect city employees. This measure was omitted because it was seen as unnecessary since city employees are protected by Florida's whistle-blower law.

These measures suggest that Tampa is moving forward with its intent "to elevate the level of ethics in local government, to provide honest and responsible service to the citizens, and to maintain the confidence and trust of the public that this government serves."[10] The ethics management approach taken in Tampa parallels those found in so many other cities—"know what the city defines as acceptable behavior to stay out of trouble" and, if in trouble, here's what can happen to you. Tampa is engaged in a limited form of ethics management.

Chicago

Historically, ethical governance and Chicago are not known to go together. The "city of big shoulders" with its industrial, blue-collar past and hard-nose machine politics often meant votes and more were for sale. While this reputation has receded some in recent years, problems remain. In 2004 a bribery case involving the city's trucking contracts grew into a full-scale federal investigation of political patronage and influence. Twenty-three persons had been convicted by mid-2005, and more were awaiting trial. Eight of Mayor Richard M. Daley's cabinet members and other top officials have either resigned or been fired as a result of accusations that they rigged hiring tests to ensure jobs for campaign workers (Wilgoren 2005).

Ethics management in the City of Chicago is legalistic in its orientation with substantial authority granted to the Board of Ethics to launch investigations and ensure compliance with the Governmental Ethics Ordinance. This is indeed impressive for city government, but like city- and state-level counterparts, this approach emphasizes a minimalist strategy.

City efforts to prevent wrongdoing actually began in earnest with the creation of the City's Board of Ethics in 1987. A seven-member Board of Ethics whose members are appointed by the mayor and confirmed by the city council is supported by a nine-member professional staff. The board is "responsible for helping to ensure public confidence in Chicago government" (Chicago

Board of Ethics, *Annual Report 2003–04*). Board programs include education and training, advice and guidance, regulation, and financial disclosure.

Ethics Training

The Governmental Ethics Ordinance sets forth an ambitious educational requirement that all fifty aldermen, aldermanic staff, and senior executive service employees attend ethics training every four years.[11] The ordinance also requires all new employees subject to attend an ethics training program within 120 days of entering service and once again every four years afterward. Those who fail to attend are subject to a $500 fine. About 3,800 officials and employees, or approximately 10 percent of the workforce, are covered by this training requirement in the Governmental Ethics Ordinance. In other words, the vast majority of the city workforce is not subject to ethics training.

More than two dozen classes for more than 800 employees were conducted in 2003 by the board's ten member staff. In addition, the board offers other ethics training programs for city and non-city personnel upon request. Presentations were provided as well to visiting foreign dignitaries from Bosnia-Herzegovina, Bulgaria, the Czech Republic, Malaysia, and the People's Republic of China. Like the U.S. federal government, each agency has a Designated Ethics Officer (DEO) who serves as the primary liaison with the Board of Ethics and assists agency employees in understanding and complying with the Governmental Ethics Ordinance.

Advice

The board's advice and guidance program consists of two categories of assistance—inquiries and cases. An inquiry is a request for information or professional advice in which the inquiring person does not ask for a written response. In 2003–2004, more than 1,900 inquires were acted on. A case is a written complaint or a request for an opinion. Fifty-two cases were acted on in 2003–2004, and 140 reports were issued as a result of investigations. The subject matter of the inquiries and cases are shown in exhibit 4.5. Financial interest disclosure, gifts, and lobbying were the subjects most often addressed by inquiries and complaints in 2004.

Investigation and Enforcement

Regulation and enforcement activities encompass campaign financing, financial disclosure, registration of lobbyists, and investigations, complaints, and preliminary inquiries. The Campaign Financing Ordinance limits the amount of money that can be contributed to an individual seeking elected

Exhibit 4.5

Chicago Board of Ethics Inquiries, 2002–2004

	2002	2004
Outside employment	46	37
Post-employment	43	108
Gifts/travel/honoraria	102	131
Lobbying activity/disclosure	166	110
Conflicts/improper influence	34	26
Employment of relatives	13	31
Financial interest disclosure	768	975
City property	4	26

Source: Annual Report 2003–2004.

city office—especially contributions from lobbyists. Between 9,000 and 12,000 employees and officials are required to file statements of financial interest with the board each spring. Failure to file a financial disclosure can result in a fine. Lobbyists are required to register with the board and pay a $200 fee doing so. They must reveal who their clients are and report all lobbying-related compensation and expenditures. Nearly 400 lobbyists were registered in 2004, representing more than 1,000 clients. The board maintains a list of registered lobbyists and their clients on its Web site at www.cityofchicago.org/Ethics.

The board also has considerable authority to investigate alleged wrongdoing. Unlike most boards, it can initiate an investigation on its own. However, this authority is limited in the case of a complaint against an alderman. A complaint of an alleged violation of the Governmental Ethics Ordinance by an alderman must be signed and sworn, in which case, it is authorized to initiate an investigation. The board also has subpoena power. All investigations are treated as confidential. For the most recent reporting year, 2003–2004, the board received fifteen written complaints, three of which alleged violations involving the unauthorized use of city property and one each with respect to post-employment, conflicts of interests, fiduciary duty, and employment of relatives. The board also conducted 107 investigations of city employees who failed to file statements of financial interests within the time prescribed by law. Thirty-five investigations into campaign violations were closed that had been filed in the previous year.

New York City

The "big apple" has a history of scandal and corruption that few cities can rival. It has an equally long history of reform intended to prevent wrongdoing. Anechiarico and Jacobs (1996) in their account of "the pursuit of absolute integrity" cite four periods in which corruption and reform waxed and waned in the city and around the nation. The period 1870–1900 focused on the "spoils" or "patronage" period when big city political machines were at their height.

The period 1900–1933 witnessed the *Progressive Era* in which the effort to root out corruption was the complete reform of the political system. The rise of non-political, merit-driven civil service along with non-partisan elections was central to making government more effective, if not more ethical. The separation of politics from administration was the key, so Progressives argued. In the decades that followed, 1933–1970, the *science of administration* came to the fore with an emphasis on organizational efficiency and economy. Embedded in scientific administration was the view that bureaucratic corruption could not be controlled internally, that is, by bureaucrats themselves. What was needed was external controls, that is, auditing and investigatory agencies to watch over other agencies.

The fourth period, 1970–1990s, experienced a *hardening of comprehensive surveillance and investigation strategies* that were sown in the previous period. Anechiarico and Jacobs (24) label this period as the "panoptic" era in which public employees are "akin to probationers in the criminal justice system." The end result is an ethics management system run amok. The pursuit of absolute integrity, one in which everyone is presumed guilty of wrongdoing, has turned New York City into an ungovernable enterprise. Corruption control in this manner does not produce good governance; rather, it results in ineffective governance according to Anechiarico and Jacobs. Not everyone, of course, would agree with this assessment.

Panoptic is a term used to describe a prison in which the architecture features a control tower at the center of a circular cell house. Thus the cells, inmates, and staff would be completely visible to the watcher (Anechiarico and Jacobs 1996, 24).

Let's take a closer look at the specific measures taken by New York City to combat corruption and promote ethical governance. The starting point was the establishment in 1959 of a Board of Ethics, an advisory body that was created along with the city's first code of ethics. A *New York Times* front-page story on August 21, 1959, proclaimed boldly that a strict city code was passed by the Board of Estimate after two years of deliberation. On September 3, 1959, Mayor Robert F. Wagner signed the ethics ordinance into law. The code, the *New York Times* reports, covers 225,000 officials and employees who will be held to rigid standards of conduct. Several months later, in January 1960, the then mayor Wagner swore in the city's new five-man Board of Ethics and charged it with administering "the finest Code of Ethics of its kind in the United States" (Bennett 1960). The principal author of the 1959 code, S. Stanley Kreutzer, described this landmark event in the following way:

> City administrations change, but the fundamental concepts of ethics as written into law are ageless because they have inherent in them the object of government in our Republic—to be fair to the people who serve and who are served by our municipality. (McFadden 2005)

Conflict of Interest Board[12]

Three decades and, regrettably, more scandals later, good government reformers called for a major overhaul of city government. Charter amendments were passed that, among other things, replaced the Board of Ethics with the Conflicts of Interest Board (COIB). The new board's powers were expanded significantly. No longer an advisory body only, the renamed board was empowered to impose fines up to $10,000 per violation, which, Executive Director Mark Davies (2005) claims, is the only ethics board in the country that has this power. At the same time, the COIB does not have the authority or power to conduct investigations. This power is lodged in the city's Department of Investigations.

The five-member board is appointed by the mayor with members serving staggered six-year terms. A staff of eighteen in 2004 tended to the daily business, which included monitoring the work of over 300,000 city employees. While a major emphasis is on dealing with conflicts of interest such as accepting gifts, moonlighting (working full-time for the city and also part-time elsewhere), and ownership in firms doing business with the city, the ethics law (chapter 68) also covers post-city employment, disclosure of confidential information, political activities, and relationships between employees and supervisors. A separate city whistle-blowing law offers protection for employees who report possible ethical violations.

The COIB is an independent agency, subject only to budgetary constraints imposed by the mayor and city council. Any citizen can file a written complaint that triggers an assessment by the staff. In 2004, the COIB received 307 complaints with six disposed that imposed fines amounting to more than $8,000. Since 1990, when the COIB was created, it has levied nearly $241,000 in fines. Like many ethics agencies, if the board concludes that there is probable cause to believe that a public servant has violated the ethics law, it is empowered to "direct the department of investigation to conduct an investigation." Further steps include the possibility of a confidential hearing in which the accused official may defend himself or herself.

The COIB also issues advisory opinions requested by an employee or supervisor. Opinions are disclosed to the public without the disclosure of the identity of the person requesting the opinion. In 2004, the COIB received 535 written requests for advice and more than 2,633 telephone requests.

Other duties include overseeing the city's financial disclosure law and providing training programs. The disclosure law was reformed in 2003 to narrow the criteria for those who must comply with it. It now states that "only public servants at risk for conflicts of interest" must file annual financial disclosure reports. City employees are not required to attend ethics training offered by the COIB staff, but many do, as the statistics for 2004 show that 14,470 employees attended 288 classes. The COIB offers some vendor training as well.

Ethics management in New York City is a substantial enterprise involving as well a Web site and media outreach, an annual seminar on ethics in city government, and visits by international delegations. In 2003, the board cooperated with the United States Office of Government Ethics and the Department of State to host visitors from Argentina, Bulgaria, China, Gaza, Haiti, Indonesia, Kenya, Pakistan, South Korea, Thailand, and Zimbabwe, among others.

King County, Washington

Among America's 3,034 counties that have policies and procedures for dealing with unethical conduct, King County (Seattle) in the State of Washington might have the oldest. The county enacted a code of ethics in 1972 in response to corruption. The code focused on conflicts of interest, placed restrictions on business transactions between former members of the county council and sitting council members, and required financial disclosure statements by commissioners and senior county managers. A three-member appointed ethics board was established to enforce the code. In its initial seventeen years of existence, "the board held only one major public hearing [and] very few county employees knew of the code's existence" (Dobel 1993, 164).

After still another series of scandals erupted in 1986–1987, the code and its enforcement were further strengthened. A new ethics code went into effect in 1990, which, unlike its predecessor, presented "a positive vision of public service" and emphasized its role in building legitimacy and respect for government as well as its support for independent judgment and public trust (171). The revised code was accompanied by the establishment of an ombudsman's office and a full-time ethics administrator that reports directly to the county council and the Board of Ethics. The revision also increased the board membership from three to five members.

Board of Ethics

In 1994, the board began an intensive education and training program to familiarize county employees with the code and "provide them with the decision-making skills necessary to resolve routine ethics issues within the workplace."[13]

How effective has the King County ethics program been over the past decade? A true measure of effectiveness is difficult to construct. Some output data are available (see exhibit 4.6).

The Board of Ethics has not conducted an ethics audit or carried out an organizational survey to measure the ethical climate of county agencies. However, it initiated an ethical awareness campaign in 2003 that included, among other things, the development of a voluntary survey quiz in 2004. The quiz was distributed by e-mail and hard copy to the county's 13,802 employees and was completed by two of every ten employees. The survey was placed online in 2005 and elicited responses from more than 2,300 persons. The online interactive survey sought "to determine the extent to which employees understand basic provisions of the Code of Ethics, and the quality of the employee's experience and effectiveness of the contact when seeking information from the ethics office" (14). The questionnaire is online at www.metrokc.gov/ethics/ethicssurveyquiz.aspx#quiz. (Accessed July 7, 2006.)

Office of Ombudsman

The Ombudsman Office was established in 1968 when county voters approved the Home Rule Charter. The ethics code revisions of 1990 reassigned the responsibility for ethics code violations from the ethics board to the ombudsman. Alleged violations of the county's whistle-blowing ordinance are also under the authority of the ombudsman as are complaints about the administrative conduct of executive branch employees.

The office is staffed with four professionally trained ombudsmen, including the Ombudsman-Director, and a support staff of two. The ombudsman cannot initiate investigations under the ethics code but does have subpoena power to compel sworn testimony and retrieve records or material relevant to an investigation. If the ombudsman finds reasonable cause for a violation of the code of ethics, the respondent may appeal the ruling to the Board of Ethics. The civil penalty for a violation by one of King County's more than

---

Exhibit 4.6
Ethics Training in King County, Washington

- In 2004, Over 2,220 employees including board and commission members received ethics training in 2005, of which 58 percent were new employees. New employees are required to sign a statement that they have received a copy of the summary of the ethics code. Ethics training is mandatory for supervisors every eighteen months. In 2005, 688 supervisors and their deputies received ethics training.
- Post-employment provisions were amended in 2004 that ban for one year a former employee becoming a contractor or subcontractor on any county action for which he or she had responsibility as a county employee.
- From 1991 through 2005, the board issued 149 advisory opinions and 746 staff informational responses which are written responses to employee inquiries on situations where the code and advisory opinions have already been applied to an analogous issue.
- In 2005, statements of financial disclosure were filed by 2,411 elected officials and employees and approximately 300 contractors and vendors.

Sources: King County Board of Ethics 2004 and 2005 *Annual Reports.*

13,000 officers or employees can range from a slap on the wrist or suspension without pay for one month to termination of employment. The criminal penalty is a fine not to exceed $1,000 or imprisonment in the county jail not to exceed ninety days, or both. The ombudsman can recommend disciplinary action but cannot compel an agency to take disciplinary measures. The Board of Ethics is equally lacking in enforcement authority. "The employee's management makes the ultimate determination as to whether disciplinary action will be implemented" (Conquergood 2005).

The *2004 Triannual Reports of the Ombudsman* show that the Ombudsman's Office received 1,385 inquiries for information, 311 requests for assistance, and 128 complaints. There were nine completed investigations of complaints alleging violations of the ethics code and twelve complaints of retaliation for reporting improper governmental action protected under the whistle-blowing code. Four of the nine cases alleging violations of the ethics code were resolved by the ombudsman and five were found to be unsupported.

King County may be the only county in the United States that divides the responsibility for ethics management between a Board of Ethics staffed by one professional and a much larger Office of Ombudsman. The ombudsman's duties, of course, include much more than dealing solely with complaints of unethical behavior.

Salt Lake County, Utah

Reform measures to foster ethical governance in Salt Lake County, Utah, were launched in 2004 as a result of a scandal in which then county mayor Nancy Workman was forced from office, accused of felony charges that she had misused public funds. It was alleged in court documents that Mayor Workman had misused health department funds to hire bookkeepers at a Boys and Girls Club where her daughter was the chief financial officer. The scandal set in motion a call for ethics reform. The county council set to wrangling about specific measures and failed to come up with a coherent proposal. Then, the deputy mayor, standing in for Mayor Workman, put together a set of proposals for consideration as a whole. Democratic mayoral candidate Peter Corroon (then mayor-elect) offered a similar list of proposals, with some additions. In combination, the measures can be seen in exhibit 4.7.

Not all proposals in Exhibit 4.7 were adopted but many have been. They include:

1. adopting an ethics statement that all county officials and employees must read and review;
2. requiring ethics training for all county officials and employees every two years;
3. encouraging county officials to hold open records and meetings consistent with state statutes and county ordinances;
4. requiring the disclosure of outside interests and conflicts of interest;
5. prohibiting employees from accepting or soliciting gifts, honoraria, or requests for employment;
6. banning for one year county officials and employees from directly communicating, for compensation, with his or her former county agency for the purpose of influencing any matter pending before that county agency;
7. appointing or hiring a relative to any county position except for seasonal employment;
8. prohibiting officers and employees from engaging in political activities, including the solicitation of political contributions, during the hours of employment;

Exhibit 4.7
Salt Lake County, Utah, Ethics Reform Proposals

- Audit all County Departments under the county mayor's jurisdiction to prevent abuse and mismanagement. Salt Lake County is a mayor-council form of government with a nine-member council, three of whom are elected at-large. All elections are partisan. There is one elected constitutional officer district attorney and seven independently elected statutory officers—assessor, auditor, clerk, recorder, sheriff, surveyor, and treasurer.
- Establish a bipartisan ethics panel to review ethics policies and complaints as well as to review redistricting proposals.
- Ban all gifts accepted by elected officials and employees unless reasonably necessary to perform their duties.
- Prohibit high-level county employees from accepting employment as an officer or director of a major county vendor or contractor for at least a year after leaving county employment.
- Prohibit county employees from using county facilities or equipment for any personal business or outside employment.
- Require written disclosures of conflicts of interest.
- Publish a list of all county contractors on a citizen-accessible Web site.
- Prohibit cars and car allowances as benefits of employment and restrict the use of county vehicles for county business purposes only.
- Require lobbyists to file registration forms and declare their clients.
- Open cabinet meetings of the executive branch to the public.
- Limit campaign-financing contributions from any one donor to $5,000 for countywide races and $2,000 for council district races.
- Formalize ethics training requirements and make training a prerequisite to employment. This requirement specifies that all county elected officials, appointed officers, and employees will attend one hour of training every two years "regarding their ethical duties." Employees are awarded four hours of additional vacation during the year the training is received.
- Require all county employees to subscribe to an ethics statement.

Source: Jensen 2004; Anderson 2004.

9. prohibiting employees from using county resources in connection with any political activity. (See Chapter 2.07 County Ethics Code, Salt Lake County, Utah, at ordlink.com/codes/saltlkco/ for more details.)

These measures have placed Salt Lake County on a solid ethics management path. They acknowledge that ethics and integrity in governance are important and require the commitment of county resources to building a strong ethical climate. While they take a legalistic approach to ethical governance they recognize that this approach is not sufficient, thus the requirement for ethics training for all officials and employees.

It is difficult to say whether Salt Lake County leaders have learned from ethical failure, although the signs are promising. Will they be enough to instill a vibrant ethical culture in Salt Lake County governance? Maybe. But it will take time, perhaps a decade, before a firm conclusion can be drawn.

Cook County, Illinois

Cook County is the fourth-largest county in the United States with a population of more than five million, of which 2.9 million reside within the city limits of Chicago, the county seat. In addition to Chicago, some 132 municipalities also call Cook County home. The county is governed by a seventeen-member Board of County Commissioners and an at-large elected (commissioner) county president who serves as the board's chief executive officer. Other independently elected county officials include the assessor, Board of Review commissioners, county clerk, clerk of the circuit court, recorder of deeds, sheriff, states attorney, and treasurer.

Like the city, the county has not enjoyed a reputation for ethics and integrity. Stories of patronage, political payoffs, and other skullduggery are legendary. Among the more infamous events was the FBI's Operation Greylord, an undercover operation in the 1980s that brought to justice seventeen county judges, forty-eight lawyers, eight policemen, ten deputy sheriffs, eight court officials, and one state legislator for receiving or giving bribes.[14]

By 1993, the county recognized the need for an ethics infrastructure by adopting Ethics Ordinance 04–0–18, which has been amended three times— most recently in 2004. The Ethics Ordinance covers gifts and proper disclosure of gifts, conflicts of interest, improper influence, dual employment, confidential information, campaign contributions, nepotism, political activity, post-employment, and use of county-owned property. The 2004 amendment brought the county into line with the recently (2003) enacted Illinois State Officials and Employees Ethics Act. It also reinstates the Board of Ethics authority to initiate investigations and mandates ethics education of senior administrative staff and elected officials.

The board is composed of five members appointed by the president of the County Board of Commissioners, with the advice and consent of the County Board. The Board of Ethics is under the jurisdiction of the president's office and is responsible for implementing and enforcing the Ethics Ordinance (93–0–29). Staff performs this responsibility by investigating complaints, issuing advisory opinions, and conducting employee training seminars. Monthly public meetings are held to discuss cases and issues brought to its attention.[15]

Advisory Opinions

City employees, contractors, and officials and candidates for office can obtain advisory opinions based on real or hypothetical situations from the board. Citizens cannot make a request for an opinion unless they have personal or direct involvement in the subject matter of the request. This provision eliminates the possibility of a citizen acting on hearsay or a media story. The name of the person making a request as well as any person named in the request is treated as confidential by the board. Advisory opinions are made public, although the names of the individuals involved are not disclosed.

Investigations

A written complaint is required to initiate an investigation into alleged wrongdoing. The executive director then decides if there is reasonable cause to initiate an investigation. Once reasonable cause is determined, an investigation, which could include interviews and the issuance of subpoenas, is initiated. The board may call for a hearing if it deems it helpful to the investigation. Upon finding a violation, a report is prepared and presented to the person who is the subject of the complaint and appropriate officials or administrators. Disciplinary recommendations are also forwarded to the president or other county official.

This ethics infrastructure—ordinance, board, advisory opinions, investigation—has put the county on a footing for deterring and reacting to wrongdoing. However, there are gaps in the county's ethics management. These include limited transparency (for example, no annual reports or statistical information are made available on the county's Web site) and no county protection for or encouragement given to potential whistle blowers. The advisory function of the Board of Ethics is impressive, but the confidentiality blanket makes it difficult for the public to know what is happening. The ethics management initiatives remain a work in progress.

Unified Government of Wyandotte County and Kansas City, Kansas

In 1997, the voters of Wyandotte County (population 157,091) and Kansas City (population 146,866) overwhelmingly voted in favor of consolidation. As the population figures indicate, the vast majority of Wyandotte County residents live in Kansas City proper. Motivating the reformers was the widespread view that both city and county governments were corrupt. The Unified Government (UG) replaced the seven-member city council and three-member county commission with an eleven-member Board of Commissioners, with the eleventh member elected countywide as the mayor. The mayor has veto power, can vote in the event of a tie on the commission, and appoints the county administrator with the consent of the commission.

Ethics Commission

The 1997 governmental reform created a five-member ethics commission with an appointed part-time ethics administrator. The commission and the administrator are completely independent of the UG. The commission members are appointed by the administrative judge of Wyandotte County District Court, and the Ethics Administrator is appointed by the legislative auditor. The UG contracted with the University of Kansas to serve as the Ethics Administrator. Professor H. George Frederickson, a well-known ethics specialist, was appointed the administrator.

The Unified Government adopted a Code of Ethics by ordinance (Number 0–25–98) on May 21, 1998. The code covers all UG elected officials and employees. The topics covered are conflicts of interest, gift solicitation and acceptance, post-employment, gratuities, nepotism, political activities, and whistle blowing. Alleged violations of the code are investigated by the Ethics Administrator when directed by the commission to do so. The commission may subpoena documents and witnesses and render a decision regarding a violation. Once a violation is determined, the administrator is empowered to recommend corrective action to the legislative auditor in the form of a censure. Such corrective action can include recommendations for demotion or other administrative measures and/or referring the matter to the district attorney if there is reasonable belief that a crime has been committed. The Ethics Administrator is also authorized to render advisory opinions when requested in writing. Opinions when rendered are binding. A popular confidential ethics hotline is an additional tool employed by the Ethics Administrator to provide UG "officials and employees with a reliable source of advice on ethical dilemmas" (Manske and Frederickson 2004). The hotline also serves as a medium for reporting allegations of wrongdoing.

Ethics Training

The Ethics Administrator is also responsible for ethics training for all UG officials and the 2,200 employees. Training is mandatory for new employees and newly elected officials within one year of assuming their position. Moreover, all employees and elected officials must undergo "refresher" ethics training once every three years. While the training emphasizes the UG Code of Ethics, it goes beyond the typical, narrow "gotcha" approach. The Ethics Administrator and a colleague describe the curriculum for the ethics education program as

> carefully constructed to facilitate meaningful instruction in ethical conduct. The formal language of the code of ethics has been restated in an easy-to-understand format, and ethical-dilemma cases have been developed to present clear—yet challenging—vehicles through which practical application may be enhanced. (Manske and Frederickson 2004, 20)

The continuing education of officials and employees emphasizes topical, in-depth analysis of current ethical issues. "Employees," Manske and Frederickson (20) assert, "do not simply relearn the previous lessons."

An additional innovative aspect of the strategy adopted by the UG is the ethics pledge and oath. The pledge contains ten items that, when signed by the official and/or employee, signifies his or her commitment to honor the pledge. It obligates the employee to treating his or her office as a public trust—a true Jeffersonian legacy. The oath is a brief signatory statement:

> I do solemnly swear that I will support the Constitution of the United States and the Constitution of the State of Kansas, and faithfully discharge the duties of _____ , and to abide by and adhere to the provisions of the Code of Ethics of the Unified Government of Wyandotte County-Kansas City, Kansas. So help me God.

Although it may be premature to pass judgment on the success of the strategy adopted by the Unified Government of Wyandotte County, the indicators are very positive. County Administrator Dennis Hays claims that

> since the consolidation of governments in 1997, the public's trust and confidence in the government have increased dramatically. I am proud that there has been no public wrongdoing; however, should something arise with the proactive avoidance through the ethics program, a swift and unbiased judgment will be made. (Manske and Frederickson 2004, 21)

And, former Kansas lieutenant governor Gary Sherrer says:

> Throughout my public life and private life, I have never been part of such a dramatic political, social, and economical change as what has occurred in Wyandotte County. While ethics alone would not have produced all that has been achieved, all that has been achieved would not have been accomplished without the strong emphasis on ethical behavior. (Manske and Frederickson 2004, 22)

The secret of a sound local government ethics program, according to Manske and Frederickson (22), rests on an integrated approach that contains four essential elements:

1. Independence and autonomy, which, in the case of the UG, is completely outside of the government.
2. Confidentiality in the treatment of allegations and investigations.
3. Trust by citizens, officials, employees, and unions that the administrators of the ethics program are approachable, fair, just, and reasonable.
4. An approach that promotes good and honest local government rather than an approach that emphasizes an attitude of "gotcha" when misconduct occurs.

Jacksonville–Duval County, Florida

Duval County (817,480) merged with the City of Jacksonville (735,617) government in 1968. The merger was triggered by political corruption and scandal involving a city commissioner who was indicted by a Duval County grand jury for accepting bribes to influence city purchases of mechanical equipment. The new consolidated City of Jacksonville government coexists alongside four municipalities that were not included in the consolidation.

The charter also set forth a Code of Ethics (Article 20) that applied to all officers and employees of the new government, including the Duval County board of public instruction. The key components of the code were (1) conflicts of interest, including the improper disclosure of confidential information to advance the financial interest of an officer or others, (2) financial disclosure of interest in any contract or matter pending before the consolidated government, (3) use of public property for personal benefit prohibited, and (4) employees participation in political campaigns disallowed during duty hours.

The seven-member civil service board was designated as the Board of

Ethics and charged to enforce the code. The Board of Ethics could issue advisory opinions, hear and investigate complaints alleging violations of the code, subpoena witnesses, administer oaths, and take testimony. An officer or employee found guilty of violating the code could be reprimanded, suspended, reduced in rank, or removed from office. The board could not, however, remove an elected official. This power was reserved for the city council.

This minimalist, "gotcha" approach in Jacksonville did not produce much in the way of ethical governance. In the early 1980s, corruption once more in city hall became the focus of a federal investigation. Further mischief in the late 1980s resulted in the state attorney convening a grand jury to investigate wrongdoing. Several years later, the state attorney was elected mayor on a platform of ethics reform. Thus, in the mid-1990s, a committee of lawyers hammered out a new code that was enacted in June 1999. The code's authors asserted that the new code "will position Jacksonville as a national leader in governmental ethics." Highlights of the code are:

- The establishment of aspirational goals for the conduct of city employees. The development of ethics in city government, the code states, must be more than the "avoidance of criminal behavior but the creation of a government that has the trust and respect of its citizens."[16] City employees "are considered stewards of the public's trust and should aspire to the highest level of integrity and character."[17]
- The creation of an Ethics Officer who has responsibility for encouraging compliance with the code, coordinating ethics training, and developing citywide programs for achieving the aspirational goals (see exhibit 4.8).
- The initiation of ethics training for city employees and an "Ethics in Government Program" for elected officials.
- The restructuring of the Ethics Commission into a quasi-independent nine-member body with term limits and the expansion of its role "in monitoring compliance with training requirements and financial and gift disclosure reporting requirements."

Ethics training is a high priority in Jacksonville's consolidated government. All new employees are trained on the first day of employment. "We also train existing employees monthly through our Departmental Ethics Officers," says Co-Ethics officer Carla Miller (2005). "We pick a topic, like campaign laws, discuss it in our Departmental Ethics Officer meetings," and then the Ethics Officers get it out to their staff. The Jacksonville Ethics Commission Annual *Compliance Report 2004* notes that the training department offered two ethics classes, one on "Character Counts" and the other an "In-

> **Exhibit 4.8**
> **Jacksonville Ethics Officer's Responsibilities**
>
> - Conduct periodic meetings with the department director, senior management, and employee groups to discuss or provide advice on ethics issues.
> - Conduct a review of and disseminate within his or her department the appropriate city and department policies and regulations that relate to the Code of Ethics for employees.
> - Assist the city ethics officer(s) in the formulation of ethics awareness training sessions, conferences, and seminars that are developed for and presented to department employees.
> - Assist the department head in the development of an overall internal ethics plan.
> - Report compliance with the ethics code to the city ethics officer(s).
> - Make recommendations for improvement in training to the city ethics officer.
> - Accomplish such other duties as are delegated by the city ethics officer(s), including conducting investigations or complaints as authorized by the city ethics officer(s).
>
> *Source:* www.coj.net/Departments.

troduction to Ethics." Additionally, a two-day seminar on "Ethics in Public Service" was presented by a well-known ethics expert, Michael Josephson of the Josephson Institute of Ethics.

Enforcement of the Code of Ethics is the responsibility of the Ethics Commission, and while the commission has wide latitude to investigate possible violations of the standard of conduct for city officers and employees, the commission has no authority to levy penalties. "The ethics commission," Miller asserts, "was not given power to handle specific violations—only to investigate generally and recommend legislation to city council." As the Internal Operating Rules of the Jacksonville Ethics Commission state, "the Ethics Commission is not vested with the authority to determine whether specific violations have occurred for purposes of entering sanctions or penalties." Who then does have this authority? The answer is the state attorney. How many code violations has the state attorney handled over the past five years? None. Does this mean that the new code with its emphasis on aspirational goals is working well? Perhaps. The consolidated government does appear to be on the road to strong ethics management.

The ethics management approach launched in 1999 has put the City of Jacksonville on a forward looking path toward recognizing that ethical governance requires more than laws and penalties. Co-Ethics officer Carla Miller, who also served as the first chair of the revitalized Board of Ethics, notes that "it is easy enough to lecture people about the laws in existence, but much harder to instruct on the basics of ethics and ways to develop an ethical culture" (2005).

Georgia's Cities of Ethics

The Georgia Municipal Association (GMA) initiated an innovative, voluntary program in 1999 to encourage Georgia's 531 cities and towns to seek certification as a "City of Ethics." There are 173 cities (as of June 2006) that have received this designation. Georgia Municipal Association executive director Jim Higdon explains that this "indicates that cities in Georgia are committed to honest, ethical government" and wish to earn and maintain the public's trust in government.[18]

What does a city have to do to qualify as a "Certified City of Ethics?" They must (1) adopt a resolution subscribing to specific ethics principles and (2) adopt an ethics ordinance. The resolution must embrace five ethics principles recommended by a GMA task force of public- and private-sector leaders (see exhibit 4.9).

The GMA Board requires that the ethics ordinance "contain definitions, an enumeration of permissible and impermissible activities by elected officials, due process procedures for elected officials charged with a violation of the ordinance and punishment provisions for those elected officials found in violation of the ordinance."[19] Some Georgia cities have given their ethics boards the power to fine offenders, although there is uncertainty about whether such sanctions are beyond the legal authority of the board. The GMA contends that while "this punishment might seem obvious and even fitting given that the ethics board polices conflicts of interest and misappropriation," it may be the more prudent position for a board of ethics to provide for public reprimands (Georgia Municipal Association 2005, 44).

To help small and large cities develop a resolution and ordinance, the GMA has made available a sample resolution and recommends that municipalities fashion an ethics ordinance that best fits their community. City leaders are advised to consult the model provided by the International Municipal Lawyers Association and those in other Georgia municipalities such as Marietta, Roswell, and Smyrna. Once a municipality passes an ethics resolu-

---

Exhibit 4.9
The Five Ethics Principles Recommended
by the Georgia Municipal Association

- Serve others, not ourselves.
- Use resources with efficiency and economy.
- Treat all people fairly.
- Use the power of our position for the well-being of our constituents.
- Create an environment of honesty, openness, and integrity.

Source: Georgia Municipal Association

---

tion and ordinance, it submits these documents to the GMA for review and approval by the Executive Committee of the GMA City Attorneys Section. When certified as a City of Ethics, a municipality receives "a plaque and a logo which can be incorporated into city stationery, road signs and other materials at the city's discretion."[20]

The Georgia Municipal Association's Certified City of Ethics program is a creative and innovative effort to promote ethics and integrity in local governance. Indeed, the popularity of the program is reflected by the 173 cities that have received this designation since 1999 when the program was initiated. Moreover, this statistic is testimony to the interest and commitment that city officials have in strengthening local governance. But are a resolution and an ordinance sufficient? Perhaps, but there are other challenges that must be met to put into place a truly effective, comprehensive ethics management program, one of which is building an ethical organizational culture.

Challenges to Ethical Governance in Cities and Counties

Five challenges must be overcome to bring about ethical governance in cities and counties. First, city and county leaders must *acknowledge* that ethics and integrity in governance are important. This challenge may appear to be "so what." After all, isn't this a given? No, many local government officials and others presume that since cities and counties are often subject to state ethics laws, there is no need to be especially attuned to ethics and integrity in governance. State ethics laws typically cover nepotism, conflicts of interest, and financial disclosure. In short, most states have enacted ethics laws that are minimal in their coverage and consequences. Thus, insofar as cities and counties do not set ethical standards higher than the state requires, they are on the low road to ethics and integrity in governance. Both cities and counties need to move beyond the low standards established by state laws in order to be responsive to citizen expectations and to meet the demands of modern professional management.

The second challenge is to *recognize* that ethics and integrity in local governance are not limited to a single organization or a single category of employees. American counties in particular, with few exceptions, are loosely coupled collections of organizations with many different kinds of employees, administrators, and elected officials. This hydra-headed reality means that a piecemeal approach to ethical governance is not likely to succeed. That is, it is not sufficient to put forward a code of ethics or training or orientation program that covers only one of a county's many units such as the administrative staff or the clerk's office or the sheriff's office or the auditor's office or the assessor's office or the property appraiser's office. Employees, appointed professional administrators, and elected officials must be included in a comprehensive approach to ethics. This approach also ensures equal treatment of all those who work in county government, regardless of position and power.

The third challenge is to *commit* sufficient resources to building and sustaining integrity in local governance. Neither city nor county governments are in the business of producing ethical governance. Rather, they are producers of valuable public services ranging from those mandated by the state—taxation, property assessment, roads, and vital statistics to those services demanded by citizens, for example, parks and recreation, marinas, golf courses, solid waste collection and disposal, and air and water quality. These goods and services consume the vast majority of local revenues. Moreover, these service needs and demands are in competition with one another for vital resources, and there are typically never sufficient funds in a city or county budget to meet all of the services that are needed or desired. In other words, local officials can and often do feel that spending scarce tax dollars on ethics and integrity is a low priority when funds for vital services are in real or imagined short supply. This view, of course, ignores the distressing reality that corruption is a major cause of a waste of resources.

The fourth challenge is to *avoid* a narrow rules and regulations approach to ethics in local governance. Remember the old saw "there ought to be a law!" Problems, this old bromide suggests, can be best dealt with by passing a law. Laws, ordinances, codes, and new or stricter personnel policies are too often viewed as quick fixes or solutions to problems that occur. Cities and counties that move along this path and do nothing more are candidates for "feel good ethics." A comprehensive management strategy that fosters ethical governance demands more than a new ordinance or a revised personnel manual. Rather, what is required is an integration of standards into all aspects of management and policy as well as unquestionable leadership commitment to the new culture of invigorated ethics standards.

The fifth challenge is to *learn* from ethics failures. Governance is a people-driven enterprise. Yes, technology, machinery, and more are the tools needed to carry out the work of governance, but it is human beings who make decisions day in and day out—24/7—that affect the lives of residents. And human beings have ethical lapses, sometimes egregious and other times minor or modest. These failures are part and parcel of modern organizational life. Cities and counties that are truly committed to building and sustaining ethical governance must be able to learn from failures and scandal and be able to take corrective actions. Responding to even scandal as a one-time occurrence may result in short-term fixes but will not be sufficient in building and sustaining a culture that embraces ethics and integrity in local governance. Public officials must adopt an open mind and learn from ethics failures. Scandal might trigger ethics reform, but if reform measures simply become standard bureaucratic operating procedures, little can be achieved in effecting genuine change. Organizations that do not learn do not grow and do not become agents for building integrity in local governance.

Next Steps

What more should local government leaders do to meet the challenge of ethical governance? Above all, they must commit themselves to a comprehensive strategy, and they must stay the course. An ethics summit or other forum could be arranged as a first step in recognizing that ethics and integrity in governance are important. Additionally, a Code of Ethics and/or a statement of principles should be adopted that applies to all employees, elected and appointed. At the county level, this group of employees should include all agencies, including the constitutional officers. The development of a code and/or statement of principles should strike a balance between ethical aspirations and the practical reality of day-to-day work.

Management should emphasize training and employee development programs. Employees in all types of organizations are vulnerable to ethical lapses. Thus, a continuous, ongoing training program amplifies the message that ethics matters. Managers must provide organizational members with clear guidelines for proper behavior, what the bottom line is if an ethical lapse occurs, and how to make ethics behavior an ordinary work habit.

An ethics audit could be equally valuable, perhaps invaluable as a benchmark for tracking changes in the organizational culture. An audit, whether based on a survey of employees or an assessment of occupational vulnerability, should be conducted periodically. City Manager Steve Bonczek (1998) strongly supports the use of an audit to let employees know the positive as well as the negative effects of their efforts.

Government leaders must advocate and embrace transparency in the work of national, state, and city-county offices and agencies. Sunshine laws and whistle-blowing ordinances can contribute to transparency but are often insufficient. Top officials must encourage subordinates to carry out their work with full disclosure, citizen access, and a tolerance for competing claims.

Conclusion

Two key themes identified in chapter 1 are amply illustrated in this chapter. First, scandal is the trigger that motivated ethics management initiatives in many local governments. Scandals that plagued Tampa, Chicago, New York City, King County, Jacksonville, Miami-Dade County, Cook County, and Salt Lake County motivated public officials to take corrective action. Second, ethics management strategies vary a great deal among the local governments examined here. But nearly all share a strong legal compliance orientation. There are exceptions, however, with the Unified Government of Wyandotte County and Kansas City, Kansas, being the most notable.

Is ethical local governance achievable? Without question. Indeed, many local governments, as evidenced by the 173 communities in Georgia, embrace ethics and integrity in governance. Yet more can and must join in to ensure that democracy, justice, and the pursuit of happiness are more than hollow words. Local governance is, after all, the bedrock upon which the American experiment with democracy rests.

Ethics Management Skill Building

Practicum 4.1. What to Do?

Imagine that you are the county sheriff in a large (one million) urban, high-growth county where you have served as a popular, elected county sheriff for twenty years. To your dismay, you are informed that one of your sergeants who has served the county for many years is charged with 129 counts of falsification of official documents, 144 counts of failure to follow standard operating procedures, and conduct unbecoming a member of the sheriff's office—charges made by your internal affairs investigators. The deputy, as it turns out, coordinates all the work at the port authority and is in a position to log off-duty assignments for himself at the port that far exceed regular work-week hours. The investigators charge that the sergeant knowingly cooked the books and overrode computer programs to prevent others from knowing what he did.

The sergeant's supervisor wants him suspended for thirty days and reduced to the rank of deputy. The disciplinary review board wants him fired. You are about to retire and don't need to worry about being reelected. The allegations against the sergeant have been published in the local newspaper.

Questions

1. What would you do with the sergeant? Would you put a letter of reprimand in his personnel file? Ban him from working any off-duty assignments? Suspend him? Reduce him in rank? Fire him?
2. How would you size up the implications of your decision for the morale of the uniformed officers under your command?
3. What are the implications for the ethical climate of your organization?

Practicum 4.2. Ethics Challenges in Disasters[21]

On August 29, 2005, Hurricane Katrina made landfall near New Orleans. A day or two later, the levees protecting the city (New Orleans actually sits below sea level) were breeched and water spewed into the streets and residences, flooding nearly all of the city with some water levels reaching eighteen to twenty feet. As conditions worsened, law and order broke down. Looters sacked stores and gangs roamed the streets. The New Orleans police force of 1,500 was overwhelmed by the lawlessness with scores of police officers off duty or cut off by the storm and floodwaters. Some police officers, estimated to be as many as 500, either walked off of their posts in the days after the storm or otherwise couldn't be accounted for. Many experienced enormous stress and distress as the rising floodwaters endangered their lives as well as the lives of their families and loved ones. Other officers reported dodging sniper bullets as they rescued victims. The city's police superintendent put it this way: "I had officers in boats who were being shot at as they were pulling people out of the water." Two officers committed suicide.

Questions

1. Assume you are the New Orleans Chief of Police. What explanations do you have for the failure of some police officers to carry out their duties? Was this an ethical failure of the individuals? The NOPD? Something else?
2. How would you deal with the stress experienced by NOPD officers?

Raise their pay? Hire counselors? Send them to Las Vegas for a five-day vacation? Give them time off to visit relatives? None of the above?

3. What would you do to discourage desertions by police officers in the event of a disaster? Would you launch a major ethics training program? Emphasize a code of ethics? Hire a consultant to assess the organization's culture? Nothing, as this is a matter of duty?

Notes

1. This section draws in part from Menzel (2006).

2. See www.kcmo.org/index.htm. Accessed June 23, 2006.

3. See www.sannet.gov. Accessed June 23, 2006.

4. See www.losgatosca.gov/ Accessed June 23, 2006.

5. See municode.com/Resources/gateway.asp?pid=12870&sid=14. Accessed June 23, 2006.

6. See www.metro.net/about_us/ethics/codes.htm. Accessed June 23, 2006

7. See www.mta.info/mta/procurement/vendor-code.htm. Accessed June 23, 2006.

8. Sec. 2–548, Division 2.Conflicts of Interest, City of Tampa Ethics Code.

9. Sec. 2–621, Division 2.Conflicts of Interest, City of Tampa Ethics Code.

10. Sec. 2–501, Purpose and Legislative Intent, Division 1.Generally, City of Tampa Ethics Code.

11. Chapter 2–156, Municipal Code of Chicago.

12. The statistics reported here are drawn from the 2003 and 2004 Annual Report of the City of New York, Conflict of Interest Board. www.Nyc.gov/ethics. Accessed June 23, 2006.

13. See www.metrokc.gov/ethics/history.aspx. Accessed June 23, 2006.

14. See www.fbi.gov/page2/march04/greylord031504.htm. Accessed June 23, 2006.

15. See www.co.cook.il.us/secretary/HomePage_Links/whats_cookin_in_cook_county_book. Accessed June 23, 2006.

16. City of Jacksonville Ethics Code, I.

17. Part X, 602.1001, City of Jacksonville Ethics Code, I.

18. See www.gmanet.com/general/default.asp?pagetype=cities_of_ethics_certified&menuid=CitiesOfEthicsID. Accessed March 6, 2006.

19. See www.gmanet.com/data/html/cities_of_ethics.html. Accessed June 23, 2006.

20. See www.gmanet.com/data/html/cities_of_ethics.html. Accessed June 23, 2006.

21. Treaster and Desantis (2005).

5

Federal and State Ethics Management

"As I look back over the years, I see that
I had lost sight of my ethical judgment."
—former Connecticut governor John G. Rowland

Ethics management in the U.S. government and the American states is like a two-sided coin. On one side is the effort to discourage and deter unethical behaviors and practices; on the other is the effort to encourage and inspire ethical behaviors and practices. All too often, however, the discourage-and-deter side is emphasized while little attention is given to the encourage-and-inspire side. The result is a spate of laws and statutes with lengthy accompanying rules and regulations that prescribe and proscribe acceptable behaviors and what might happen to those who dare, wittingly or unwittingly, to cross over the "do not do" line.

This chapter surveys legislative and administrative measures taken by the U.S. government and the fifty states to promote ethics and integrity in governance. And, where possible, an assessment is offered about how well or poorly these efforts have fared. We begin with a look at the actions emanating from the federal government and then move to the states, with a close look at three states—Florida, Illinois, and New York.

Federal Ethics Laws

A variety of statutes govern the conduct of federal employees with the oldest statute, dating from the Civil War era, aimed at curbing abuses in government procurement. A variety of executive branch agencies, including the Executive Office of the President, the U.S. Department of Justice, Inspectors General, the Merit Systems Protection Board, the Office of Special Counsel, the General Services Administration, the Office of Personnel Management, the Federal Elections Commission, and the General Accountability Office, have ethics responsibilities,

The two most significant federal statutes are the Ethics in Government Act of 1978 and the Ethics Reform Act of 1989. The 1978 act followed on the heels of the Watergate crisis of the early 1970s. This legislation established the U.S. Office of Government Ethics within the Office of Personnel Management and "charged it with providing overall leadership and direction for the ethics program within the executive branch" (Gilman 1995a). The 1978 act also "established a comprehensive public financial disclosure system for all three branches of the Federal Government" (1995a). Additionally, this legislation authorized the president to appoint an independent special prosecutor to investigate high-profile cases. Do you recall Ken Starr and the Clinton/Lewinsky scandal?

The Ethics Reform Act of 1989 expanded previous legislation in several areas. Post-employment restrictions were applied to members of Congress and top congressional staff. Moreover, the public financial disclosure system was strengthened by "authorizing all three branches of government to implement a system of confidential financial reporting" (Gilman 1995a). The prohibition on solicitation and acceptance of gifts was expanded to include all three branches. Yet other provisions dealt with limitations on outside earned income and compensation received for service as an officer or board member of an association or corporation. Further, the 1989 act placed restrictions on the compensation that a federal official might receive for teaching without prior notification and approval of the appropriate ethics office.

Other federal legislation that should be noted is the Office of Government Ethics Reauthorization Act of 1988, the Whistleblower Protection Act of 1989, and the Lobbying Disclosure Act of 1995. The Lobbying Disclosure Act (P.L. 104–65) was signed into law by President Clinton on December 19, 1995, and took effect January 1, 1996. The act expanded the definition of who a lobbyist is, thereby greatly "increasing the number of registered lobbyists and the amount of information they must disclose" (Tenebaum 2002). Failure to comply with the act can result in a civil fine up to $50,000.

The Whistleblower Protection Act of 1989 established the Office of Special Counsel (OSC) as an independent agency within the executive branch to receive complaints and "safeguard the merit system by protecting federal employees and applicants from prohibited personnel practices, especially reprisal for whistleblowing."[1] The OSC is a small agency with 106 employees who are primarily personnel management specialists, investigators, and attorneys. The act was amended in 1994 with the passage of Public Law 103–424, which expanded the coverage to some government corporations and employees in the Veterans Administration.

Some critics point out that while the U.S. whistle-blowing regulatory system is a positive development, there is still much room for improvement. The current approach, according to Groeneweg (2001), is based heavily on how much money is saved by blowing the whistle on misconduct, fraud, or abuse of authority. She asserts that the U.S. system is reactive, not proactive, and therefore puts the whistle blower's career in a precarious situation. Most important, "at its core, the U.S. model displays the failure to focus on the spirit of whistleblower protections" (15). Roberta Ann Johnson (2003, 21) in *Whistleblowing* adds: "Studies of whistleblower protection suggest that the protection offered is far from perfect."

The U.S. Office of Government Ethics

The Office of Government Ethics Reauthorization Act of 1998 is significant because it removed the Office of Government Ethics (OGE) from the Office of Personnel Management and established it as a separate executive agency. The director is appointed to a five-year term by the president with the consent of the Senate. The office has no investigatory powers and does not serve the legislative or judicial branches of government. OGE has three primary functions: (1) to manage the public financial disclosure reporting system for presidential appointees confirmed by the Senate and Designated Agency Ethics Officials, (2) to conduct program reviews of "headquarters and regional offices to determine whether an agency has an effective ethics program tailored to its mission," and (3) to "develop and provide ethics training courses and materials for executive branch departments and agencies"[2] (see exhibit 5.1).

Each executive agency has a Designated Agency Ethics Official (DAEO) tasked with supporting the agency's ethics program and with whom OGE primarily deals. There are 125 DAEOs who provide guidance on how to interpret and comply with conflict-of-interest regulations, standards-of-conduct regulations, and financial disclosure policies and procedures. As might be surmised, knowing how to stay out of trouble in the executive branch of the U.S. government has become a major challenge given the numerous rules and regulations regarding unacceptable practices and behaviors. Thus, a primary mission of the OGE is to help federal employees comply with those rules and regulations so that they can avoid intentional and unintentional ethical lapses.

The development of a clear set of ethical standards for officers and employees of the executive branch was initiated in January 1989, when President George H. W. Bush issued Executive Order (EO) 12668. The president's EO established the Commission on Federal Ethics Law Reform that in turn produced a report, "To Serve with Honor." The report made twenty-seven recommendations, including a recommendation that a "1965 executive order prescribing the standards of conduct be revised and that the Office of Government Ethics be directed to consolidate all executive branch standards of conduct in a single set of regulations" (Gilman 1995a). A second Executive

---

Exhibit 5.1
Who Is Responsible for Investigating
the Alleged Misconduct of Federal Employees?

The inspector general of the department or agency involved and, when necessary, the Federal Bureau of Investigation of the Department of Justice. The sixty-four inspectors general (IG) in the executive branch of the U.S. government conduct the majority of investigations into government wrongdoing. In addition they also coordinate investigations with their regular financial and management audits of federal agencies and programs. The coordinating body for the inspectors general is the President's Council on Integrity and Efficiency (PCIE), of which the Office of Government Ethics is a member.

Source: www.usoge.gov/pages/misc_files/faq.html.

Order 12674 (April 12, 1989—See exhibit 5.2) set forth fourteen principles of ethical conduct for government officers and employees and directed the Office of Government Ethics to "promulgate a single, comprehensive, and clear set of executive branch standards of conduct that shall be objective, reasonable and enforceable" (Gilman 1995a). In August 1992, the OGE issued a final rule promulgating standards of conduct for executive branch employees, effective February 3, 1993.

The ethics infrastructure in place in the executive branch of United States government is built on rules, regulations, enforcement, education, and more. There is both good news and bad news here. Rule-driven ethics management with its legal compliance overtones is regarded by many ethicists as reactive and punitive—a minimalist approach. Moreover, it can cause major disruptions in an agency. Consider the National Institutes of Health initiatives offered by Director Elias A. Zerhouni in early 2005 to force NIH staff to divest their holdings in drug and biotechnology companies. Six thousand employees among the agency's 18,000 would have been affected had the director not backed off of the rules in August 2005. Threats of high-level defections and 1,300 mostly critical comments by employees about the proposed rules motivated the director to loosen the conflict-of-interest rules (Connolly 2005). Rules are inescapable, but a more comprehensive and inclusive approach requires officials to lead with integrity and find avenues to motivate public service employees and professionals "to serve with honor," as the 1989 President's Commission on Federal Ethics Law Reform report reads.

Exhibit 5.2
Principles of Ethical Conduct for
Government Officers and Employees

By virtue of the authority vested in me as President by the Constitution and the laws of the United States of America, and in order to establish fair and exacting standards of ethical conduct for all executive branch employees, it is hereby ordered as follows:

Part I. Principles of Ethical Conduct

Section 101. Principles of Ethical Conduct. To ensure that every citizen can have complete confidence in the integrity of the Federal Government, each Federal employee shall respect and adhere to the fundamental principles of ethical service as implemented in regulations promulgated under sections 201 and 301 of this order:

(a)   Public service is a public trust, requiring employees to place loyalty to the Constitution, the laws, and ethical principles above private gain.

(b)   Employees shall not hold financial interests that conflict with the conscientious performance of duty.

(c)   Employees shall not engage in financial transactions using nonpublic Government information or allow the improper use of such information to further any private interest.

(d)   An employee shall not, except pursuant to such reasonable exceptions as are provided by regulation, solicit or accept any gift or other item of monetary value from any person or entity seeking official action from, doing business with, or conducting activities regulated by the employee's agency, or whose interests may be substantially affected by the performance or nonperformance of the employee's duties.

(e)   Employees shall put forth honest effort in the performance of their duties.

(f)   Employees shall make no unauthorized commitments or promises of any kind purporting to bind the Government.

(g)   Employees shall not use public office for private gain.

(h)   Employees shall act impartially and not give preferential treatment to any private organization or individual.

(continued)

Exhibit 5.1 *(continued)*

(i)   Employees shall protect and conserve Federal property and shall not use it for other than authorized activities.

(j)   Employees shall not engage in outside employment or activities, including seeking or negotiating for employment, that conflict with official Government duties and responsibilities.

(k)   Employees shall disclose waste, fraud, abuse, and corruption to appropriate authorities.

(l)   Employees shall satisfy in good faith their obligations as citizens, including all just financial obligations, especially those such as Federal, State, or local taxes that are imposed by law.

(m)   Employees shall adhere to all laws and regulations that provide equal opportunity for all Americans regardless of race, color, religion, sex, national origin, age, or handicap.

(n)   Employees shall endeavor to avoid any actions creating the appearance that they are violating the law or the ethical standards promulgated pursuant to this order.

Source: Executive Order 12674 of April 12, 1989 (as modified by E.O. 12731).

Presidents[3]

Do the "Principles of Ethical Conduct for Government Officers and Employees" apply to presidents? Surely, one might think. But life in the White House can be more challenging than one might suppose. Consider President Lyndon B. Johnson (1963–1968) and the conduct of the Vietnam War. The military buildup in Vietnam proceeded steadily in the 1960s despite repeated claims by the president that the United States did not want to escalate the conflict. As Daniel Ellsberg, a member of the State Department who gained notoriety when he leaked the Pentagon papers to the *Washington Post*, recalls: "On election day 1964 I spent the day with an interagency working group to expand the war—contrary to Lyndon Johnson's assertion that the administration seeks no wider war" (Ellsberg 2004). Did President Johnson lie to the American public?

LBJ's successor, President Richard M. Nixon, had his own problems when he engaged in a conspiracy to cover up the trail of misdeeds and criminal wrongdoing when political operatives broke into the Democratic headquar-

President John F. Kennedy made ethics a major policy theme of his administration. An ethics czar was appointed to work with the head of the Civil Service Commission. Executive Order 10939, issued May 5, 1961, established conflict-of-interest standards for presidential nominees and appointees, including members of the White House staff.

ters at the Watergate Hotel in 1972. Two years later, in August 1974, President Nixon resigned from office rather than face impeachment by the House of Representatives.

Fast-forward to the 1980s. President Ronald Reagan found himself in a difficult position as his administration attempted to aid Contra rebels in Nicaragua who were attempting to oust the Socialist-led government. Reagan's national security advisor John Poindexter and Poindexter's underling Lt. Colonel Oliver L. North took it upon themselves to sell arms to Iran to secure money to support the Contra rebels—a clear violation of law. Did President Reagan know about this transaction? He claims he didn't. The Iran-Contra controversy certainly raised the possibility that President Reagan lied.

President Bill Clinton (1992–2000) took the ethical high ground immediately upon taking office by requiring senior members of his administration to take a "five-year" pledge that they would not represent private parties in dealing with the government after leaving office. Executive Order 12834, "Ethics Commitments by Executive Branch Employees," President Clinton hoped, would put an end to the employment revolving door and the lingering perception that the federal government was "hostage to special interests" (Gilman 1995b). Alas, a few years later, the president found himself in a legal and political morass of his own making when it became known that he had a sexual tryst with young White House intern Monica Lewinsky. The scandal grew into a political firestorm when President Clinton testified under oath that he did not have sex with Ms. Lewinsky. Many members of Congress concluded that the president lied. Consequently, the Republican-controlled House proceeded to impeach President Clinton. The Senate, however, did not convict him, that is, vote to remove him from office. Did President Clinton lie? So it would seem. Was lying under oath sufficient grounds for removal from office? No. Not surprisingly, the 2000 presidential campaign of George W. Bush promised to restore dignity to the office of the president.

President Bush has had his share of ethical issues as well. The list includes the invasion and occupation of Iraq, stem cell research, privacy rights, government secrecy, domestic spying by the National Security Agency without court approval, and charges that his administration sought political revenge by leaking information that revealed the name of CIA undercover agent

Valerie Plame. The administration's contention that Saddam Hussein possessed weapons of mass destruction, which was the rationale for the invasion, turned out to be untrue. Nor was a credible link found to exist between Iraq and the terrorists attacks of September 11, 2001. Many citizens have asked, "Did President Bush lie to the American public?"

The investigation into who leaked information about the CIA agent resulted in the indictment in 2005 of I. Lewis "Scooter" Libby, Vice President Cheney's former chief of staff, and has threatened to bring down Karl Rove, President Bush's chief political advisor. (On June 13, 2006, it was announced that special prosecuter Patrick J. Fitzgerald would not bring charges against Rove.) The CIA leak prompted President Bush in late 2005 to order mandatory ethics training for all White House staff.

President Bush, his critics assert, has turned the ethics management clock in the federal government backward as evidenced by appointments of individuals to high-ranking positions who have used their office to advance the president's political agenda over the objections of senior managers. One example can be found in a General Accountability Office report that top officials in the Food and Drug Administration ignored the recommendations of an independent advisory committee and the agency's own scientific review staff to reject an application to allow over-the-counter sales of morning-after birth control pills (Harris 2005). Similar intervention by top Department of Justice officials is reported to have taken place in the decision to reject senior staffers' advice that the redistricting of congressional districts in Texas in the early 2000s, spearheaded by House Majority Leader Tom DeLay (R), diluted minority voting rights.

No president is above the law, but these cases point to the fine line between telling the truth and knowing when to do so is in the public interest. Americans expect the president to do both. And, in the case of President George W. Bush, an increasingly skeptical public is raising its voice. A *Washington Post*–ABC News national survey conducted in October 2005 found that six in ten Americans have doubts about the president's honesty and personal integrity. *Washington Post* reporters Richard Morin and Dan Balz (2005) note that "Bush's approval ratings have been in decline for months, but on issues of personal trust, honesty and values, Bush has suffered some of his most notable declines."

Congress

While federal ethics statutes have steadily expanded the coverage of the law over the past several decades, Congress has also found it necessary to ensure that their members and top staff are engaged in appropriate behavior. As noted in chapter 2, the Founding Fathers designed a system of government that separated and divided power among institutions and officeholders. Horizontally, the separation of powers between the Congress, the president, and the judiciary sought to prevent the concentration of power. Similarly, the division of power between the central government and the states created multiple power centers. The Founding Fathers understood that men and women of ambition would seek the power of public office and, unless checked in some manner, could threaten the well-being of the republic.

House of Representatives

Over time it has become evident that other measures besides checks and balances would be needed to prevent the misuse and/or abuse of public power. For example, the Congress has found it necessary to constrain the unacceptable behavior of its own members. The Committee on Standards of Official Conduct, a ten-member bipartisan committee, is the ethics enforcer of the House of Representatives. Complaints brought to the committee are investigated if a majority finds probable cause to do so. In the event of a 5–5 Republican-Democrat deadlock, investigations automatically resume in forty-five days. In January 2005, the Republican-controlled House by a vote of 220 to 195 changed this provision so that in the event of a deadlock, ethics investigations are dismissed. The politics behind this change had to do with the behavior of the House majority leader, Representative Tom DeLay (R-Texas), who was admonished three times in 2004 for egregious behavior. By changing this deadlock rule, Republicans claimed that the House will be able to protect the members from what could be purely partisan attacks.

Democrats strongly disagreed, arguing that this change would largely make the Ethics Committee impotent. By the end of April after new revelations surfaced about Mr. DeLay's international travel supported by a lobbyist and the Democrats' vocal resistance, Speaker of the House J. Dennis Hastert of Illinois relented. By a vote of 406 to 20, the House approved a resolution that restored the rules that were in place at the beginning of the year.

The House disciplinary procedures for dealing with an alleged violation of the ethics rules are shown in exhibit 5.3.

Several highly visible members of the House from both the Democratic and Republican parties have been investigated and punished over the years. They include Newt Gingrich, Republican Speaker of the House 1994–1997, and Representative James C. Wright, Jr., a Democrat of Texas who resigned in 1989 over improper lobbying on behalf of a constituent. Flamboyant Representative Adam Clayton Powell, Jr., Democrat of New York, was fined $25,000 and excluded from his seat following his reelection to the 91st Con-

Exhibit 5.3
U.S. House of Representatives Procedures
for Handling an Ethics Complaint

Step 1. A complaint is filed in writing and submitted to the Committee on Standards of Official Conduct.

Step 2. The committee chairman and ranking minority member have fourteen days to determine if the complaint meets rules that define a complaint.

Step 3. If the complaint is deemed legitimate by the chair and ranking minority member, the full committee must decide to either investigate or drop the case.

Step 4. Investigations are carried out by subcommittees that can lead to a sanction hearing to determine the level of punishment, if any. The possible sanctions include:

- expulsion
- censure
- reprimand
- fine
- limitations of rights or privileges, or
- other as determined by the committee such as the letters of admonishment sent to Representative Tom Delay

Source: www.house.gov/ethics/ethicschap1.html.

gress in 1967. He appealed the House's action to the U.S. Supreme Court, which ruled that his exclusion was unconstitutional. Powerful Chicago Democratic congressman Dan Rostenkowski used his office for many years to secure political favors. In 1994, he was indicted for corruption and failed to be reelected. In 1995 he pleaded guilty to mail fraud and was sentenced to seventeen months in federal prison. He served fifteen months before President Bill Clinton pardoned him in 2000.

The House of Representatives was stunned in 2005 when a popular senior California Republican, Randy Cunningham, who was also a decorated combat pilot in Vietnam, resigned his seat after admitting that he received more than $2 million in money and favorable considerations from a defense contractor. In November 2003, for example, the contractor MZM purchased Cunningham's Del Mar house for $1,675,000, put it back on the market for the same price where it sat for nearly nine months until it sold for $975,000—a hefty $700,000 loss, or gain, depending on your point of view. Representative Cunningham sat on the House Defense Appropriations Subcommittee. In December 2005, Speaker of the House J. Dennis Hastert proposed that lawmakers receive ethics training.

Senate

The U.S. Senate has assigned responsibility for ethics investigations to a six-member bipartisan Select Committee on Ethics. A 542-page *Senate Ethics Manual* guides the deliberations of the Select Committee and provides rules for gifts, conflicts of interest, outside earned income, financial disclosure, political activity, use of frank and Senate facilities, employment practices, and more. The review and investigative process followed by the Senate Select Committee is similar to that followed in the House.

> Senate perks include traveling to political fundraisers on corporate jets. Senate rules require that the plane's owners are reimbursed at first-class rates, which are considered to be a bargain rate. Newly elected Senator Barack Obama (D-Illinois) has stopped traveling on corporate jets because it creates an appearance of wrongdoing.

A four-member majority must vote in support of moving an investigation forward. Letters of admonition are also used by the Senate Select Committee on Ethics. For example, Senator Robert G. Torricelli (D-New Jersey) was severely admonished for violating Senate rules for gifts he received. The committee of three Republicans and three Democrats wrote in a three-page letter, "Your actions and failure to act led to violations of Senate Rules (and related statutes) and created at least the appearance of impropriety, and you are hereby severely admonished."[4] Some critics regarded this punishment as little more than a "slap on the wrist."

Judiciary—Federal and State

Judges are widely viewed as ethical public officials. Yet, it has long been recognized that judges need ethical guidance and advice as much as other public officials. Federal judges receive lifetime appointments when approved by the U.S. Senate in its capacity to "advise and consent." The Code of Conduct for United States Judges sets forth seven canons to which all federally appointed judges must subscribe.

Canons are a body of standards, rules, or principles accepted as universally binding.

As can be seen in exhibit 5.4, the canons are both proscriptive and prescriptive. Judges are admonished to "uphold the integrity and independence of the judiciary" while also "avoiding the appearance of impropriety in all activities" and "refraining from political activity." Judges who find themselves in ethically questionable situations can seek advisory opinions from the Committee on Codes of Conduct of the Judicial Conference. The Judicial Conference serves as the principal policy-making body concerned with the administration of the United States courts.

State judges are not subject to the U.S. Code of Conduct, but each state has a judicial commission that deals with complaints of judicial misconduct, with most commissions established in the past thirty years.[5] Judicial commissions typically have the power to sanction a judge and to require a judge to retire or resign. Commission findings are almost always appealable to state courts.

Exhibit 5.4
Code of Conduct for United States Judges

Canon 1. A Judge Should Uphold the Integrity and Independence of the Judiciary

Canon 2. A Judge Should Avoid Impropriety and the Appearance of Impropriety in All Activities

Canon 3. A Judge Should Perform the Duties of the Office Impartially and Diligently

Canon 4. A Judge May Engage in Extra-Judicial Activities to Improve the Law, the Legal System, and the Administration of Justice

Canon 5. A Judge Should Regulate Extra-Judicial Activities to Minimize the Risk of Conflict with Judicial Duties

Canon 6. A Judge Should Regularly File Reports of Compensation Received for Law-Related and Extra-Judicial Activities

Canon 7. A Judge Should Refrain from Political Activity

Source: www.uscourts.gov/guide/vol2/ch1.html.

State judges are selected in a variety of ways—partisan election, nonpartisan election, appointment and then reelection on a ballot that permits citizens to vote to retain or not retain the judge, and merit selection by appointment or with a commission. Eight states (including Illinois and Kansas) select judges through partisan elections, thirteen (including California and Florida) choose judges through nonpartisan election, fifteen states (including Massachusetts and Utah) use merit selection with a nominating committee, nine states (including South Carolina) choose judges through merit selection combined with other methods, and two states (New Jersey and Virginia) authorize the governor and/or legislature to select judges.[6]

The kaleidoscope of selection methods and accountability mechanisms poses its own ethical challenges in the states. Consider the case of Judge John Renke III, a Florida circuit court judge. In 2002, then candidate Renke defeated two others vying for a seat on the Pasco-Pinellas circuit court. The election was very competitive, with Renke accused of nine counts of campaign misconduct. The Florida Judicial Qualifications Commission heard the case in 2005 and ruled that Renke brought disrepute to the judiciary as a result of his misconduct. The misconduct included an illegal contribution of $95,800 from his father. The commission recommended a public reprimand and a $40,000 fine but not removal from office. Evidence collected by the commission indicated that Judge Renke had done an excellent job as a circuit court judge, presiding mostly over domestic cases. Judge Renke's future is in the hands of the Florida Supreme Court and the voting public in 2008 when he stands for reelection (Jenkins, C. 2005).

Judges who break the law pose a special challenge for judicial ethics. Ohio Supreme Court Justice Alice Robie Resnick, for example, was convicted of drunken driving and therefore charged with violating the state's judicial code of conduct. Canon 2 of the Ohio code states that "A Judge Shall Respect and Comply with the Law and Shall Act at All Times in a Manner That Promotes Public Confidence in the Integrity and Impartiality of the Judiciary."[7] A thirteen-member panel of state appellate judges heard her case and decided that Justice Resnick had indeed violated Canon 2. The panel publicly reprimanded her for professional misconduct. No other discipline, such as suspending her law license or removing her from the bench, was recommended.

Ethics Management in the States

The states have also taken measures to strengthen ethics and integrity in governance, although there is considerable variation among them. Some states do a great deal while others do very little. New York passed the first major

Exhibit 5.5

Better Government Integrity Index, 2002
(states ranked from highest to lowest)

The index represents combined scores on laws dealing with Freedom of Information, Whistle-blower Protection, Campaign Finance, Gifts-Trips-Honoraria, and Conflicts of Interest.

Wisconsin	1	Georgia	26
Rhode Island	2	Utah	27
Kentucky	3	Virginia	28
Hawaii	4	New York	29
California	5	Nevada	30
Nebraska	6	Arkansas	31
South Carolina	7	Michigan	32
West Virginia	8	Mississippi	33
Texas	9	Indiana	34
Maryland	10	Missouri	35
Washington	11	New Hampshire	36
New Jersey	12	Wyoming	37
Connecticut	13	Delaware	38
Ohio	14	North Dakota	39
Massachusetts	15	Pennsylvania	40
Colorado	16	Illinois	41
Minnesota	17	Idaho	42
Florida	18	Iowa	43
Oregon	19	Tennessee	44
Arizona	20	Montana	45
Kansas	21	Louisiana	46
North Carolina	22	Alabama	47
Alaska	23	New Mexico	48
Maine	24	Vermont	49
Okalahoma	25	South Dakota	50

Source: www.bettergov.org/IntegrityIndex_10.22.02.pdf.

ethics law in 1954. Other states have moved more slowly in launching ethics reform initiatives with many doing so in the 1970s on the heels of the Watergate scandal. Contrary to public perception, states a recent report issued by Council on Governmental Ethics and Laws, the ethical climate of the states has improved substantially in recent years.[8]

Another report issued by the Better Government Association (BGA), a Chicago-based civic watchdog group, is less optimistic. In 2002, the association compiled a state Integrity Index (see exhibit 5.5) based on how well each state addressed laws dealing with freedom of information; whistle blowing; campaign finance; gifts, trips, and honoraria; and financial conflicts of interest. "The BGA Integrity Index revealed a troubling trend: All states performed poorly in an absolute sense."[9] While some states performed much better than others in a relative sense, the best state—Wisconsin—still fell far short of high performance as measured on a scale of 0–100. The worst state, South Dakota, received zero marks for freedom of information laws and laws that covered gifts, trips, and honoraria.

The ethics problems facing state governments are not insignificant and all too often cross over into the criminal domain. In March 2005, former Connecticut governor John G. Rowland (R) was sentenced to one year and one day in federal prison for accepting $107,000 in gifts from people doing business with the state and not paying taxes on them. Rowland resigned in July 2003, halfway through his third term in office. Another governor, James McGreevey (D-New Jersey), was forced out of office in 2004 as a result of an adulterous affair with a former aide, a man who was given special employment consideration by the governor as an advisor to the state Office of Homeland Security.

In Illinois in 2001, former Republican governor George Ryan chose not to seek reelection after one term in office as a result of the "licenses-for-sale" scandal. The scandal involved bribes paid to state officials to issue commercial driver's licenses. The bribe money was laundered into Governor Ryan's campaign for governor in 1998. Federal investigators brought indictments against seventy-nine persons and secured convictions of seventy-five persons, including Ryan. After a lengthy, complex trial lasting more than five months, the former governor was found guilty of eighteen felony charges that ranged from racketeering conspiracy, mail fraud, tax fraud, and making false statements to the Federal Bureau of Investigations (Davey and Ruethling 2006).[10]

Not every governor who has ethics lapses is subject to criminal proceedings. Governor Bob Taft (R) of Ohio failed to report fifty-two gifts, including golf outings, hockey tickets, and meals, on his annual financial disclosure reports from 1998 to 2004. The gifts amounted to nearly $6,000. Under Ohio law, gifts worth more than $75 must be reported. Governor Taft admitted that he had failed to disclose the gifts. The judge ordered him to pay $4,000 in fines and write a letter of apology to the people of Ohio (Dao 2005).

State Ethics Laws

States differ in the content and coverage of ethics laws, although all states provide some protection from retaliation for employees who blow the whistle on government fraud, waste, or abuse of power. (See exhibit 5.6 for subject matter coverage in selected states.) All fifty states also require lobbyists to file disclosure reports that identify persons seeking to influence legislation as well as the expenditures made by lobbyists. Gift restrictions on legislators

Exhibit 5.6

Operating Size and Jurisdiction of Ethics Commissions in California, Florida, New York, and Texas

	Operating size		Jurisdiction over . . .		
	Budget	# Employees	Legislators	State elected officials	Local government employees
California	$6 mil	60	Yes	Yes	Yes
Florida	$2.1 mil	23	Yes	Yes	Yes
New York	$1.5 mil	20	No	Yes	No
Texas	$2 mil	25	Yes	No	No

Source: COGEL Blue Book 2004 Ethics Update.

Exhibit 5.7

Advisory Opinions, Investigations, and Training in California, Florida, New York, and Texas, COGEL

	Advisory opinions		Investigations		Training required
	Authority to issue	# per year	Authority on own initiative	# per year	
California	Yes	300–400	Yes	892	Yes
Florida	Yes	23	No	107	No
New York	Yes	5–10	Yes	60	No
Texas	Yes	10	Yes	76	Yes

Source: Blue Book 2004 Ethics Update.

vary substantially with some states limiting the monetary value of gifts at $3 while other states allow gifts valued as much as $500. Thirty-seven states have campaign finance contribution limits, with twenty-seven states placing restrictions on the contributions that legislators can receive from lobbyists. Restrictions on former legislators from lobbying are in place in twenty-six states, with nineteen states restricting former legislators from lobbying for one year after leaving office and six states imposing a two-year ban on this revolving door. Some states prohibit legislators from receiving honorariums if offered in connection with a legislator's official duties.[11]

State Legislative Ethics

Members of the fifty state legislatures, like members of Congress, are subject to ethical lapses. Indeed, some critics assert that legislative ethics is an oxymoron. There is no shortage of lobbyists in Tallahassee, Albany, Spring-field, or Sacramento, all seeking to influence lawmakers—legally but all too often unethically. Campaign contributions flow freely from the clients of lobbyists, and conflicts of interest are a constant peril. Most efforts to curb unethical behavior among state legislators in the pre-Watergate period fo-cused on enacting anti-bribery laws.

States began tightening their ethics laws following the Watergate ethical meltdown that drove a sitting president from office. "Eleven states that had not enacted any laws regulating legislative conflicts of interest before 1972 took decisive action during the short period from 1973 to 1976" (Rosenson 2005, 91). Other states—North Carolina and Texas—strengthened their brib-ery statutes, and still others—California, Minnesota, and Wisconsin—added financial disclosure to their ethical restrictions. Eight states, including Florida and Kansas, set up independent ethics commissions to monitor legislators' financial disclosures and investigate allegations of wrongdoing (91). By 1996, thirty-six states had taken steps to strengthen their legislative ethics laws.

A handful of states have been even more aggressive in enacting restrictive ethics laws. Beth A. Rosen in *The Shadowlands of Conduct* (2005) points to California, New Jersey, and Illinois as placing "substantive restrictions on legislators' activities, including limits on lawyer-legislators' appearances before state agencies, limits on gifts, limits on legislators becoming lobby-ists after leaving office, and mandatory financial disclosure" (65). And in 2005, the Republican-controlled Florida legislature enacted what is prob-ably the most restrictive gift law in the nation. Effective January 1, 2006, "no lobbyist or principal shall make, directly or indirectly, and no member or employee of the Legislature shall knowingly accept, directly or indirectly, any expenditure . . ."

The devil, of course, is always in the details. Consequently, the legislative leadership drafted "Interim Lobbying Guidelines for the House and Senate." The guidelines advise that, among other things, a legislator cannot accept a subscription to a newspaper or periodical that is paid for by a lobbyist or a client, free health screening by an association that is a principal, payment for travel expenses to deliver a speech, or a drink at the bar without verifying that the person picking up the tab is not a lobbyist or a client of one. The law does permit a lobbyist or principal to buy a legislator a meal if the legislator "contemporaneously provides equal or greater consideration . . ." So, if a lobbyist puts out $50 for a legislator's dinner but the legislator buys a $75 bottle of wine, all is well.

The law exempts political fundraising. A legislator can accept food or drink paid for by a lobbyist or principal who sponsors a fundraising event. Moreover, the law does not prohibit expenditures made by lobbyists or principals to influence legislative action through oral or written communication. Nor are local legislative bodies—city councils and county commissions—covered by the gift-ban law.

Investigations of alleged ethics violations by members of a state legislature are typically handled by a standing legislative ethics committee. Every state except Colorado and Connecticut has a standing legislative ethics committee. In Colorado and Connecticut, a committee is appointed by the speaker of the House and Senate president when a complaint is lodged against a lawmaker (Rosen 2005, 114). Ethics commissions in states where they exist may also be involved if the complaint alleges a violation of state law.

Ethics Commissions and Boards

The principal agency for overseeing a state's ethics laws is a commission or board. These boards generally act as regulatory watchdogs. Thirty-six states have an ethics commission or board that administers and enforces ethics codes and rules for public officials, state employees, and lobbyists. Louisiana was the first state to establish an independent ethics commission in 1964. The commissions vary enormously in size and capacity, with some states (for example, Montana) having a single commissioner to other states (such as West Virginia) having twelve commissioners. Budgets vary from as little as $5,000 in Michigan to $7 million in California. State ethics laws typically cover local government employees, although not all do. These agencies can issue advisory opinions, provide training and information regarding the state's ethics laws, and adjudicate allegations of unethical behavior. The more powerful agencies can initiate investigations, subpoena witnesses, and levy civil fines. Decisions reached by ethics commissions are subject to judicial review.[12]

Even in states with strong ethics commissions, there are calls to strengthen the enforcement of the ethics laws. For example, the chairman of the New York State Ethics Commission, Paul L. Schechtman, says his commission needs more muscle. "The Ethics Commission does have teeth, and does sanction those who stay around; the problem is we're missing a tooth or a molar" (Finn 2005). Mr. Schechtman is referring to the fact that state officials accused of unethical behavior can and do walk away from ethics investigations upon resigning from office.

Effectiveness

How effective are state ethics laws, enforcement, and education or training? It is not easy to determine as the evidence is sparse and somewhat anecdotal in nature. Moreover, the legalistic and rule-driven approach taken by most states emphasizes ethics management as a legal process, thus training, for example, turns mostly around interpretations of the law—what the law says and what can happen to those who break the law. And, of course, state ethics regulatory commissions and agencies are mindful of the need for due process in all rulings.

There were and are other limitations—even loopholes—in some ethics laws. The New York State law, which is often touted as one of the oldest and strongest, had allowed officials charged with an ethics violation to stop the New York State Ethics Commission from investigating once the official leaves public office. The loophole in the law that "grants most employees immunity when they leave the state payroll—no matter what their actions while on the job"—was closed in 2005 (Slackman 2005). About fifty cases in New York were voided over the past decade when an employee walked. The cases involved a high-ranking university official (the president of SUNY at Albany), a Long Island Rail Road administrator, and a former general counsel in the Department of Transportation. They simply walked away from an ethics investigation, although the SUNY president claims that was not the reason she moved on. The Long Island Rail Road administrator said she chose to retire rather than spend a lot of money to prove her innocence. The general counsel said he left state government for personal reasons. Still, a loophole is just that.

A handful of studies have attempted to assess the effectiveness of state ethics laws and agencies. Among them is Smith's (2003) study of Connecticut, Florida, and New York. These states have established commissions that, as ethics watchdogs, take as their primary mission the enforcement of ethics laws. All were created as a result of scandal, with the Connecticut and Florida Ethics Commissions established in 1978 and 1977, respectively. The New York State Ethics Commission was created in 1987. All issue advisory opinions, provide training, and conduct investigations, although the Florida Commission cannot initiate investigations on its own nor can it directly levy civil penalties; it can recommend penalties but needs an executive order to implement a recommendation. Smith concludes that "ethics commissions play a positive role in the states" (293). "Enforcement actions," he asserts, "send a message to violators or would-be violators to be mindful of ethics transgressions . . ." and therefore acts as an effective deterrent.

Other investigators are not so confident. Herrmann (1997) contends that ethics commissions face serious problems. They are not effective regulatory agencies and need to be empowered with adequate funding, greater operating autonomy, and vigorous enforcement authority. He describes commissions as houses built with bricks without mortar, that is, agencies with weak organizational structures. Mackenzie (2002) claims that the enactment of

numerous ethics laws and ordinances—federal, state, and local—have tried
to make government scandalproof, but there is little evidence that this approach has succeeded. Indeed, he goes so far as to suggest that ". . . some
ethics deregulation will improve the overall quality of the public service and
of government performance with no discernable impact on public integrity"
(164–165). Williams' (1996) study of the Florida Commission on Ethics also
lends little support to the contention that ethics agencies are effective. He
found that the commission is weak in education and training initiatives to aid
public officials understand what the state's ethics laws and rules are, is totally reactive in responding to complaints, and does little to improve the ethical climate of Florida. Williams suggests that commission practices may
actually detract from the ethical climate in the state.

Florida[13]

Menzel's (1996a) investigation of the Florida Commission on Ethics rein-
forces the view that the state's ethics, legal, and organizational infrastructure
is not adequate. Indeed, there is a disturbing possibility that the Ethics Commission unwittingly contributes to the "trust deficit" facing the nation. What
is the evidence for this claim? Menzel gathered data on the complaint-making process in Florida in the early 1990s from more than 300 residents who
filed ethics complaints with the Commission on Ethics and 555 officials who
had complaints filed against them. The survey information focused on the
experiences of each group in dealing with the Commission on Ethics.

Public officials reported a much more positive experience with the way in
which the commission handled complaints than did citizens. For example,
50 percent of the complainants rated staff courtesy as "good" or "excellent"
whereas 75 percent of the public officials reported a similar rating. At the
other end of the courtesy scale, one of every four citizen complainants rated
the staff's courtesy as "poor" or "unacceptable." The pattern is even more
pronounced for the promptness with which the staff dealt with complaints.
More than 50 percent of the complainants said that staff promptness was
"poor" or "unacceptable" in contrast to a majority of public officials who
said that staff promptness was "excellent" or "good."

Other findings were equally disparate, with public officials generally much
more positive about the work of the Ethics Commission than were citizens.
Consider the following assessment written by a citizen:

> The public city managers and high-ranking employees of local govern-
> ment in Florida strongly believe that the Florida Commission on Ethics is
> ineffective and usually does nothing or very little about unethical conduct

of local officials. I believe this directly contributes to elected local officials' and public managers' attitudes that they can misuse their power—they are above ethical laws, so to speak.

Still another citizen remarked in a lengthy three-page letter:

> As one moves thru the labyrinth of government offices one cannot escape the contempt in which the public is held by the officeholders. A great fear rests within each and every citizen as to whether or not they should speak out . . . what will happen to them? Is it worth the risk?

Public officials who had complaints filed against them, while more positive about their experiences than citizens, can be alienated by the process nonetheless. Consider the experience of a city commissioner who had a complaint filed against her. The complaint was dismissed, yet she still found the experience unsatisfactory. She wrote:

> I was very dissatisfied with the outcome of this complaint—not because it was dismissed due to legal insufficiency and a finding of no probable cause. That I was very happy about because I knew I had done nothing wrong. The fact that an elected official has to take such abuse and has no recourse to do anything is why I was dissatisfied with the outcome. I really feel that a person can file a complaint with malicious intent and there is absolutely nothing you can do about it. It comes with the territory of being an elected official, I was told.
>
> It seems like you have to take it as an elected official and that is not fair . . . let's keep the complaints to legitimate reason, not to get even, make another candidate look better, to get your friend in or any other frivolous or malicious intent. The persons that make those kinds of complaints are guilty of ethical wrongdoing and are costing the government thousands of dollars each year to investigate.

Other officials view the complaint-making process as a gauntlet of malcontent citizens armed with invectives and baseless accusations. Consider the fact that once a complaint is filed, the complainant can go public with it. That is, an elected official has no media protection from an allegation of wrongdoing if the complainant wishes to make the complaint public information, which can be done by simply calling a local newspaper reporter. Could citizen complainants be "civic terrorists"? Or, could they be ethical zealots or whistle blowers who hold worldviews vastly different than others in their community and are therefore more likely to have a "bad" experience following the filing of a complaint, no matter what the final outcome is?

The experiences of several officials led them to conclude that the process invites complaints by "ill-tempered and disgruntled persons" who seek revenge, retaliation, harassment, or political harm. Others claim that political ambition and "grandstanding" motivate the filing of complaints. Yet another respondent found the complaint-making experience so disheartening that he abandoned his aspirations to run for the mayor of his community and said he planned to retire from local political life when his term of office concluded.

Comments by both citizens and officials suggest that Florida's presumed well-intentioned ethics laws and infrastructure, the Ethics Commission, may be widening rather than closing the trust deficit. Ethics and trustworthy government go hand in hand. They are essential components of democracy whose very survival rests on public trust and confidence. Robert Bellah and colleagues (1991, 3) in an important book on social institutions claim that "democracy requires a degree of trust that we often take for granted . . . [but] it is much harder to build trust than to lose it." And, in the United States, "we have begun to lose trust in our institutions; the heritage of trust that has been the basis of our stable democracy is eroding" (4). Although there may be many conditions and circumstances that destroy trust in public authorities and government, none is likely to do it more quickly or effectively than the unethical conduct of public officeholders. Closing the trust deficit cannot be accomplished easily, quickly, or without painful change in the way things are done in the states.

Alas, the behavior of some Florida state legislators has done little to change the public's waning trust and confidence in state government. In 2005, State Senator Mandy Dawson (D) solicited $2,500 from lobbyists to pay for a trip to South Africa. Senator Dawson solicited the funds with a letter drafted on the Senate's official stationary. Dawson denied doing anything unethical and challenged detractors to file an ethics charge. She claimed that she was unfamiliar with ethics rules, even though she served on the Senate Ethics and Elections Committee. Her colleague, Republican state senator Victor Crist, enjoyed a $5,000 reception in his honor funded by a lobbyist representing tow truck operators just as he was sponsoring legislation the operators supported. Unethical? Not according to Senator Crist as he did not know who bankrolled the event (*Tampa Tribune* Editorial 2005).

Skepticism of the state's ethical culture surfaced once more when the Florida Commission on Ethics ruled in late 2005 that it was okay for members of the state Public Service Commission to have attended a conference in Miami Beach partially paid for by the same companies that they regulate. What had been thought by many as a slam-dunk case of unethical behavior got turned upside down when the Florida legislature changed the law to make it perfectly legal for Florida's utility regulators to "hobnob" with the companies they regulate, says columnist Howard Troxler of the *St. Petersburg Times* (2005). In Troxler's view, "in politics, what's unethical today is legal tomorrow!"

Illinois

Illinois has been battered by scandal and official misdeeds that have caused a steady decline of public trust and confidence in state government. The Better Government Association Integrity Index places the state near the bottom among the fifty states in enacting laws that encourage a high degree of integrity in state government. Nonetheless, efforts to rebuild the ethics infrastructure were launched in 1998 when the legislature passed and then governor Jim Edgar signed into law the State Gift Ban Act. The act banned the giving and receiving of gifts to and by officials and employees of all government entities in Illinois. The law also contained significant political campaign disclosure requirements that identifies who gives how much to whom. Moreover, it required all local government entities to pass "gift ban" ordinances consistent with state law. Finally, the law called for seven separate statewide ethics commissions. Two years later, after much maneuvering and legal challenges, Will County Circuit Judge Thomas Ewert threw out the law, ruling that it was so vague and filled with so many exemptions that it was unenforceable. Thus Illinois became lawless to prevent abuses in gifts given to and received by public officials.

> Gift bans attempt to limit the influence of interested parties, including lobbyists, on decisions of public officials. Some "bans" set specific limits and circumstances while others are "zero tolerance" bans, that is, no gifts are allowed under any circumstances.

This condition was finally brought to an end with the 2002 election of Governor Rod Blagojevich (D) who issued Executive Order 3 on January 2003 to create the Office of Inspector General (OIG). The OIG's power and duties were expanded to include jurisdiction over all state agencies except the Attorney General, Secretary of State, Comptroller, and Treasurer. As an independent agency reporting directly to the governor, the OIG has subpoena power and is authorized to investigate complaints of fraud, abuse, or misconduct. When OIG reports a finding of wrongdoing, disciplinary action is then recommended to the governor and the appropriate agency director. If the recommended disciplinary action is not acted on, the OIG can take the finding to the newly established Executive Ethics Commission for a ruling.

Illinois went a step further in strengthening its ethics infrastructure when the legislature enacted and the governor signed into law on December 9, 2003, the State Officials and Employees Ethics Act (Public Act 93–0617). The law provides for both civil and criminal penalties with fines up to $10,000 and/or one year in prison for some violations. Key provisions of this landmark legislation are:

- The establishment of the Executive Ethics Commission, a body of nine commissioners appointed by the State Constitutional Officers and the governor. The commission receives complaints, conducts administrative hearings, prepares and publishes guides regarding the ethics laws, issues subpoenas, and makes rulings and recommendations in disciplinary cases. The commission has jurisdiction over the employees and officers of the executive branch of government.[14]
- Legislators and constitutional officers are forbidden from using public money to pay for billboards, bumper stickers, and other paraphernalia bearing their name or image. These practices have been widely used by public officeholders to gain greater name recognition.
- State employees are banned for one year after leaving the state payroll from taking jobs with companies about which they made regulatory, licensing, or contracting decisions.
- State workers are prohibited from soliciting political contributions on state property and from performing political work—another widespread abuse in years past.
- Units of local government—including park districts, municipalities, special purpose districts, school districts, and community colleges—are required to adopt an ordinance or resolution that is no less restrictive than the act.
- Unpaid advisors to the governor and other state officials must file economic disclosure statements if they act on behalf of the officials.
- Perks such as golf outings and tennis matches paid for by lobbyists are not permitted, but lobbyists may spend up to $75 per day per official for drink and food, provided they are consumed on the premises from which they were purchased, prepared, or catered.
- Ethics training for all state employees and constitutional officers is required annually.
- Lobbyists are required to register with the secretary of state, and the law broadened the definition of a lobbyist.

Have these provisions and others put Illinois on the path to integrity and sound ethics management? The evidence is skimpy but promising. Among other things, a twenty-four-hour ethics hotline has been established by the

Office of Executive Inspector General, and more than 3,000 calls have been received. An online ethics training program has trained over 115,000 state employees. Nearly 1,800 complaints have been received with more than 500 investigated and closed. Eighty-five instances of wrongdoing have been found with recommendations made for disciplinary action. The OIG, however, has not found it necessary to appeal a single case of wrongdoing to the Executive Ethics Commission.

> Online ethics training is growing in popularity in government because it provides a means of reaching many employees and is inexpensive. Its effectiveness, however, has not been established.

Ethics management in the State of Illinois is underway in a manner similar to that found in most other states. In all likelihood, it has deterred willful and non-willful acts of wrongdoing by public officials and government employees. However, it is not possible to know how many or what kinds of unethical behavior have been prevented. Nor is it possible to assess the consequences of the online ethics training program. The vast majority of training programs in both the private and public sector are people-to-people, hands-on experiences. The approach taken by Illinois is clearly reaching a large number of government managers and workers, but the effectiveness of online training is unknown.

New York

New York State was the first state to adopt an ethics law in 1954 after a series of scandals surfaced involving the bribery of public officials by organized crime. Yet it would be thirty more years before the state could claim it had an effective law. Prompted once more by scandal in which lawmakers placed no-show workers on their payrolls, the state legislature passed a sweeping reform measure—the Ethics in Government Act of 1987 (Rosen 2005, 99). The act created the State Ethics Commission and gave it jurisdiction over officers and employees of the executive branch. The five-member commission can initiate its own investigations and levy civil fines (not to exceed $10,000)—both powerful tools compared to those of many other states. The commissioners are appointed by the governor; with one member each nominated by the state attorney general and another by the state comptroller.

Other duties of the commission include rendering advisory opinions that interpret and apply the laws; distributing, collecting, and auditing financial disclosure statements; issuing rules and regulations to implement and enforce the Ethics in Government Act; and conducting training. The commission is supported by a nineteen-member staff, which includes four investigators.

Advisory Opinions. The commission issues two types of advisory opinions, formal and informal. A formal opinion is issued when a state officials requests it in writing. The opinion is binding on both the commission and the person making the request. Formal opinions are made public, but the name of the requestor is held in confidence. An informal opinion merely advises the person making the request about issues previously decided by the commission and is not binding. The opinion is not made public. The commission has issued on average eighteen formal advisory opinions over the past sixteen years, with one-half as many formal opinions issued on average per year over the past five years. The commission has issued on average 119 informal advisory opinions per year since 1987.[15]

Investigations and Enforcement. The commission on average conducts sixty-two investigations per year, with a much smaller number of alleged violators put on notice that the commission believes they may have violated the law. On average, the commission has issued ten notices of reasonable cause per year since 1990. The Notice of Reasonable Cause is a letter sent to a state employee or officer that provides detailed information regarding why the commission has cause to believe that a violation of the Ethics Law has occurred. The accused employee has a right to a hearing to resolve the allegations or can opt for an agreement with the commission to not proceed further with enforcement proceedings. Sixteen notices were issued in 2004 with eight resolved by a disposition agreement. Most of the alleged violations had to do with the employee receiving gifts such as a golf outing or meals or tickets to social events from clients doing business with the state. The largest settlement in the commission's history was $30,000 from two former state employees "when they appeared and gave testimony as paid witnesses for a health care project in which they were directly concerned while in State service" (New York State Ethics Commission 2004).

Education and Training. An online training program was put into place in 2003 to "explain New York's ethics laws in easy-to-understand language, with laws followed by a series of 'real life' examples to test individuals' understanding."[16] Nearly 500 persons took the course in November and December 2003. Other training was offered to state employees in 2003, with some fifty-three sessions providing general information on the ethics law. In recognition of outstanding commitment to ethics in government, the Theodore Roosevelt Ethics Award is given to an agency each year. The 2003 award winner was the Office of General Services.

New York State's approach to ethics management mirrors those found in other states—legalistic, reactive, and largely punitive in nature. Robert W. Smith (2003, 293–294), who has conducted in-depth research on New York, Florida, and Connecticut, makes a number of recommendations to improve the functioning of state ethics commissions. They include:

- Removing any partisan considerations for determining who serves on the commission.
- Enhance the education and training function of commissions.
- Provide for independent investigatory power.
- Empower commissions to impose substantial fines.
- Provide adequate base-level funding.
- Provide for a uniform ethics structure, not a fragmented structure.
- Expand the discretion of commissions to interpret how the law should be applied in certain circumstances.

The New York State Ethics Commission as judged by these recommendations has a distance yet to go before it can be as effective as Smith suggests it should be. This conclusion is reinforced by the Better Government Association's Integrity Index which places New York in the lower 50 percent tier of states. While the BGA Index scores the state highly in laws regulating financial conflicts of interest, it scores New York near the bottom in laws that regulate gifts, trips, and honoraria.

A Patchwork of Laws and Regulations

This chapter has shown that the states vary a great deal in how they attempt to deter wrongdoing and encourage ethical behavior. There is little uniformity across states in their ethics infrastructure. "What has emerged," says Elder Witt (1992, 343), "is not a clear system of rules, but an inconsistent and confusing patchwork." The Better Government Association uses similar language in asserting that "states have taken a patchwork approach towards promoting integrity which indicates a lack of the proper amount of concern regarding integrity and corruption" (2002, 5).

Ethics management is more than laws, rules, and regulations and the processing of ethics complaints. Obeying the law and following ethics regulations may keep state officials and employees out of legal difficulty, but abiding by the law is not sufficient to ensure ethical governance. Many states have ethics statutes, commissions with investigatory powers, and training programs, but there is little evidence that states employ the full complement of ethics management tools available to them.

The federal government's ethics management approach can also be described as a patchwork. There are many laws, agencies, and rules and regulations that define in a Byzantine manner the government's effort to discourage unethical behavior and encourage ethical behavior. The federal effort is also underpinned by a compliance orientation that puts the accent on the low road of "gotcha" ethics.

Ethics Management Skill Building

Practicum 5.1. FEMA and Hurricane Katrina

As director of the U.S. Federal Emergency Management Agency (FEMA), you have the responsibility of employing FEMA's resources (people, funds, technology) to assist communities and states devastated by natural disasters such as Hurricane Katrina, which struck the Gulf Coast states in late August 2005. Your agency is not a first-responder, as this responsibility belongs to local authorities. Moreover, significant FEMA resources cannot be deployed until the president declares that a county or region is in a state of emergency.

President George W. Bush issued such a declaration two days before Katrina, with deadly winds in excess of 150 miles per hour, made landfall on August 29, 2005. Soon after hurricane winds pummeled New Orleans and flooding occurred with the breech of the levees protecting the city (New Orleans actually sits below sea level), law and order broke down with looters sacking vacated stores and gangs roaming the streets. The New Orleans police force of 1,500 were overwhelmed by the flooding, a breakdown in communications, and internal stress caused by floodwaters that endangered their lives as well as the lives of their families and loved ones. Some police officers resigned, others deserted, and some simply couldn't report in because of the chaos.

Under these circumstances, the National Guard is typically deployed. Unless federalized, however, the decision to deploy the National Guard of a state resides with the governor. In Louisiana, Governor Kathleen Babineaux Blanco (D) activated the guard, although nearly half were serving in Iraq and therefore were unavailable. More would be needed to restore law and order.

Questions

1. As director of FEMA, you urge the president to federalize the National Guard for deployment to New Orleans, but you are unsure about the authority the president has to do this without an invitation from Governor Blanco. Due to emergency conditions, should you

advise the president to act immediately and federalize National Guard troops from other states for deployment to Louisiana?

2. If Governor Blanco challenges the president's authority to take control of the Louisiana National Guard, what would you recommend that he do, especially in light of the fact that disorder and life-endangering conditions are worsening each day?

3. What is the morally and/or ethically correct course of action?

4. What is likely to be the impact on FEMA if:
   a. the president acts quickly?
   b. the president acts slowly?
   c. the president doesn't act at all?

Practicum 5.2. Getting a Code Adopted

As a newly arrived senior manager in a large state agency, you are dismayed to find that the agency has never adopted a code of ethics or considered requiring employees to sign an oath stating something like: "I do solemnly swear that I will support the Constitution of the United States and the Constitution of the State of Linconland, faithfully discharge the duties of my office, and abide by and adhere to the provisions of the agency's Code of Ethics. So help me God."

Convinced that codes and oaths contribute to ethical workplaces, you appoint a committee drawn from many different departments to draft a code and an oath for your agency. Six months later the committee chair reports that the committee is hopelessly deadlocked over whether the code should specify appropriate behavior that could be monitored and therefore sanctioned when violations occur or whether a statement of values and principles might suffice.

Questions

1. What advice would you offer the committee chair? Would you send him back to the committee with the charge to try once more? Would you disband the committee and start anew? Would you appear before the committee and attempt to persuade them to adopt an enforceable code and a stringent oath? A values statement? Neither?

2. What arguments would you put forward for the adoption of an enforceable code and oath? A values statement?

3. What course of action would produce the best outcome?

Notes

1. Introduction to the OSC, www.osc.gov/intro.htm. Accessed January 2, 2006.

2. www.usoge.gov/pages/about_oge/agcy_prg_serv.html. Accessed January 2, 2006.

3. For an insightful historical perspective on presidential ethics, see Gilman (1995b).

4. The letter of admonishment can be found at http://ethics.senate.gov/downloads/pdffiles/torricelli.pdf. Accessed January 3, 2006.

5. www.law.cornell.edu/wex/index.php/Judicial_ethics. Accessed June 24, 2006.

6. www.pbs.org/now/politics/choosingjudges.html. Accessed June 24, 2006.

7. www.sconet.state.oh.us/Rules/conduct/#canon2. Accessed January 2, 2006.

8. The State of State Legislative Ethic. www.ncsl.org/programs/press/2002/legethics02.htm. Accessed January 2, 2006.

9. The BGA Integrity Index. http://bettergov.org/pdfs/IntegrityIndex_10.22.02.pdf. Accessed January 2, 2006.

10. www.cnn.com/2003/LAW/12/17/ryan.ap. Accessed June 24, 2006.

11. OLR Research Report State Ethics Organizations. www.cga.ct.gov/2004/rpt/2004-R-0881.htm. Accessed January 2, 2006.

12. OLR Research Report State Ethics Organizations. www.cga.ct.gov/2004/rpt/2004-R-0881.htm. Accessed January 2, 2006.

13. This section draws in part on Menzel (1996a).

14. www.ag.state.il.us/government/ethics.html. Accessed June 25, 2006.

15. New York State Ethics Commission, *2003 Annual Report to the Governor and the Legislature.*

16. New York State Ethics Commission, *2003 Annual Report to the Governor and the Legislature.*

6

Ethics Management Internationally

"The integrity of politicians and public servants
is a critical ingredient in democratic society."
—Alice Rivlin

International ethics management is a rapidly evolving reality with many countries placing considerable emphasis on anti-corruption initiatives. A recent study of the twenty-six member countries of the European Union notes that "the focus in national public administrations and the media is on corruption, fraud and conflicts of interest, but much less on unethical behaviour in general" (Bossaert and Demmke 2005, 3). This chapter provides a broad overview of worldwide efforts to adopt ethics management strategies that encourage ethical behavior and combat corruption.

> Corruption is the (mis)use of public office for private gain. Common forms of corruption are extortion, bribery and graft, influence peddling, insider deals, and kickbacks.

International Organizations

International bodies, including the United Nations, Transparency International, the Utstein Group (United Kingdom, the Netherlands, Norway, Sweden, Canada, and Germany), and the Organization for Economic Cooperation and Development (OECD) have launched a number of anti-corruption initiatives. The U.N., for example, promulgated an International Code of Conduct for Public Officials in 1996 (see exhibit 6.1). Additionally, the United Nations International Centre for Crime Prevention has developed an Anti-Corruption Tool Kit to "help U.N. Member States and the public to understand the insidious nature of corruption, the potential damaging effect it can have on the welfare of entire nations and suggest measures used successfully by other countries in their efforts to uncover and deter corruption and build integrity."[1]

Exhibit 6.1
U.N. General Principles of the International Code for Public Officials

1. A public office, as defined by national law, is a position of trust, implying a duty to act in the public interest. Therefore, the ultimate loyalty of public officials shall be to the public interests of their country as expressed through the democratic institutions of government.
2. Public officials shall ensure that they perform their duties and functions efficiently, effectively, and with integrity, in accordance with laws or administrative policies. They shall at all times seek to ensure that public resources for which they are responsible are administered in the most effective and efficient manner.
3. Public officials shall be attentive, fair, and impartial in the performance of their functions and, in particular, in their relations with the public. They shall at no time afford any undue preferential treatment to any group or individual or improperly discriminate against any group or individual, or otherwise abuse the power and authority vested in them.

Source: www.un.org/documents/ecosoc/res/1996/eres1996-8.htm Accessed June 28, 2006.

Transparency International and the Utstein Group

Transparency International (TI), the only international non-governmental organization devoted to combating corruption, seeks through information and education to discourage corruption and foster integrity in governance. TI publishes a Bribes Payers Index, a Global Corruption Report, and a Corruption Perceptions Index (CPI) that track corruption in 158 countries. The 2005 CPI reports that Iceland, Finland, New Zealand, Denmark, and Singapore are the five most corruption-free countries in the world. The five most corrupt countries, according to the CPI, are Chad, Bangladesh, Turkmenistan, Myanmar, and Haiti. The United States is ranked number 17, one spot ahead of France and one spot behind Germany.

Transparency International also publishes guides and books that promote integrity in governance. A National Integrity System source book, available in over twenty languages, offers "a holistic approach to transparency and accountability and embracing a range of accountability 'pillars,' democratic, judicial, media and civil society."[2]

The Utstein Group, with headquarters in London, was established by the ministers of international development from Germany, the Netherlands, Norway, and United Kingdom when they gathered at the Utstein Abbey in Norway in 1999. The group has created an online resource center at www.u4.no/

about/utsteinagencies.cfm that lists studies, reports, and anti-corruption projects currently underway throughout the world.

OECD

The Organization of Economic Cooperation and Development (OECD) with thirty member countries and a history dating to the early 1960s has long been in the forefront of promoting good governance. The OECD was instrumental in putting forward the 1997 Anti-Bribery Convention that is "the first global instrument to fight corruption in cross-border business deals."[3] Thirty-six countries, including six non-OECD members, have enacted anti-bribery laws based on the OECD Convention. Estonia is the most recent party to the convention.

In 1998, the OECD also adopted a recommendation to improve ethical conduct in the public service that contains twelve "Principles for Managing Ethics in the Public Service" (see exhibit 6.2). These principles, the preamble to the OECD recommendation states, are intended to be a point of reference for member countries "when combining the elements of an effective ethics management system in line with their own political, administrative and cultural circumstances." The extent to which these principles have been drawn on by member countries and other countries to develop an effective ethics management system is difficult to say. Nonetheless, the twelve principles are noteworthy, and the intention is certainly meritorious.

Exhibit 6.2
OECD Published Principles for Managing Ethics
in the Public Service

1. Ethical standards for public service should be clear. Public servants need to know the basic principles and standards they are expected to apply to their work and where the boundaries of acceptable behaviour lie.
2. Ethical standards should be reflected in the legal framework. The legal framework is the basis for communicating the minimum obligatory standards and principles of behaviour for every public servant.
3. Ethical guidance should be available to public servants. Guidance and internal consultation mechanisms should be made available to help public servants apply basic ethical standards in the workplace.
4. Public servants should know their rights and obligations when exposing wrongdoing. Public servants also need to know what protection will be available to them in cases of exposing wrongdoing.

(continued)

Exhibit 6.2 *(continued)*

5. Political commitment to ethics should reinforce the ethical conduct of public servants. Political leaders are responsible for maintaining a high standard of propriety in the discharge of their official duties.
6. The decision-making process should be transparent and open to scrutiny. The public has a right to know how public institutions apply the power and resources entrusted to them.
7. There should be clear guidelines for interaction between the public and private sectors. Clear rules defining ethical standards should guide the behaviour of public servants in dealing with the private sector, for example regarding public procurement, outsourcing, or public employment conditions.
8. Managers should demonstrate and promote ethical conduct. An organizational environment where high standards of conduct are encouraged by providing appropriate incentives for ethical behaviour . . . has a direct impact on the daily practice of public service values and ethical standards.
9. Management policies, procedures, and practices should promote ethical conduct. Government policy should not only delineate the minimal standards below which a government official's actions will not be tolerated but also clearly articulate a set of public service values that employees should aspire to.
10. Public service conditions and management of human resources should promote ethical conduct. Public service employment conditions, such as career prospects, personal development, adequate remuneration, and human resource management policies should create an environment conducive to ethical behaviour.
11. Adequate accountability mechanisms should be in place within the public service. Accountability should focus both on compliance with rules and ethical principles and on achievement of results.
12. Appropriate procedures and sanctions should exist to deal with misconduct. Mechanisms for the detection and independent investigation of wrongdoing such as corruption are a necessary part of an ethics infrastructure.

Source: www.oecd.org/dataoecd/60/13/1899138.pdf.

Exhibit 6.3 **The Integrity-Compliance and Public Administration–Managerialism Dimensions**

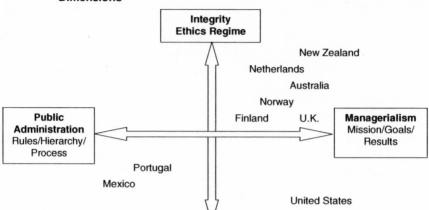

The principles are consistent with the OECD's recommendation that countries build their ethics infrastructure "to regulate against undesirable behaviour and to provide incentives to good conduct."[4] A well-built ethics infrastructure would include politicians who are advocates and exemplars of ethical governance; an effective legal framework; accountability mechanisms; workable codes of conduct, education, and training, and an active civic society. Admirable? Without question. Doable? Not easily.

As a working model, OECD classified nine countries along two dimensions —an integrity-compliance dimension and a public administration–managerialism dimension (see exhibit 6.3). The United States is characterized as having an ethics infrastructure that is a mix of compliance-based ethics and managerialism, that is, the emphasis is on "getting the job done" while at the same time complying with ethics rules and regulations.

Ethics Laws and Codes Internationally

Ethics laws and codes of conduct are widely used tools in the international ethics manager's toolbox. For example, Australia's Northern Territory placed a code of conduct in the 1993 Public Sector Employment and Management Act. Neighboring New Zealand passed a nationwide code of conduct in 1998 that emphasizes obligations generally expected of civil servants in their professional lives. Each agency has been encouraged to develop specific codes of conduct consistent with the standards set out in the national code. The United Kingdom Committee on Standards in Public Life, known as the Nolan

Exhibit 6.4
U.K Committee on Standards in Public Life:
Seven Principles of Public Life

Selflessness: Holders of public office should take decisions solely in terms of the public interest. They should not do so in order to gain financial or other material benefits for themselves, their family, or their friends.

Integrity: Holders of public office should not place themselves under any financial or other obligation to outside individuals or organizations that might influence them in the performance of their official duties.

Objectivity: In carrying out public business, including making public appointments, awarding contracts, or recommending individuals for rewards and benefits, holders of public office should make choices on merit.

Accountability: Holders of public office are accountable for their decisions and actions to the public and must submit themselves to whatever scrutiny is appropriate to their office.

Openness: Holders of public office should be as open as possible about all the decisions and actions that they take. They should give reasons for their decisions and restrict information only when the wider public interest clearly demands.

Honesty: Holders of public office have a duty to declare any private interests relating to their public duties and to take steps to resolve any conflicts arising in a way that protects the public interest.

Leadership: Holders of public office should promote and support these principles by leadership and example.

These principles apply to all aspects of public life.

Source: www.public-standards.gov.uk/default.htm.

Committee, promulgated the "Seven Principles of Public Life" that have been incorporated into codes of conduct by various agencies (see exhibit 6.4).

In Brazil, the Public Ethics Committee was established in 1999 to promote ethical behavior in the federal executive branch. The committee is also responsible for the implementation of the Federal Code of Conduct of High Administration and oversees and coordinates decentralized ethics initiatives in order to ensure the adequacy of the Brazilian administration's ethical standards. Another part of the agency's duties is to ensure that the relevant rules and procedures are known and understood, which includes publicity and training for officials and guidelines and help in dealing with ethical dilemmas.[5]

South Korea adopted a code of conduct for maintaining the integrity of public officials in 2003. This code specifies the standards of conduct to be observed by both state and local public officials and covers conflicts of interest, the use of one's office for private purposes, and the obligation of officials to exercise neutrality and impartiality in their agencies.

The Philippines enacted a Code of Conduct and Ethical Standards for Public Officials and Employees in 1989. The standards include upholding the public interest over and above personal interest; discharging duties with the highest degree of excellence, professionalism, intelligence, and skill; acting with justness and sincerity; not discriminating against anyone, especially the poor and the underprivileged; and leading modest lives appropriate to their positions and income. Moreover, officials are admonished to not indulge in an extravagant or ostentatious display of wealth in any form. The code also emphasizes positive incentives for exemplary behavior, stating that incentives and rewards to government officials and employees may take the form of bonuses, citations, directorships in government-owned or controlled corporations, local and foreign scholarship grants, and paid vacations. Public officials so honored are automatically promoted to the next higher position with the commensurate salary suitable to their qualifications.[6]

One ethics management tool under development by the Philippines Civil Service Commission is an Ethics-Based Personality Test. The commission believes that an ethics-based personality test will result in the "recruitment of the right people in all aspects and dimension" (Valmores 2005). The test will "determine the behavioral tendencies and personality profile of a job applicant . . . [to] . . . address the long standing problem of hiring otherwise qualified people who are deficient on the moral and ethical requirements of public service."

Codes in Central and Eastern Europe

Perhaps the most active regions of the world today in the development and implementation of codes of ethics are Central and Eastern Europe where many countries are in transition from authoritarian regimes to democratic regimes. A recent study by Palidauskaite (2006), a scholar from Lithuania, tracked the approaches taken in ten countries—Albania, Bulgaria, the Czech Republic, Estonia, Latvia, Lithuania, Poland, Macedonia, Romania, and the Slovak Republic. She reports that two trends are discernable—some countries focus on the behavior of public servants through laws and codes while other countries rely on statutory regulation only. The implementation of ethics codes and/or laws follows one of two paths. The first path is the use of an impartial council or board much like that found in the United States and the United Kingdom. The second path is left up to the individuals themselves "to interpret and apply the code of ethics" (45). The latter approach is consistent with the professional norm of self-enforcement, which is central to the codes adopted by many professional societies in the United States.

Ethics codes and statutes are not, of course, sufficient tools to ensure ethical governance. As Mike Nelson (1999) notes,

> the problem with Codes of Conduct is that it is easy to stick them on the wall, but hard to make them stick in practice . . . without an effective development and implementation strategy which is integrated and engages with the heart and bowels issues of concern to the organization, the net result seems consistently the same: that the Code of Conduct remains a mere piece of paper, displayed or appealed to when convenient, but ignored the rest of the time.

In assessing the role of codes in European Union countries, Bossaert and Demmke (2005, 7) conclude:

> Despite their popularity, codes of ethics make little sense unless they are accepted by the personnel, and maintained, cultivated and implemented with vigour. . . . Codes are useless if staff are not reminded of them on a regular basis and given continuous training on ethics. Codes are only effective if they are impressed upon the hearts and minds of employees.

Alas, even with a vigorous implementation strategy, a code may still not deter unethical behavior.

Whistle-Blowing Laws

Whistle-blowing laws and practices vary enormously throughout the world. The United States has numerous laws that encourage and protect individuals who blow the whistle on those who engage in corruption, waste, fraud, and abuse of power. And, there is a high incident of whistle blowing. Like those of the United States, Israel's laws provide extensive protection for whistle blowers, although there is a low incident of whistle blowing. India, the largest democracy in the world, has no statutes that encourage or protect whistle blowers. "In fact, whistle blowing is technically illegal, according to civil service rules, and might even be personally dangerous" (Johnson 2005, 1057). Still, there is a growing grassroots movement in India to expose government wrongdoing.

Until the collapse of the Soviet Union, whistle blowing in Russia was encouraged as a form of spying that enabled the government to sustain itself and control its citizens. This historic and unique Russian history, Roberta Johnson contends, is changing as there is evidence that a new breed of whistle blowers is emerging who are motivated to serve the public interest (1056). Johnson's case study of the United States, Israel, Russia, and India has led her to conclude that there is no direct correlation between the law and the incident of whistle blowing. Rather, she contends that the "cultural context, more than any other factor helps explain why in some countries whistleblowers play an important role in opposing corruption and in other countries they do not" (1051).

To further assess ethics management internationally, we turn next to a more in-depth look at developments in Europe and Asia.

Europe

The founder of Transparency International and an activist European lawyer, Jeremy Pope, notes that when TI was launched in the early 1990s, the guiding philosophy was to fight corruption by building a country's "national integrity system." More than a decade later, he concluded that no matter how hard people work trying to strengthen public institutions and implement international standards, little seems to change. The bottom line is that "it does not really matter how strong one's institutions are if the wrong people are inside them" (Pope 2005). An individual's ethics, however acquired and influenced, cannot be ignored. Thus education and training programs are essential to building an individual's ethical infrastructure.

Moreover, he points out that the differences between ethics "best practices" in Western Europe and the United States are apparent. He suggests that the American approach can be seen in a famous cartoon in which a company's ethics advisor is shown addressing his board of directors: "My role," the advisor says, "is to draw a line between what is acceptable, and what is not. And then get the company as close to that line as possible." Drawing the line and then getting as close to it as possible?—a risky and low

low-road proposition. The Western European approach to ethics management is not, as Jeremy Pope puts it, "simply a case of 'lawful conduct.'"

Still, lawful conduct has a place in Europe. Seventeen of the twenty-six E.U. countries prohibit accepting gifts and invitations, with eight of those countries prohibiting gifts above a certain amount—United Kingdom, Austria, Cyprus, Latvia, Lithuania, Italy, Slovenia, and Sweden. All but five E.U. countries—Luxembourg, the Czech Republic, Germany, Denmark, Belgium —require public officials to disclose financial interests (Bossaert and Demmke 2005, 105). Seventeen E.U. countries provide for punitive measures for those who violate ethics rules.

Russia, a non-E.U. country, is struggling with rampant corruption in many sectors. A recently completed two-year study funded by the World Bank reports that Russians pay about $37 billion each year in bribes and unofficial fees.[7] Bribes paid by businesses are mostly directed at low-level local officials to secure licenses and fix the bidding for contracts. Higher-level officials, however, are not immune as some businessmen claim that they pay monthly bribes to federal ministries. Russian native and scholar Jasmine Martirossian (2004, 105) describes the situation in this way:

> Russia, today, has been likened to America's "wild west." Criminal elements seem to be unchecked and it appears that people believe that efforts to expose wrongdoing are fruitless because corrupt public institutions and agencies will fail to act upon complaints, or, if they are acted upon, that the apparatus of corrupt practices will spring into action, bribes will change hands, favors will be exchanged, and no punishments will be meted out.

We turn next to an examination of ethics management in two countries— the United Kingdom and the Netherlands.

United Kingdom

The United Kingdom is a unitary government, although local governments exercise a great deal of autonomy. Nonetheless, the Seven Principles of Public Life put forth by the Nolan Committee in 1995 (see exhibit 6.4) provided a starting point for more aggressive efforts to deal with ethical challenges in government. This landmark event found expression in the 2000 Local Government Act that set forth three principal components for ethics management in the United Kingdom:

1. A requirement that every local authority adopt a Code of Conduct that all councilors must sign up to;

2. A requirement that authorities set up a standards committee to over-see ethical issues and provide advice and guidance on the Code of Conduct and its implementation; and,

3. The establishment of an independent body (the Standards Board) with responsibility for investigating alleged breaches of a Council's Code of Conduct and promoting and maintaining high standards of conduct (Committee on Standards in Public Life 2004).

The Standards Board became operational in March 2001 and has regula-tory responsibility for 386 local authorities, 8,000 parish councils, 31 fire and civil defense authorities, and 44 police authorities. It also covers the Greater London Authority and other regional assemblies. More than 4,000 complaints have been received by the Standards Board, with less than half investigated. Michael Hunt describes this number of complaints as very high (Hunt 2005). A significant number of complaints deal with a failure to register a personal or financial interest. Other complaints allege councilors bring disrepute on their community and do not treat others with respect. Eighty-two councilors have been disqualified from holding office and fifteen members suspended follow-ing a hearing by the Adjudication Panel. The panel is an independent judicial tribunal that hears and adjudicates serious matters concerning the conduct of elected officials (Committee on Standards in Public Life 2004, 13–14).

Another agency, the Audit Commission, is also involved in ethics man-agement. The commission describes itself as an "independent body respon-sible for ensuring that public money is spent economically, efficiently and effectively, to achieve high-quality local and national service for the pub-lic."[8] The commission's approach is not to define ethical governance but to include it as part of an overall definition of governance in the public sector. That is, it is expected to audit the ethical standards and practices of local governments. The audits can result in a Public Interest Report that focuses on any governance issue, including failure to maintain high ethical standards.

Of central importance to the Audit Commission is determining whether poor ethical governance adversely affects performance—a very difficult task. Indeed, the commission's more traditional focus has been on performance compliance and risk assessment. However, it has developed a toolkit, *Chang-ing Organisational Cultures*, that tests "the operation of ethical standards." This includes an assessment of officers' understanding of the local authority's code of conduct.

In 2004, the commission conducted ethical audit reviews of thirty-eight local authorities and concluded that "it is questionable as to whether or not the problems identified by these audits will lead to service failure or poor quality services" (Fawcett and Wardman 2005, 10). At the same time, more than 1,700 middle and senior managers completed the *Changing Organisational Cultures* exercise and were quite positive about their local government's commitment to combating fraud and corruption.

These meritorious efforts were strengthened even more in 2006 when the head of the civil service, Sir Gus O'Donnell, published the new Civil Service Code. Among other things, the code calls for greater transparency, responsiveness, and professionalism in government. "Creating a culture of excellence," Sir Gus exclaims (2006), is an achievable goal. "My vision is for a civil service that exudes pride, pace, passion and professionalism" undergirded by the core values of honesty, objectivity, integrity, and impartiality.

Altogether, the approach taken to ethics management in the United Kingdom is not as heavily compliance-driven as that in the United States, but may be moving in that direction, despite Sir Gus' vision for a revitalized civil service. Jeremy Pope points out that should a litigation culture take hold in the United Kingdom and Western Europe like that in the United States, "the ethics scene here may well shift to that of the United States"—adversarial and "gotcha" oriented (Pope 2005, 6).

The Netherlands

The Netherlands, a decentralized unitary state with a population of 16.5 million, has begun to shift its ethics and integrity policy from a strong compliance focus on rules and regulations to one that emphasizes personal integrity and moral judgment (Hoekstra, Belling, Van Der Heide 2005). This has been described by senior policy advisors in the Ministry of the Interior and Kingdom Relations as going "beyond compliance." That is, the government recognizes the need for rules and regulations but also recognizes that these are not sufficient to ensure ethical governance. Thus, the emerging strategy is one that combines "structure and rules on the one hand and of culture and awareness on the other" (7). This shift in emphasis began slowly in the 1990s but has moved rapidly since 2003, when an investigation into the building industry found that many attempts were made to bribe civil servants. Responding to this situation, lawmakers amended the Civil Servants Act in 2005. The act obligates government bodies to adopt a code of conduct for civil servants and requires all new civil servants to take an oath of office.

The central government's commitment is reflected as well in the establishment in 2005 of a Bureau for Ethics and Integrity Stimulation in the Dutch Ministry of Interior and Kingdom Relations. The bureau provides guidance to managers on the development and implementation of ethics management programs, supports various studies, and analyzes trends and international developments in this field.

The Netherlands Tax and Customs Administration is suggestive of a Dutch agency's attempt to go beyond the establishment of a code of ethics. In 2000, the Tax Administration embarked on an ambitious project to infuse its 30,000 employees with values inherent in the nature of the agency's work. As the director general of the Tax Administration states, "Due to the nature of their work, employees of the Tax Administration can easily find themselves in uncertain or even precarious situations . . . where guidelines and rules alone are not sufficient" (Van Blijswijk et al. 2004, 725). Tax employees must deal with the public fairly and apply the rules in a consistent manner. But this is not always easy to do on a case-by-case basis. Thus rules are not enough. Other necessary steps include (1) training new and current employees on how to handle dilemmas, (2) appointing integrity counselors who will "serve as the first line of inquiry to employees' questions with regard to integrity," (3) creating reflection groups from among integrity counselors to "discuss real-life cases and what actions have been taken," and (4) offering intranet group discussion opportunities for employees (723). The integrity project in the Netherlands points to the value of striking a balance between codifying ethics and meeting the day-to-day challenges of acting with integrity.

Asia

Asian values with an emphasis on personalism, paternalism, and particularlism are sometimes asserted to be different from Western values, which have an emphasis on impersonalism, merit, and rationalism. Thus the giving of gifts in return for favors, for example, is commonplace in much of Asia. Indeed, bribing public officials for favorable considerations is not uncommon. Consider the small Pacific island country of Vanuatu located about three-quarters of the way from Hawaii to Australia. With a tiny population of 205,754, one might expect high ethical standards to prevail. Apparently, this is not so according to Marie-Noelle Ferrieux-Patterson (2003), the president of Transparency International, Vanuatu. She asserts that there is no recognizable moral or ethical code to define right and wrong in the public sphere. Conflicts of interest are especially rampant as people are linked by strong tribal allegiances and "take actions or decisions to pay back past favors or to store up future favors or rewards, such as jobs or contracts."

The situation in all Asian countries is certainly not as dire as suggested by Vanuatu's experience. There is a strong movement to embrace the rule of law throughout the Pacific, Asia, and Southeast Asia. Many countries are putting into place legal and institutional barriers to combat corruption and promote ethical governance. Let's look at what's happening in China and Japan.

China

"We should combine the rule of law with the rule of virtue in order to build a lofty . . . ethical foundation for maintaining a good public order and practice," asserted President Jiang Zemin in 2001.[9] Law and virtue in combination would indeed be a powerful antidote to corruption and unethical behavior. China, with a population of 1.3 billion and more than six million persons in the civil service, has long strived to break the grip of corruption. Since 1981, five major anti-corruption campaigns have taken place. Alas, the struggle continues. The 2005 Corruption Perceptions Index published by Transparency International places China 78th among 158 countries. In 1995, the first year that TI published the index, China placed next to last among the forty-one countries surveyed.

Building organizations of integrity among China's 29 ministries of the central government, 32 provincial governments, 1,735 counties, and 48,000 townships is a substantial challenge. Nonetheless, it is one that officials are committed to meeting. China is a single-party–dominated government. Thus both the Communist Party as represented by the Central Disciplinary Committee and government Ministry of Supervision share responsibility for disciplining civil servants who engage in illegal and unethical acts. The approach taken by China, according to Robert W. Smith, is strikingly similar to that in the United States, although more formalistic. That is, there are fewer opportunities for informal, negotiated settlements of cases in China than there are in the United States.

Smith (2004) also asserts that China has many anti-corruption and ethics entities, perhaps more than any other country (311). Audit bureaus, centers for reporting corruption, offices of general inspection of financial and fiscal discipline, and nonofficial corruption monitors and bureaus of anti-graft and bribery have been established at various levels of government. These bodies possess strong investigatory and sanctioning powers and invoke harsh penalties, even death penalties, on offenders. In 1999, 4,322 public servants were found guilty of ethics violations, among whom were fifty-eight senior officials. In corruption cases, the death penalty "has been exercised with great frequency during the past few decades . . ." (314).

In 2005, four years and thirteen drafts later, the Chinese national legislature approved a law featuring a code of conduct that outlines the rights and obligations of civil servants. The law, however, stopped short of requiring top civil servants to disclose their personal financial obligations, which critics assert is a significant omission. "There should be no doubt that the public's right to know should weigh more heavily than officials' right to privacy," a news article in the *China Daily* asserts.[10] As this criticism suggests, mainland

China's approach to ethics management is limited in scope and focuses almost exclusively on corruption.

Whistle blowing is encouraged in some Chinese provinces. The Guangdong provincial government, for example, began rewarding whistle blowers in 1995 to root out corruption. Financial rewards were paid out to fifty-five whistle blowers totaling 140,000 yuan—approximately $18,000 U.S. dollars (Gong 2000). Whistle blowing can be done by telephone, letter, or personal visits. Whistle blowing centers also exist in many localities that provide toll-free hotlines for reporting wrongdoing. The effectiveness of whistle blowing in China is difficult to estimate. Ting Gong, who has studied whistle blowing in the Chinese culture, claims that many potential whistle blowers remain silent because corrupt officials "are often protected by an organizational network involving lower and higher ranking officials and sometimes even people in anti-corruption agencies. They collaborate with each other to cover up their corrupt activities" (1915).

Public Service in China

Efforts to instill a public service ethos in the Chinese civil service face significant obstacles. Among other things, there is little evidence that universities are undertaking this Herculean task. Ninety-two Chinese universities offer graduate study in public administration (compared to 250 U.S. universities).[11] The course subject matter for the MPA (master's of public administration) degree includes two courses with heavy ideological content—the construction of socialism and Marxist theory. Other subjects include those commonplace in the West—public policy analysis, management, information technology, administrative law, and economics. Courses on ethics are noticeably absent. However, this deficiency has been recognized, and Chinese scholars have called for curriculum reform. Lan Xue and Zongchao Peng (2004, 26) assert that "we should improve students' ethical self-cultivation and their ethical analysis ability in the public administration process."

Calls have also been made to strengthen the competency training of Chinese public servants. Currently, the training emphasis is more knowledge oriented than competency oriented (Wang 2004). Moreover, Zukun He (2004, 148) claims that "the government should care about public servants' moral and ethical education, strengthen their sense of responsibility and sense of service; only in this way can the efficiency of the government's responsiveness be better."

Hong Kong

Hong Kong, a former crown colony of Great Britain until 1997, is a Special Administrative Region (SAR) in China with a population of seven million.

Scholars describe the prevailing brand of administrative ethics in Hong Kong as "a curious mix of modern Weberian notions on the one hand and traditional Confucian values on the other" (Lui and Scott 2001, 650). Hong Kong civil servants are expected to be competent administrators who subscribe to the values of neutrality and loyalty to the hierarchy—Weberian notions. Confucian values enter in as well, stressing virtue and rule by scholar-officials. That is, good government depends on the kindness and wisdom of those who rule. This is a form of "rule by man," whereas the Weberian notions emphasize the "rule of law." The result, according to Lui and Scott, is that the Hong Kong bureaucracy "operates as a corporate moral entity" (657). As the authors note,

> The individual official remains a faceless, anonymous bureaucrat, a cog in a machine who has no moral identity outside his place in the collectivity. An "ethical" civil servant is one who abides by the norms of the organization and the orders of his superiors (657).

Hong Kong civil servants do not espouse values "beyond what the bureaucracy has inculcated in them" (653). Although rules and regulations abound, "they are largely designed to facilitate efficient organizational operations rather than to prescribe norms of moral behavior" (653). While Hong Kong has an ombudsman and an anti-corruption body, the Independent Commission Against Corruption, they have not been capable of drawing much attention to the significance of administrative ethics (653). Professionally oriented codes of conduct also exist but are not well publicized and are nearly unenforceable (Lui 1988).

Ethics management in China as well as in Hong Kong is at a nascent stage with much distance to go before a claim to ethical governance can be asserted. At the same time, there is promise of a more professional civil service as the management of civil servants is increasingly merit oriented with an emphasis on performance, character, ability, self-discipline, and achievement as the basis for promotion and reward (Zhu 2000). Nonetheless, administrative behavior is dependent on self-control as there are few significant controls outside the institution of government (1961).

Japan

Japan has 4.4 million public employees of whom one-quarter work for the national government and the remaining three-quarters for local governments in prefectures, cities, towns, and villages. School teachers are considered public employees and constitute one-fifth of the public-employee workforce.

Exhibit 6.5
General Ethical Principles in Japan's National
Public Service Ethics Law

1. Employees shall not give unfair, discriminative treatment to the public . . . and shall always engage in their duties with fairness, recognizing that they are servants of the whole nation and not of any group thereof.
2. Employees shall always distinguish between public and private affairs and shall not use their duties or positions for private gain for themselves or the organization they belong to.
3. Employees shall not take any actions that create public suspicion or distrust against the fairness of public service while performing their duties, such as receiving a gift from entities influenced by their duties.

Source: 72.14.209.104/search?q=cache:J6djWtg-XnQJ:unpan1.un.org/ intradoc/groups/public/documents/APCITY/UNPAN019109.pdf+japan% 27s+national+public+service+law&hl=en&gl=us&ct=clnk&cd=1&client= firefox-a. Accessed June 26, 2006.

Ethics management in Japan is a work in progress. In 1999, the Japanese Diet (the National Assembly) enacted the National Public Service Ethics Law. This law set in motion a limited but nonetheless important approach to advancing ethics and integrity in the governance of Japan. Among other things, the law set forth three general ethical principles, established an Ethics Board in the national administration, created ethics supervisors, called for the promulgation of a National Public Service Officials Ethics Code (see exhibit 6.5), and provided for the introduction of ethics management in local government.

The Ethics Board was placed in the National Personnel Authority, an independent agency whose mission is to ensure fairness in personnel management and develop personnel management policies. The board comprises a president and four members. All members of the board are appointed by the Cabinet. A fifteen-person staff supports the work of the board (Kudo and Maesschalck 2005). The board's central ethics management responsibilities include:

- Preparing and revising standards for disciplinary action against employees who violate ethics principles or rules.

- Planning and coordinating ethics training programs within and across ministries and agencies.
- Investigating alleged violations of the Ethics Law and taking disciplinary actions against violations or requesting ministers to do so for violations in their ministry.

The law also called for the appointment of an ethics supervisory officer in each ministry or agency. The ethics supervisory officers are expected to provide guidance and advice to co-workers on ethics issues and to establish management systems that foster ethical behavior consistent with directions provided by the National Public Service Ethics Board.

The Ethics Code incorporated the three earlier mentioned ethical principles and added two more standards for ethical behavior:

- Employees shall, in performance of their duties, aim at increasing public interests and exert their utmost efforts.
- Employees shall always behave recognizing that their actions may influence the trust in the public service, even outside of their official hours.

Following the inclusion of these two principles, the code then becomes "very specific and in fact focuses on only one issue of ethics management: whether or not public servants can accept favours (presents, hospitality, benefits, etc.) from individuals or entities" that could be affected by the actions of government officials during the course of their work (Kudo and Maesschalck 2005, 13–14).

The National Personnel Authority is responsible for the development of training programs, which consist of two basic types: general training for improvement of administrative duties and professional training that focuses on specific skills and techniques. Ethics sensitivity training is available to junior and mid-level managers, although senior-level administrators are exempted.[12] Training for ethics managers is organized by the Ethics Board and is typically a "detailed explanation of the Ethics Law and Ethics Code and the discussion of specific cases, including actual case of violations against the Law or the Code" (Kudo and Maesschalck 2005,15). The Ethics Board has also published and distributed an ethics handbook that explains ethics regulations.

In summary, ethics management in Japan is narrowly focused on compliance with the Ethics Law and Ethics Code as evidenced by the fact that, among other things, it is directed at curbing expensive wining and dining of senior bureaucrats by those who seek favors from them. The approach taken in Japan parallels closely the legalistic approach taken by many American states with an emphasis on prescribing and proscribing acceptable behavior.

Moving Forward

Are nations around the globe embracing ethics management strategies? Yes, but primarily from the perspective of combating corruption through laws, rules, and regulations. The limitations of this approach are straightforward. It reduces ethical behavior to a minimalist conception (don't break the law or regulations) and encourages a narrow, legalistic approach to defining acceptable behavior.

However, there is reason to be optimistic about a change in direction. Kenneth Kernaghan (2003), a Canadian ethics scholar, points to changes in Australia, New Zealand, the United Kingdom, and Canada. He suggests that these countries are moving toward a value-driven approach to strengthening the ethical culture of their governments. He points to the 1999 *Vision and Values Statement* intended to complement the U.K. Civil Service Code as evidence. In Canada, he notes that the Office of Values and Ethics, which was established in 1999, published a *Values and Ethics Code for the Public Service* (2003). In New Zealand, the State Services Commission put the accent on core values in public service with the publication of *Walking the Talk: Making Values Real* (2001). This guide encourages public servants to uphold core values such as trust and integrity in their decisions and actions. Australia, Kernaghan asserts, "is the most notable for its recognition of the central importance of leadership to effective integration of the right values into public service" (718).

Conclusion

Ethics management worldwide is important. Indeed, the United Nations has been at the forefront in encouraging countries to embrace ethics and integrity in governance. At a 1997 conference on Public Service in Transition held in Greece, more than twenty countries from Eastern and Central Europe and representatives from international organizations such as the European Commission gathered to discuss what can be done to facilitate "capacity building in the broad areas of governance, public administration and finance" (United Nations 1999, 15). Ranked near the top of the list was the critical importance of probity and integrity. The raising of ethical standards and performance in government would require more than combating corruption. "Public service ethics encompass a broad and widening range of principles and values . . . objectivity, impartiality, fairness, sensitivity, compassion, responsiveness, accountability, and selfless devotion to duty" (2). More than anything else, the conference participants concluded, "the transition to a free and open society calls for rededication to democratic values, the respect of human rights and belief in the service of citizens and of the common good" (2).

There is little question that corruption impedes the possibility of a universal public service ethic and, therefore, international agreement on the adoption of effective ethics management strategies. There is another important reason why a universal public service ethic has yet to emerge. It is the belief that cultural and religious norms and traditions strongly influence the ethics of a society. Consequently, what is an acceptable ethical practice or behavior in one society may not be acceptable in another. This culturally deterministic definition of ethics suggests that right and wrong behavior is relative, not universal. Put differently, ethical norms and behaviors are embedded in and defined by a country's culture. But does this mean that there are no values that transcend the cultural diversity of societies? Not necessarily, Gilman and Lewis contend. "There are fundamental values—treated at a high level of abstraction—that are closely associated with democracy, market economy, and professional bureaucracy" (Gilman and Lewis 1996, 518). These fundamental values include respect for human dignity, freedom from oppression, fairness, and truth and honesty in civic life.

Ethics Management Skill Building

Practicum 6.1. The Greater Good

As a contract manager for the U.S. Department of Defense with an office located in Saudi Arabia, your job is to ensure that contracts are managed properly so that the procurement of goods and equipment reaches American military forces in a cost-effective and timely manner. Several months ago the U.S. Air Force ordered more than $250,000 worth of equipment that is now sitting at the customs agency on the other side of the country. The Saudi customs agency has held up delivery for some unknown reason, perhaps a technicality. The politics of the situation is such that the United States does not want to rock the boat by challenging Saudi officials.

As the contracting officer, you feel obligated to get the equipment released as quickly as possible. To accomplish this you know it is necessary to secure a release document notarized by a high-ranking U.S. official. The document is time sensitive. To your dismay you discover that the finance officer dropped the ball and will delay securing the signature by one day. To make matters worse, the release document will become null and void if not secured immediately.

Frantic, you make every effort to reach the official whose signature is needed but discover that he is not available. What should you do under these circumstances?

Although you have no authority to do so, you decide to call the legal officer at the western end of the country and request that he redo the whole document. Furthermore, you encourage him to do whatever needs to be done, including changing the date. He asks a bunch of questions, so you instruct him on how to cut, paste, and copy and redo the official seal—in essence to falsify the document.

You rationalize that you had no choice. The process of negotiations to even get to the point of getting the equipment out of customs would take several months. Lining up and coordinating all of these agencies would be very time consuming, and you contend, "I am not about to blow it on a stupid piece of legally required document."

Furthermore, you muse, there are only two of us who will ever know the document is falsified—myself and the attorney. Your success in securing the release of the equipment motives DoD to give you an award. Further reflecting on what you did, you say to yourself—"I did not pay for those goods, U.S. taxpayers did. And if it were my money, I'd have done the same. If I had not been able to secure the release of the equipment, it was going to go into the country's local market. They were not going to return it to the vendor."

Musing further, "Every situation violates some person's ethics, so, whose do we choose? And at what point do we as administrators determine that our ethics are above that of another employee's? There are obvious ones in which, generally speaking, we say never to do—knowingly falsifying documents for one. But, I'm thinking . . . you know, there may be a situation in which doing that particular thing would be more ethical than not doing it."

Questions

1. Do you think it is ever ethical to falsify a document?
2. Did falsifying the document to secure the release of U.S. Air Force equipment justify the act?
3. Are there career risks for falsifying a document?

Practicum 6.2. Religious Expression in the Workplace

You are the chief of the State Division of Vehicular Licensing with 1,250 employees located at six district offices. The director of District 2 approaches you about a thorny problem—what to do about providing employees who are Muslims a suitable time of the day to worship. The problem began on October 30, when the state shifted from Central Daylight Savings Time to Central Standard Time. As it turns out, the "fall back" of the clock pulled the Muslim sunset prayer back into the work hours.

A group of Muslim workers requested that the district office allow them to conduct their sunset prayer at 5 P.M. The district office closes at 6 P.M. The group said that they would be willing to work from 6:00 P.M. to 7:00 P.M. to make up for the time lost.

The director is unsure what other districts have done and does not know if state law requires public agencies to accommodate employees' religious beliefs. It is, of course, clear to all that public agencies cannot promote religious beliefs and practices, but this is not quite the same thing.

As the division chief, you inform the director that other district offices have not faced this issue before. Moreover, state law is reasonably clear—employers (public and private) must accommodate employees' religious beliefs as long as the requests are reasonable and do not create a hardship for the agency.

Questions

1. Is the request by the workers reasonable?
2. Would shifting the sunset prayer hour to 5 P.M. create a hardship for the District Office of Vehicular Licensing? (Remember that the primary work of the District Office is to issue licenses to the public on a first-come, first-serve basis.)
3. Would agreeing to the request be viewed as favoritism toward one group of employees? If so, would this create morale problems?
4. What recommendation would you, as division chief, make to the district director?

Notes

1. www.u4.no/document/toolkits.cfm. Accessed January 3, 2006.
2. www.transparency.org/sourcebook/00-about.html. Accessed January 3, 2006.
3. www.oecd.org/dataoecd/43/8/34107314.pdf. Accessed January 3, 2006.
4. www.oecd.org/dataoecd/59/60/1899269.pdf. Accessed January 3, 2006.
5. www.transparency.org/ach/pub_sector/conduct/implementation.html. Accessed January 3, 2006.
6. www.lawphil.net/. Accessed June 25, 2006.
7. www.templetonthorp.com/fr/news31. Accessed January 3, 2006.
8. www.audit-commission.gov.uk/aboutus/index.asp. Accessed January 3, 2006.
9. www.news.xinhuanet.com/English/20010726/433649.htm. Accessed August 2, 2005.
10. www2.chinadaily.com.cn/english/doc/2005–04/29/content_438416.htm. Accessed January 3, 2006.
11. In parallel with the schools of administration in China, there is a system of Communist Party training schools that have a much longer history. Programs at party schools, while focusing more on political and ideological areas, are increasingly management oriented (Wang 2004, 36).
12. www.jinji.go.jp/english/fig/fig_15.htm. Accessed January 3, 2006.

7

Ethical Governance in the Twenty-First Century

> *"Most of the things worth doing in the world had been declared impossible before they were done."*
> —Justice Louis Brandeis

What emerging issues and challenges should we focus on to ensure that ethical governance moves forward, not backward, in the twenty-first century? There are many. Among them are privatization, the Information Age, the global pursuit of economic well-being and democratic governance, and ethics education. The future, it so often seems, is here with the historic boundary between public and private sectors a vast blur. Equally blurred is the time line between the past, present, and future. The time warp of cyberspace and instantaneous worldwide communication has all but collapsed our calendars. In this concluding chapter, we take a close look at these challenges that must be overcome to foster ethical governance.

The Privatization Challenge

The privatization of public services and facilities is in full force worldwide. Governments of all sizes and descriptions are redefining their roles and responsibilities in providing and delivering public services. Cities, counties, states, and the U.S. government are entering into new relationships with private-sector organizations—profit and nonprofit—to "create a government that works better and costs less," to borrow the title of the *Report of the National Performance Review* (1993). In some instances, the result has been load shedding—disengaging entirely as a governmental service provider. In other instances, government contracting with a private profit-making firm or a nonprofit organization to deliver public services has been the preferred modus operandi.

When David Osborne and Ted Gaebler issued their clarion call in *Reinventing Government: How the Entrepreneurial Spirit Is Transforming the*

Public Sector (1992), the response was nearly instantaneous and widespread. The reinventors endorsed privatization and called for public managers to be entrepreneurial in leading their agencies. Precious little was uttered about what privatization or entrepreneurialism might mean for ethical management. Indeed, there is no mention of ethics in their book. Perhaps Osborne and Gaebler believed there is little to be concerned about since they are not calling for managers to engage in illegal activities—merely to manage differently within the law.

Laura Abbott (2006) who worked for twenty-six years as a uniformed officer of the U.S. Public Health Service in the Department of Health and Human Services describes her experience with contractors in this way:

> It has been frustrating because even if the legal means are available to force contractors to meet their deliverables, at least in my department, the will to enforce them is seriously impaired or perhaps intentionally ignored. As government has turned to greater and greater use of contractors, supposedly for support functions, the chain of accountability and sense of common purpose has been much diminished. . . .

H. George Frederickson (1997, 194) pulls no punches in asserting that the privatization movement will eventually collapse or, at a minimum, retreat on the heels of greed and corruption amid renewed "calls for administrative competence in government." Contracting in particular, Frederickson (193) reminds us, has "always made a tempting environment for kickbacks and fraud. Doesn't anyone remember why Spiro Agnew resigned as vice president?" Frederickson's indictment is unflinching. "As more privately inclined people are appointed to governmental positions and as more governmental services are based on the enterprise model," the more likely it is that we will experience corruption and unethical behavior (180).

Linda deLeon takes a more optimistic view of ethics, privatization, and public management entrepreneurship. She (1996, 496) argues that "public entrepreneurship can be, and at its best is, ethical." She acknowledges, however, that the values commonly associated with successful private-sector entrepreneurs—egotism, selfishness, waywardness, domination, and opportunism—if not adequately constrained or checked may result in norms antithetical to the public interest. Self-serving, profit-seeking, calculating public entrepreneurial managers may be able, if successful, to spot opportunities and marshal resources to produce innovation, but the trade-off may be a diminished ethical environment. Nonetheless, deLeon believes that ethical entrepreneurship is possible and should be encouraged in public organizations.

But what evidence do we have that privatization or reinvention or entrepreneurialism threatens ethical management in government or, at worst, evokes corrupt and unethical behavior? Some evidence is supplied by Cohen and Eimicke (1999) who have investigated three cases of public entrepreneurship—the Orange County financial bankruptcy case resulting from a $1.6-billion loss; a risky hotel partnership project in Visalia, California; and the successful privatization of Indianapolis's wastewater-treatment plants.

The Orange County, California case is an example of entrepreneurship gone amok ethically, crossing over into the illegal. Robert Citron, the county treasurer, invested locally pooled funds in fiscal instruments known as derivatives that produced spectacular financial gains until interest rates began to rise. When this happened, the financial bottom fell out and eventually forced the treasurer out of office and Orange County into bankruptcy in 1994. Two years later, Citron was sentenced to one year in jail and fined $100,000.

The Visalia case is more problematic as an ethics failure or success story. What is clear is that the city took risks with taxpayer dollars when its partnership with the Radisson hotel chain to build and operate a hotel on city-owned property floundered. The end result was that the city was forced into buying the hotel and assuming its debts.

In Indianapolis, the city often cited as the epicenter of municipal privatization, Mayor Stephen Goldsmith set about privatizing more than forty city services in the early 1990s. Among those services were the waste-water-treatment plants. Although the city's plants were considered efficient, the city administration decided to contract out the services. The result was that a firm based in France with 51 percent ownership by the local Indianapolis Water Company won the contract and was able to achieve significant financial savings. Based upon their examination of the experiences of these three cases, Cohen and Eimicke conclude that public entrepreneurship can be ethical, but that a large measure of care, caution, and competence should be exercised.

As a case in point Richard K. Ghere (1996) describes the arguable if not unethical results of a partnership forged between a metropolitan county in a Midwestern state and a local chamber of commerce. The county sought to promote tourism, attract convention business, and develop a regional economic development strategy that would lure international business. A 3 percent hotel/motel bed tax was earmarked for this purpose, and the local chamber of commerce was contracted with to provide these services. Suffice it to say that chamber officials were delighted with this arrangement and were energetic partners—perhaps too energetic. As time passed, a number of "irregularities" began to accrue. These included non-competitive awards made to vendors who had family connections with chamber officials, falsification of expense reports and convention business activities, golf and dinner outings for county commissioners paid for by the chamber, and questionable international travel provided by the chamber for county officials. Ghere's analysis does not detail the extent to which the chamber's practices may have permeated county government as a whole. But it is clear that the relationship or partnership at the top did little to foster an ethical climate. Indeed, this case points out how the privatization of a public function amounted to the diminishment, if not privatization, of ethical behavior ordinarily expected of public officials. The contract, of course, was the vehicle for this transformation.

Other stories of privatization challenges to ethical governance can be found in Florida. The next sections illustrate three of these stories.

Use and Abuse of Insider Information

Another contractual ethical issue is the use and abuse of insider information. Consider the State of Florida, which, under Republican governor Jeb Bush (1998–2006), has moved full force into the privatization of Florida government. Insider information was apparently used in securing a $126-million state technology contract by a private firm. An investigation by the Florida Department of Law Enforcement concluded that the company had insider information as the company easily won the contract over nineteen competitors. Here's what happened. A company employee who was hired as a consultant also served as the de facto chief of staff for the State Technology Office, the granting agency. An editorial in the *St. Petersburg Times* (2005) described the situation as "a curious work environment, one in which government employees and those hired under contract were virtually indistinguishable." The Florida Department of Law Enforcement and the state attorney, despite having misgivings about the curious work environment, decided they lacked sufficient evidence to criminally prosecute the company. One unexpected outcome, however, was the finding that Florida's ethics laws do not apply to private-sector employees when they have acted in a state agency executive capacity.

Private Contracting for Prison Management

In 2004, thirty-four American states awarded contracts to private profit-making firms to operate prisons. Florida was one of those states. The state contracted with private firms in 1993 to manage its prison system. The law also created the eight-member Correctional Privatization Commission to oversee the contractors who manage five prisons at a cost of $106.4 million a year. A decade later, however, dissatisfaction with the lack of management oversight by the commission had reached the point where the Florida legislature said "enough." In 2005, the Florida legislature terminated the Correctional Privatization Commission (CPC) and transferred all of its powers and duties to the Florida Department of Management Services (DMS). What happened?

A review by the Florida Office of the Inspector General (2005) of the financial transactions of the CPC uncovered sordid details about this particular form of private-public cooperation. It seems as if the two for-profit prison companies overbilled the state by $12.7 million during this period. The commission paid the two contractors—Corrections Corporations of America and the GEO Group—for guards that did not exist at the prisons. The overbilled funds were then remitted back to the CPC's Grants and Donations Trust Fund to enable the CMC to pay staff salaries. As it turns out, the legislature eliminated the commission's budget in 2001 but not the commission. Thus the commission found a creative, entrepreneurial way to keep its ten-member staff employed. Is it any wonder that the CPC failed at overseeing the contractors?

Privatizing Home Building Reviews and Inspections

The privatization of home building plan reviews and inspections to ensure that codes are met illustrates another side to public-private cooperation in Florida. Many communities are experiencing a significant building boom. Consequently, the building departments of local governments have not been able to process permits and conduct inspections in a manner deemed timely by the building industry. Some building departments take up to six weeks or more to turn around a building permit. Thus the Florida legislature came to the rescue. In 2002, the legislature enacted the "Private Provider Law" (FS 553.791), which enables a building owner to use a private provider to satisfy building code compliance plans and carry out inspections for the structural, mechanical, electrical, and plumbing components of a building. The law requires the builder to notify the local government of the owner's intent to use a private provider. The local building official must then issue the requested permit or provide written notice to the permit applicant identifying the specific plan features that do not comply with the code within thirty business days. If the local building official does not provide a written notice of the plan's deficiencies within the thirty-day period, the permit application is deemed a matter of law and the permit must be issued by the local building official on the next business day.

The Private Provider Law has resulted in a new industry with several engineering firms hiring plan reviewers and inspectors whom, by law, must be state certified and licensed. The president of Capri Engineering, whose firm has ten offices throughout Florida, asserts that "the private provider law came along at the right time. It's a wonderful opportunity for the public and private sectors to work for the benefit of the community." Others are not so sure, describing the situation as the classic "fox in the hen house." One county building official put it this way: "They are a for-profit business. Our duty is to serve the public—they're not doing this as a public service. We are here to protect the public in that sense." The verdict is still out regarding how successful the cooperation will be between the corps of private providers and local government building departments. Time will tell.

These Florida experiences illustrate the challenging nature that the privatization movement poses for public officials who want to embrace sound ethical management practices. As Frederickson (1997, 171) notes, "it is no small irony that government is moving in the direction of privatization at the same time that there is a rising concern for governmental ethics."

Information (R)Age Challenges

The privatization "rage" is occurring at a time that coincides with another "rage"—the information "rage." Americans and citizens worldwide are acquiring PCs, CD-ROMs, handheld devices, MP3 players, and "going online." The language of the Internet, the World Wide Web, browsers, search engines, e-mail, listservs, blogs, chat rooms, HTML, and more has become commonplace vocabulary. Today's workplace, whether in the central office, field office, or home, is an increasingly high-tech, information-driven workplace.

Governments throughout the United States have climbed onto the Information Highway en masse. The technical aspects of accessing the Internet pale alongside the attempt to understand and abate the undesirable, and sometimes unethical, consequences that this technology can have on group life in public agencies. A study of the negative effects of e-mail on social life in the corporate workplace found that effects, such as making the workplace less personal, were a product of two factors—the technology itself (for example, the depersonalization of social relations due to the absence of face-to-face interaction) and intentional choices by users or employees "to avoid unwanted social interactions" (Markus 1994, 119). In other words, technology is not singularly responsible for "negative" social effects in the workplace. Employees can and do make intentional choices in deciding who they do and do not want to communicate with. Managers committed to promoting a strong ethical climate are likely to find this situation especially difficult, particularly in light of our rudimentary knowledge of such behavior.

Another ethical challenge facing managers is implementing and monitoring Internet usage practices. These include surfing the Web on agency time for personal pleasure, downloading or viewing obscene material, advertising or soliciting for personal gain, making political statements, posting or downloading inflammatory racial or sexual material, waging or selling chances, and using pseudo names when transmitting electronic messages. What can be done to discourage these practices? One approach is to adopt Internet Acceptable Use policies. But what if these policies do not work and abuse occurs? Ethics management leaders may then have to take further steps. This has happened in the City of Tampa where four city parking division employees were fired after sending e-mails with discriminatory references to sex, race, and ethnicity. Human Resources director Sarah Lang said that "their e-mails were specifically directed at specific employees in a pattern of e-mails that lent themselves to sexual harassment" (Varian 2005). A follow-up investigation of employees' work habits found that other city workers, forty-four in fact, had sent e-mails that violated the city's business-only e-mail policy. Disciplinary letters were sent to these individuals with a copy placed in their personnel file. To promote the city's zero-tolerance Internet-use policy, the HR director sent letters to all personnel reminding them that it is against the rules to send personal e-mails from city-owned computers. Additionally, when employees now sign on to their computers, they are greeted with an on-screen message requiring them to acknowledge the city rule banning the personal use of e-mail.

There is an awareness that the Internet can be a vital gateway to innovative, responsive government. Thus, there is an incentive to provide employees access to and encourage experimentation with the vast storehouse of data and information on the World Wide Web. Consider the approach taken by the city manager of Sarasota, Florida, Michael McNees who created a blog to communicate with residents. His blog (srqcm.blogspot.com/) had more than 10,000 visitors during the first six months. Although opinions are mixed regarding the value of the blog as a vehicle for communicating with city residents, his willingness to use this medium to reach out to citizens earned him the 2006 "Courage in Communication" award from the Florida City/ County Management Association.

Other ethical, perhaps legal issues go beyond citizen and employee access and use of the Internet and have to do with the posture of government itself. Online governments and their leaders must position themselves to promote democratic practices such as citizen access to public information while at the same time ensuring that sensitive information is protected. It is one thing to post data about crime rates or AIDS statistics and another to allow access to names or addresses of victims. Likewise, the question might be asked: Is a public service being provided when the county property appraiser's office creates a searchable database containing property values and locations? Or is this merely making it easier for criminals to employ the same technology to target would-be victims?

Many local governments that face lean budget years might be encouraged to adopt entrepreneurial practices such as selling advertising space on their home page or endorsing a commercial product as the official product of their government. Are these practices ethical? Legal? The commercialization of the Internet is well underway. But how far should we go in commercializing government?

Finally, there is the matter of electronic communication between and among public officials and citizens. Few (small *d*) democrats would object to e-mail replacing fax messages between citizens and officials, but it may be an entirely different matter when the communication path is between officeholders. Will the Information Age, especially in its electronic form, effectively dismantle government in the sunshine? Or, will officials exercise due care, diligence, and caution before jumping on the keyboard and sending an important message to colleagues or top managers?

The Winds of Globalization

A popular saying in the 1970s was that "small is beautiful," a reaction to big government, big corporations, and big policy failures in America. Three decades later, it can truly be said that small is beautiful globally. With the advent of high-powered technology, instant communication transmissions, endless choice through direct satellite TV programming, and shrinking travel distances and time, the world has never been so small. Elected and appointed officials in places as far-flung as Beijing, Lima, Moscow, Cairo, Johannesburg, London, and Brisbane are instantly aware of the latest political and economic developments in Washington, Chicago, and Tallahassee.

The winds of globalization blew with powerful market-driven force during much of the 1990s. First thought to be only an economic force as countries such as China and Russia and Vietnam embraced market-based reforms, globalization began to expand its reach as a social and political agent of change as countries began to democratize and engage in increasingly transparent policy making. The rule of law became more than a mantra; it became a means through which political leaders envisioned the possibility of seismic shifts in improving their countries' well-being and, in some instances, lifting their people out of poverty.

Globalization writ large began to touch Americans as well. Appointed and elected officials found themselves scrambling to connect their communities with the opening and exciting opportunities abroad. Sister-city programs sprung up along with international trade delegations from cities, counties, and states traveling far and wide to explore the new world order, as it was sometimes labeled. Today, there is scarcely a large city or county that does not have an international affairs office.

Public managers soon learned that it was important for them and their organizations to "think globally." This perspective has been reinforced by professional associations such as the International City/County Management Association (ICMA) and the American Society for Public Administration. Both associations have launched initiatives that emphasis international affairs. Thus managers are increasingly confronted by the norms and ways of different cultures. This has been especially challenging in situations where the cultures vary regarding what is and is not ethical. Giving and receiving gifts among public officeholders in Asian cultures, for example, are commonplace happenings. Similar practices in the United States are viewed with suspicion, and many cities and counties have zero-gift policies.

These differences continue to be debated with one argument calling for a global ethic—a framework for defining right and wrong that knows no social, economic, or political borders. Easier said than done? No question about it. Still, the search for a global ethic is meritorious.

Worldwide ethics management is important. Indeed, the United Nations has been at the forefront in encouraging countries to embrace ethics and integrity in governance. At a 1997 conference on Public Service in Transition held in Greece, more than twenty countries from Eastern and Central Europe and representatives from international organizations such as the European Commission gathered to discuss what can be done to facilitate "capacity building in the broad areas of governance, public administration and finance" (United Nations 1999, 15). Ranked near the top of the list was the critical importance of probity and integrity. The raising of standards and performance in government would require more than combating corruption. "Public service ethics encompass a broad and widening range of principles and values . . . objectivity, impartiality, fairness, sensitivity, compassion, responsiveness, accountability, and selfless devotion to duty" (2). More than anything else, the participants concluded, "transition to a free and open society calls for rededication to democratic values, the respect of human rights and belief in the service of citizens and of the common good" (2).

Ethics Education Challenges

Education for professional public administrators is carried out primarily through 253 institutions of higher education in the United States that provide graduate or undergraduate study in public affairs and administration. As of June 2006, one hundred fifty-five graduate programs at 147 schools were accredited by the National Association of Schools of Public Affairs and Administration (NASPAA). The master's of public affairs/policy/administration (MPA) degree is increasingly viewed by the practitioner community as the degree of preference. The inclusion of professional ethics in the course of study adds considerable value to the MPA.

The teaching of ethics is a multifaceted and often controversial enterprise. It is multifaceted because the field of public administration ranges broadly within and across organizations, nations, and cultures. It is often controversial because there is little agreement on what to teach and how to teach ethics. Indeed, some persons believe that ethics cannot be taught in a traditional class or course context. Rather, the best that can be hoped for is to teach *about* ethics. Still, there is a widespread view among practicing administrators and educators that an ethical public service is essential to a well-functioning democracy. Accordingly, teaching ethics to men and women who occupy positions of public trust should and must be pursued regardless of the uncertain outcomes.

There are three approaches to teaching ethics: sensitivity and awareness, moral reasoning, and leadership and exemplar modeling.

Sensitivity and Awareness Teaching

A sensitivity and awareness approach has moved along two primary paths. The first path is legalistic and is often reflected in the advice and instruction provided by state ethics commissions to state and local public employees and elected officials. This approach puts the accent on the "do's and don'ts" of state ethics laws. These laws, as noted in chapter 3, emphasize conflicts of interest, financial disclosure, whistle-blowing protection, and confidentiality of information. This "how to stay out of trouble" approach is also embraced by the U.S. Office of Government Ethics. The bad news is that this approach often reduces acceptable behavior to the lowest level of "if it's not illegal, it's okay!"—which, as John Rohr reminds us in *Ethics for Bureaucrats* (1978), is the "low road" to public service ethics.

The second path is semi-legalistic with a focus on professional codes of ethics or agency rules of acceptable behavior. At the professional association level, for example, nearly every public service group has a code of ethics that its members are expected to support. Two associations are illustrative in this regard—the American Society for Public Administration (ASPA) and the International City/County Management Association (ICMA).

ASPA is a 8,500-member organization consisting primarily of educators, students, and public employees drawn from local, state, and federal agencies and members of nonprofit associations. The ASPA code, which was adopted in 1984, identifies five key principles: (1) serve the public interest, (2) respect the Constitution and the law, (3) demonstrate personal integrity, (4) promote ethical organizations, and (5) strive for professional excellence. Members who violate the code can be expelled from ASPA, but there has been few such actions taken (see www.aspanet.org).

The ICMA is a 7,500-member organization consisting primarily of practicing public managers in cities and counties in the United States and abroad (for example, Ireland and Australia). The ICMA code dates to 1924 and provides specific guidance on acceptable and unacceptable behaviors of local government managers. For example, it is deemed unethical for a city manager to leave her management post with less than two years of service, unless there are extenuating circumstances such as severe personal problems. It is also viewed as unethical for a city manager to endorse a commercial product that a vendor might sell to a local government. The ICMA actively enforces the code with a half dozen or more members sanctioned nearly every year for violations (see www.icma.org/go.cfm).

The teaching of ethics based on codes or administrative rules of behavior such as the preceding examples stress the contents of the codes or the rules themselves, which, unfortunately, can become ends in themselves. The teaching of codes and rules is often conducted by personnel within a governmental agency, management consultants, and college and university instructors, especially those in graduate-degree-granting programs that prepare men and women for public service careers.

Moral Reasoning

A second approach to teaching ethics in public administration is moral reasoning. The effort here presumes that one can learn to reason through a difficult moral or ethical dilemma. Learning how to act ethically in public service is just that—a learning process, which when a real-world ethical dilemma arises can be applied with desirable outcomes. The reasoning process puts the accent on decision making through ethical reflection based on the interplay of moral rules, ethical principles, self-appraisal, and justification. At the heart of this exercise is what Cooper (2006) calls exercising one's moral imagination to sort through right or wrong decision outcomes.

Another proponent of teaching ethical decision making is Carol W. Lewis who, in *The Ethics Challenge in Public Service* (1991), presents the reader with a problem-solving guide. Her guide engages the learner with real and hypothetical decision-making scenarios, self-assessment tools, and questions that stimulate ethical reflection. She contends that neither the "low" road of compliance nor the "high" road of integrity is a realistic guide for navigating the often stormy political and bureaucratic environments of public service. Rather, it is necessary to develop a two-pronged, systematic strategy that incorporates the path of compliance with both formal standards and the path of individual integrity. She labels this approach as the "fusion route" to meeting the ethics challenge in public service.

How does one learn to engage in moral reasoning? The answer is practice, practice, practice. That is, one learns how to reason and make ethical decisions by practicing; the learner can engage himself with decision dilemmas and work through them. A teacher of ethics can use scenarios and small group processes to help the learner practice ethical decision making and acquire skill in doing so. This methodology has much in common with virtue ethics espoused by Aristotle in the Age of Antiquity. Aristotle believed that one could acquire a virtue only by engaging in virtuous acts. But, he was wise to add, one does not acquire a virtue by engaging in foolhardy acts. Jumping into a lion's cage to acquire the virtue of courage is not what he had in mind! Moreover, it is the pursuit of virtue, a lifelong effort that defines the virtuous person.

Leadership and Exemplar Modeling

A third way to teach ethics centers on leadership and exemplars in public service. This approach has had a time-honored tradition in the U.S. military academies such as West Point and Annapolis and is increasingly reflected in the curricula of graduate schools that award the master's of public administration degree. A handful of schools, for example the LBJ School of Public Affairs at the University of Texas, have established centers for ethical leadership that they believe will attract men and women with a strong desire for leadership responsibilities (see www.utexas.edu/lbj/research/leadership).

The study of leadership, of course, is wide reaching, encompassing commercial, political, and educational sectors. Interestingly, the study and teaching of administrative leadership has been problematic, as Larry Terry notes in *Leadership of Public Bureaucracies* (1995). Several factors have contributed to this situation—the complexity of modern public organizations including the growing interdependency of private- and public-sector organizations, the anti-bureaucratic ethos that permeates American politics, and the challenge of distinguishing administrative leadership from political leadership.

Effectiveness of Ethics Education

What can be said about the effectiveness of ethics education in graduate PA/A programs? Are professional schools and programs preparing public administrators to be effective ethics managers? Are they making a difference? These are difficult questions to answer. There is no question that ethics educators believe they are making a difference (Menzel 1997). Survey data collected from seventy-eight of the member schools of the National Association of Schools of Public Affairs and Administration (NASPAA) that offer an ethics course showed that seven out of ten believe students find the subject matter valuable. A smaller percentage (67 percent) said they believe that students who receive ethics instruction become more ethically sensitive. And, one out of every two respondents assert that perhaps, most important, students use the ethical knowledge gained in their program of study to resolve ethical dilemmas.

These findings are encouraging for those who believe that ethics education is important and does make a difference in the lives of practitioners. Impressions, of course, can be wrong. Moreover, since many educators may bring to their task a professional advocacy (which is presumably neither a brand of moral indoctrination nor ethical zealotry), a self-fulfilling prophecy may be at work. That is, ethics educators may want to believe that they are making a difference and are therefore inclined to report such on a survey. A more definitive measure of ethics education outcomes is necessary.

Survey of MPA Graduates

Thus, another survey was conducted in 1996 that involved graduates of four public administration programs. The schools vary in size, geography, and student clientele. Perhaps most important, all require MPA-degree-seeking students to take an ethics course, and all have had that requirement in place for more than five years. Two hundred sixty-six graduates returned a questionnaire for an overall response rate of 64.7 percent. Two related questions were asked:

(1) Have you personally faced one or more ethical dilemmas on your job over the past five years?

If the respondent replied "yes," then she or he was asked:

(2) Did your ethics education help you resolve the dilemmas you faced?

Three of every four persons reported that they had faced a work-related ethical dilemma. The response to the second question for those who said they had faced an ethical dilemma was varied, with forty-three percent indicating that their graduate ethics educational experience helped them while thirty-one percent said it did not. One of every four said they were unsure.

All participants were provided the opportunity to comment on why they felt their ethics education did or did not help them deal with dilemmas. The comments of those who said that their ethics education had helped them can be placed into two broad categories: (1) value reinforcement, and (2) ethics reasoning. Many respondents said that their ethics education, especially as reflected in the ethics course they had taken, did not displace old or existing values with new or different values but clarified and reinforced those that they brought to their course of study. Consider the following comment by a white female in her forties employed by an academic institution:

> As an administrator of financial assistance, ethical issues are a regular occurrence. The values that I hold dear were acquired prior to completing an ethics course. However, the course helped me better identify ethical issues and make more objective decisions, which is often difficult to do.

Others noted that their ethics education helped them reason through difficult situations. A white female in her twenties employed by a federal agency exclaimed:

> I am in a position to provide government assistance to non-skilled, largely uneducated, lower socioeconomic individuals. My ethics education helped me suspend traditional stereotypical "knee-jerk" reactions and remember that their frame of reference may be different than mine, but that doesn't make it (or them) "wrong." Mine is not to judge.

A white male in his fifties employed by a nonprofit organization added:

> I saw some confidential information about a parent of a patient. It had implications regarding the parent's moral suitability for his job. My ethics class made me aware of the legal implications and the necessity of doing something. Although I can't be sure I did any good, I feel that at least I did do something rather than feeling unequipped to deal with the problem at all.

Among those who said that their education did not help them deal with ethical dilemmas, a number of persons commented that their ethics had been molded by their upbringing, which, for better or worse, was what mattered the most when they were faced with a dilemma. As a young white male employed by a municipality put it: "I believe that most 'ethics education' has been completed by about age ten. Formal education will not change people's ethics in grad school because your ethical foundation has already been laid and built upon during and by life experiences."

Still others who said that they had faced an ethical dilemma and had found their ethics education not influential often criticized the approach taken in their ethics course. A white female in her forties who is employed by a council of governments asserted: "We discussed academic theories of various belief systems. And, while very intellectually stimulating, it did not seem very relevant when your entry-level job depends on doing whatever is expected of you by your bosses." Another white female in her thirties and employed by a state agency said she was unsure whether her ethics education helped her deal with an ethical dilemma because "intellectually understanding a framework does not necessarily translate into behavior. Practitioners need an environment that supports or at least allows using ethical considerations as part of the criteria for decision making."

These comments and the survey statistics provide some insight into the "difference" that ethics education makes, but even more can be learned by disaggregating the data. When disaggregated by school, some interesting contrasts appear. A plurality of alumni at three of the four schools felt that their ethics education had been helpful. A plurality at the smallest school, however, felt just the opposite. On balance, there is probably more "good" news here than "bad" news. Still, the fact that majorities at all schools believe that their ethics education either did not help them or are unsure about the matter could be viewed as a concern.

Probing further, another section of the questionnaire solicited general attitudes and views of ethics education. Nearly seven of every ten respondents said that their ethics education helped them deal with job-related ethical issues. Moreover, majorities said that their ethics education was not a form of moral indoctrination. Moral reasoning as an approach to ethics education is endorsed by nearly eight of every ten respondents.

Professors as Exemplars

Attitudes toward the role of professors in the ethics education equation are interesting. While most said they learned little about ethics from watching the behavior of MPA instructors and feel that ethics instructors should not try to make students more ethical persons, seven of every ten agreed with the statement that "professors should serve as moral exemplars." An even larger number (92 percent) believe that colleges/universities should prepare MPA students to recognize and deal with ethical issues.

At face value, these findings are encouraging. MPA alumni are discriminating consumers of ethics education. They do not want instructors to be missionaries, but they do want them to teach them how to reason through ethical issues. Perhaps most significant, students and alumni want their professors to practice what they teach, and they firmly believe that higher education has an ethics education responsibility.

The "New" Ethics

The proliferation of ethics courses is an important development in what Derek Bok (1990) calls teaching the "new" ethics. The applied ethics course, he contends, "does not seek to convey a set of moral truths but tries to encourage students to think carefully about complex moral issues" (73). Continuing, "the principal aim of the course is not to impart right answers but to make students more perceptive in detecting ethical problems when they arise, better acquainted with the best moral thought that has accumulated through the ages, and more equipped to reason about the ethical issues they will face in their own personal and professional lives" (73).

The "new" ethics should also include a focus on teaching future public administrators how to be effective ethics managers. There is little evidence that professional education in public administration even touches on this subject. The irony, of course, is that the leaders of public organizations are engaged in ethics management day in and day out. The present approach is learning by the "seat of your pants." Educators and NASPAA have much to do in cultivating men and women to be ethics managers that know how to build organizations of integrity. There is no "one best way" to teach or acquire ethics, nor is there one best way to educate ethics managers. NASPAA's call for programs to "enhance the student's values, knowledge, and skills to act ethically and effectively . . . in the management of public and, as appropriate, third sector organizations" cannot be contested. The 1996 Ethics Education Survey points to the unmistakable conclusion that ethical challenges in the public service are commonplace and choices must be made. The 1996 data also point to the fact that formal training in ethics is resulting in desired outcomes. At the same time, there is evidence that other factors such as the ethical environment of the educational program are at work and must be taken into account in order to obtain a more complete understanding of ethics education outcomes.

More than a decade ago the Hastings Center released a report calling for the higher educational community to act with greater vigor and conviction in placing ethics and values in campus curricula. Their message should not be lost sight of. The report asserted that we cannot afford, wittingly or unwittingly, to be a partner in producing "a new generation of leaders who are ethically illiterate at best or dangerously adrift and morally misguided at worse" (Jennings, Nelson, and Parens 1994, 2).

Building Organizations of Integrity

The teaching of ethics in public administration has a promising future but much more effort is needed, especially in educating men and women to be effective in building organizations of integrity. The findings reported by Paul C. Light in *The New Public Service* (1999) are revealing and disturbing. Light's study focused on the graduates of the nation's leading public policy and administration programs (including Syracuse, Kansas, University of Southern California, University of Michigan, and Harvard). He reports that these graduates, regardless of current sector of employment (government, nonprofit, private), placed "maintaining ethical standards" at the top of the list of skills considered very important for success in their current job. At the same time, when asked if their school was helpful in teaching skills that would enable one to maintain ethical standards, most rated their education as insufficient. In fact, Light reports that this gap between how helpful a school is in teaching ethics and how important ethics is to one's job success was the largest of all skills listed, including such important skills as "budgeting and public finance," "doing policy analysis," "managing motivation and change," and "managing conflict."

And, as noted earlier, the National Schools of Public Affairs and Administration (NASPAA) through its Commission on Peer Review and Accreditation incorporated language in its accreditation standards (4.21) that graduates should be able "to act ethically." Standard 4.21 has encouraged schools to put into place ethics courses or otherwise demonstrate that they are teaching ethics across the curriculum. This tightening of the standards is promising but the evidence regarding the outcome is skimpy. A brief, informal survey conducted by the author in 2001 of more than 80 of the 143 accredited programs in the United States found that many (n = 32) schools have increased the emphasis placed on ethics in their curriculum but the majority (n = 44) have not. Some schools claim they have not increased their emphasis because they are already giving considerable attention to ethics—a claim that is difficult to validate. A sizeable majority of schools (n = 59) feel that Standard 4.21 is sufficient, although some express concern about its implementation and enforcement by the Commission on Peer Review and Accreditation. Only a handful of schools claim that they have developed outcome measures of their graduates' ability "to act ethically."

NASPAA has taken yet another step toward encouraging schools to emphasize ethics with its adoption in 2005 of a Member Code of Practice. The code admonishes all programs holding membership in NASPAA—not just those accredited—to integrate "ethics into the curriculum and all aspects of program operation, and expects students and faculty to exhibit the highest ethical standards in their teaching, research, and service." Perhaps the next significant step that NASPAA should take is to require all accredited programs to either (a) offer an ethics course and/or (b) place an ethics course in the core curriculum. As Dennis F. Thompson (1992, 255) has cogently remarked, "From the truth that ethics is mainly instrumental, it does not follow, as many critics seem to think, that ethics is always less important than other issues." Paraphrased differently, acquiring the ability to "to act ethically" should not be relegated to the educational rear.

NASPAA might also encourage MPA programs to adopt an ethics code for students. A student code could be useful in introducing students to professional ethics. Curious about whether any NASPAA school has such a code, I placed the following question on the NASPAA listserv—does your school have a student code of ethics? The answer was a resounding and deafening silence. Should a student code of ethics such as the one in exhibit 7.1 be adopted by MPA programs? Perhaps NASPAA should draft a model student code that academic programs could draw on to fashion their own code.

Teaching ethics is a diverse, dynamic, and challenging enterprise. There is considerable evidence that more effort to do so will occur in the decades ahead in the United States and abroad. A chapter in the *Handbook of Administrative Ethics* (Cooper 2001) tracks the emergence of administrative ethics as a field of study in the United States and leaves little doubt that more attention will be devoted to teaching ethics in public administration schools.

Promoting ethical behavior in public service is not limited to MPA programs. Many universities have established ethics centers and institutes to carry out a myriad of programs and activities. The Markkula Center for Applied Ethics at Santa Clara University in California is one of the most active (see www.scu.edu/ethics/). The center's ethics programs are quite comprehensive ranging from business ethics to global ethics to government ethics to technology ethics and more. Among the innovative government ethics programs is the "Ethics and Leadership Camp for Public Officials." This two day camp, which was launched for the first time in June 2006, attracted more than two dozen local city council members and ethics officers from California, Texas, and Arizona (Brown 2006). One novelty intended to heighten the campers sensitivity to ethics and accountability was a "moral compass" that each had slung around his/her neck. Exercises and group discussions were directed at enabling the campers to:

- Find ways to strengthen their city's ethics program
- Identify the 10 most common ethical pitfalls of cities
- Learn the best practices for city ethics program
- Fulfill California's AB1234 ethics training requirement

Exhibit 7.1
MPA Student Code of Ethics*

1. I will abide by procedures, rules, and regulations as described in the *MPA Student Handbook* and the college catalog;
2. I will respect the guidelines prescribed by each professor in the preparation of academic assignments and other course requirements;
3. I will be objective, understanding, and honest in academic performance and relationships;
4. I will strive toward academic excellence, improvement of professional skills, and expansion of professional knowledge;
5. I will neither engage in, assist in, nor condone cheating, plagiarism, or other such activities;
6. I will respect and protect the rights, privileges, and beliefs of others.
7. I will become familiar with and adhere to the standards of ethical conduct established by each of the professional societies to which I am admitted as a member.
8. I will not tolerate unethical conduct on the part of others who claim membership in a professional society of which I am a member and will take appropriate action to disclose a violation of ethical standards.

Sources: Statement of Professional Responsibility, the Wisconsin Certified Public Manager Program and the MPA Program, Florida Gulf Coast University.
*This code was developed by the author and does not represent an existing code.

In addition to university-based ethics centers, there are a number of non-profit organizations that promote ethics and integrity in the public service. The more prominent ones are the Ethics Resource Center (www.ethics.org/), the Council on Governmental Ethics Laws (www.cogel.org/), City Ethics (www.cityethics.org/index.html), International Institute for Public Ethics (www.iipe.org/), and the Government Accountability Project (www.whistleblower.org/template/index.cfm).

Public service professional associations such as the American Society for Public Administration (ASPA—www.aspanet.org/), the International City/County Management Association (ICMA—www.icma.org/), and the Government Finance Officers Association (www.gfoa.org/) place a great deal of emphasis on ethical behavior. All have professional codes of ethics. ASPA and ICMA also offer resource materials and training activities for their members. ASPA's Ethics Section is especially focused on promoting ethics and integrity in governance. The Section's Web site (www.aspaonline.org/ethicscommunity/) offers visitors access to decision scenarios, slide presentations, and an ethics compendium.

Internationally, there is considerable movement to promote ethical behavior, especially among emerging democracies that are struggling for economic and political independence. Nations like Russia and China are trying to loosen the grip of corruption and embrace the rule of law. The United Nations has stepped up its efforts to lend a hand as well. A report *Public Service in Transition* (1999) by the U.N. Division of Public Economics and Public Administration emphasizes "the critical importance of probity and integrity" of governments worldwide to conduct the public's business. The United Nations has developed an impressive Web site, UNPAN (www.unpan.org), that provides valuable advisory and training resources that can be drawn on for the teaching of ethics (see www.unpan.org/training-professionalism.asp). The United Nations is also leading by example with the establishment on January 1, 2006, of the Ethics Office. The new office has set up an ethics hotline and is counseling the U.N.'s 29,000 personnel worldwide on financial disclosure and conflicts of interest. "Other tasks will eventually include awareness training on ethics issues" (UN News 2006).

Staying the Ethical Course

Public managers are increasingly drawn into the ethical haze of privatization and the ethical time warp of the Information Age. Privatization and entrepreneurialism are here to stay (at least for a while) and cannot be ignored. Nor can we turn our heads and ignore the realities of the Information Age and the necessity to rethink what motivates the behaviors and practices of workers in local and global workplaces. We must recognize that while the individual is a moral agent and therefore responsible for his/her actions, he or she functions in a more, not less, complex and dynamic social and organizational environment.

What then are the implications for managers who wish to navigate these troubling waters? The most compelling implication is the need to think and act in terms of organizational ethics. Managers should ask themselves day in and day out: "What can and should I do to foster an ethical environment in my organization?" Leading by example is, of course, a starting point, but it is hardly sufficient. Another starting point is to recruit honest people. Easier said than done? Certainly.

How can managers foster a strong ethical environment in their organizations? Many suggestions have been provided in this book. But to truly succeed, managers must strive to instill an ethical consciousness in their organizations and in their relationships with members of other organizations, private and public. Among other things, steps should be taken to develop and implement a code or values statement, provide ethics training, establish an ombudsman, or add an ethics element to annual performance reviews. These efforts, separately and collectively, support the view of "ethics as organization development" (Zajac and Comfort 1997).

Twenty-First Century Challenges

There are several conclusions that can be drawn about the challenges facing ethical governance in the twenty-first century. First, ethics issues and efforts to deal with them are not limited to the American experience. These matters are ubiquitous. Moreover, it is clear that efforts to manage ethics internationally cannot be reduced to a "one size fits all" boilerplate. Creative solutions are needed that allow for cultural differences while at the same time not treating ethics as something that depends on the situation.

Second, building organizations of integrity is not a one-shot affair. Rather, it is an ongoing process in much the spirit of the cliché that it is the journey, not the destination, that matters. Still, the destination is very important even if never reached. What is that destination—workplaces where individuals treat each other with respect, take pride in their work, care about one another, promote accountability, and place the public interest over individual and organizational self-interest? This is the idea and ideal of an organization of integrity.

A third conclusion is that a compliance approach to building an organization of integrity is not sufficient. Indeed, in its most pernicious form it can lead to the lowest common denominator, namely, that if it's legal, it's ethical. This low-road approach will never lead to an ethical workplace. Rather, the workplace becomes one in which rule evasion and dodging go hand in hand with a "gotcha" mentality. The high road of aspirational ethics must be taken. Members of the organization must always ask themselves, "What is the right thing to do?" Rules and regulations may help answer this question, but they will never be sufficient. Each person must strive to ensure that his or her ethical compass is working correctly. A floundering ethical compass is the surest way to get lost in the quagmire of today's complex organizations.

A final conclusion offered here is that there is no checklist for building organizations of integrity. Public managers must engage in exemplary leadership, promote ethics training, support codes, conduct ethics audits, and find ways to promote an ethical climate through the use of human resources management processes such as hiring, annual evaluations, and promotion. These tactics can be powerful when coupled in a systematic, comprehensive manner. Each must be used by ethics managers in a skillful manner, perhaps similar to that of an orchestra conductor who must be able to produce harmonious music from a diversity of musicians and instruments. No single tactic is the best one to transform the sour notes of unethical behavior into the reassuring culture of an organization of integrity.

The ethical challenges facing elected and appointed public officeholders are real and ever more complex, and they must be met. The failure to do so will erode public trust and confidence in government and faith in our more than 200-year-old experiment called the United States of America. Are you ready to meet the challenges of ethics management?

Ethics Management Skill Building

Practicum 7.1. Nonprofit Contracting

As a recent retiree from the U.S. Air Force, you decide to take a position with a nonprofit agency that manages the city's federally funded low-income housing program. On four separate occasions over the next few months you are told by the city's program administrator to use money from one federal grant to pay for a project that wasn't covered by the grant. One month later you are asked to approve the expenditure of $87,150 on a private residence that would sell for $70,000.

Increasingly uncomfortable with the situation, you object, asserting that federal guidelines prohibit the city from spending that much money on low-income housing. The city administrator complains to your boss that you are not attentive, productive, or responsive to city staff. Your boss decides to remove you from the project. Frustrated but convinced that you did the right thing, you write to the mayor detailing your concerns about the misuse of federal funds. The mayor never responds.

A few months later the city's internal auditing staff reports that the city administrator has issued questionable loans, kept poor records, and awarded non-competitive bids. Housing and Urban Development (HUD) officials warn the mayor that the administrator may have misused $1.4 million in federal funds. The administrator claims that the feds are applying ridiculous rules. The mayor backs him. The administrator appears before the city council and asserts that "we do not intend to follow HUD's direction at this point." All but one member of the city council praises the administrator.

Fast-forward two years . . . a federal indictment charges that the city housing administrator used government jobs to reap thousands of dollars in gratuities. HUD requires the city to return $1,402,650 to the U.S. Treasury.

Questions

1. Did your boss do the right thing in removing you from the project?
2. Did you do the right thing in going around your boss by writing directly to the mayor?
3. What policy would you draft to prevent a city administrator from misusing federal grants for low-income housing? Would your policy apply to the director of the nonprofit agency?

Practicum 7.2. Entrepreneurialism at the Office

Jan and Bill are ambitious, energetic urban planners employed by the U.S. Department of Transportation (DOT) in Atlanta's regional headquarters. Their work on several comprehensive plans brings them much praise, including several positive stories published in the *New York Times*. One day Jan says to Bill, "Why don't we try to make some money as planning consultants? We can advertise ourselves on the World Wide Web with a Web site. The costs would be minimal, and as long as we don't contract with clients doing business with our agency, there shouldn't be any ethical or legal issues to contend with."

Bill gives Jan's suggestion a few days of thought, and a week later they have a Web site in place. On the Web page, Jan and Bill are presented as Jones & Greene Associates, Urban Planners. Services that their firm can provide include, among other things, market analysis, community planning, business site selection, and geographic information systems.

Assume you are Jan and Bill's boss at the DOT and you happen to come upon their Web site. The Web page does not identify the U.S. DOT as Bill and Jan's employer, but it does state that they have significant government experience as urban planners. Moreover, the page contains their firm's e-mail address and telephone number.

Two weeks later while at work you happen to overhear Bill talking by telephone with an apparent client about his consulting services.

Questions

1. What would you do? Would you call Bill and Jan aside and tell them that they cannot do private business while at the office?
2. Would you consult with your agency's Designated Ethics Officer?
3. Would you report them to the U.S. Office of Government Ethics?
4. Would you ignore the situation?

References

Abbott, L. 2006. Personal e-mail message July 8.

Adam, A.M. and D. Rachman-Moore. 2004. "The Methods Used to Implement an Ethical Code of Conduct and Employee Attitudes." *Journal of Business Ethics* 54: 225–244.

Anderson, G. 2004. District Attorneys Office. Telephone conversation, December.

Anechiarico, F. and J.B. Jacobs. 1994. "Visions of Corruption Control and the Evolution of American Public Administration." *Public Administration Review* 54: 465–473.

Anechiarico, F. and J.B. Jacobs. 1996. *The Pursuit of Absolute Integrity: How Corruption Control Makes Government Ineffective.* Chicago, IL: University of Chicago Press.

Barnard, C. 1938. *The Functions of the Executive.* Cambridge, MA: Harvard University Press.

Bellah, Robert N. et. al. 1991. *The Good Society.* New York: Random House.

Bellomo, T. 2005. "The Making of an Ethical Executive." *New York Times*, February 14.

Bennett, C.G. 1960. "Mayor Inducts Board of Ethics." *New York Times*, January 8.

Berman, E.M. 1996. "Restoring the Bridges of Trust: Attitudes of Community Leaders Toward Local Government." *Public Integrity Annual*, 31–49.

Berman, E.M. and J.P. West. 1997. "Managing Ethics to Improve Performance and Build Trust." *Public Integrity Annual*, 23–31.

———. 2003. "Solutions to the Problem of Managerial Mediocrity." *Public Performance & Management Review* 27 (December): 30–52.

Berman, E., J. West, and A. Cava. 1994. "Ethics Management in Municipal Governments and Large Firms: Exploring Similarities and Differences." *Administration & Society* 26 (August): 185–203.

Better Government Association. 2002. "The BGA Integrity Index."

Bok, D. 1990. *Universities and the Future of America.* Durham, NC: Duke University Press.

Bonczek, S.J. 1998. "Creating an Ethical Work Environment: Enhancing Ethics Awareness in Local Government." In *The Ethics Edge,* ed. E.M. Berman, J.P. West, and S.J. Bonczek. Washington, DC: International City/County Management Association, 72–79.

Bossaert, D. and C. Demmke. 2005. *Main Challenges in the Field of Ethics and Integrity in the EU Member States.* Maastricht, The Netherlands: European Institute of Public Administration.

Bowman, J.S. 1977. "Ethics in the Federal Service: A Post-Watergate View." *Midwest Review of Public Administration* vol. 11 (March): 3–20.

Bowman, J.S. 1981. "Ethical Issues for the Public Manager." In *A Handbook of Organization Management,* ed. William B. Eddy. New York: Marcel Dekker.

———. 1990. "Ethics in Government: A National Survey of Public Administrators." *Public Administration Review* 50 (May/June): 345–353.

Bowman, J.S. and R.L. Williams. 1997. "Ethics in Government: From a Winter of Despair to a Spring of Hope." *Public Administration Review* 57: 517–526.

Bowman, J.S. and D. Menzel. 2004. "Ethics Practices and Experiences in Graduate Public Administration Education." Paper presented at the 65th Annual Conference of the American Society for Public Administration. Portland, Oregon, March 27–30.

Brewer, G.A. and S. Coleman Selden, 1998. "Whistle Blowers in the Federal Civil Service: New Evidence of the Public Service Ethic." *Journal of Public Administration Research and Theory* 8 (July): 413–439.

Brown, S. 2005. "Managing Municipal Ethics." www.gmanet.com/event_detail/default.asp?eventid=6445&menuid=GeorgiaCitiesNewspaperID. Accessed December 29.

Brown, P.L. 2006. "At Ethics Camp, Not-So-Tall Tales from the Dark Side." *New York Times*, June 23.

Bruce, W. 1994. "Ethical People Are Productive People." *Public Productivity and Management Review* 17 (Spring): 23–30.

Brumback, G.B. 1998. "Institutionalizing Ethics in Government." In *The Ethics Edge,* ed. E.M. Berman, J.P. West, and S.J. Bonczek. Washington, DC: International City/County Management Association, 61–71.

Burke, J.P. 1986. *Bureaucratic Responsibility.* Baltimore, MD: Johns Hopkins Press.

Burke, F. and A. Black. 1990. "Improving Organizational Productivity: Add Ethics." *Public Productivity and Management Review* 14 (Winter): 121–133.

Carnevale, D.G. 1995. *Trustworthy Government: Leadership and Management Strategies for Building Trust and High Performance.* San Francisco: Jossey-Bass Publishers.

Carter, S.L. 1997. Integrity. New York: Harper Perennial.

Chan, S. 2005. "Transit Leader to Pay Fine in Ethics Case." *New York Times,* August 27.

Chicago Board of Ethics. *2003–04 Annual Report.*

COGEL. 2004. *Ethics Update.* Council of Governmental Ethics Laws. Jacksonville, FL.

Cohen, S. and W. Eimicke. 1999. "Is Public Entrepreneurship Ethical?" *Public Integrity* 1 (Winter): 54–74.

Committee on Standards in Public Life. 2004. Tenth Report. *Getting the Balance Right—Implementing Standards of Conduct in Public Life,* HMSO.

Connolly, C. 2005. "Director of NIH Agrees to Loosen Ethics Rules." Washingtonpost .com. August 26.

Conquergood, M. 2005. E-mail message to the author.

Cooper, T.L. 1982. *The Responsible Administrator: An Approach to Ethics for the Administrative Role.* Port Washington, NY: Kennikat Press.

———. 1984. "Citizenship and Professionalism in Public Administration." *Public Administration Review* 44 (March): 143–149.

———. 1986. *The Responsible Administrator: An Approach to Ethics for the Administrator Role.* 2nd ed. Millwood, NY: Associated Faculty Press.

———. 1987. "Hierarchy, Virtue, and the Practice of Public Administration: A Perspective for Normative Ethics." *Public Administration Review* 47 (July/August): 320–328.

————. 1998. *The Responsible Administrator.* 4th ed. San Francisco: Jossey-Bass.

————. 2001. ed. *Handbook of Administrative Ethics.* 2nd ed. New York: Marcel Dekker.

————. 2006. *The Responsible Administrator.* 5th ed. San Francisco: Jossey-Bass.

Cooper, T.L. and D.E.Yoder. 2002. "Public Management Ethics Standards in a Transnational World." *Public Integrity* 4 (Fall): 333–352.

Council for Excellence in Government. 1992–1993. "Ethical Principles for Public Servants." *The Public Manager* 21: 37–39.

Dao, J. 2005. "Governor of Ohio Is Charged With Breaking Ethics Law." *New York Times,* August 18.

Davey, M. and G. Ruethling. 2006. "Former Governor of Illinois Guilty of Graft Charges." *New York Times* April 18.

Davies, M. 2005. E-mail message to author. February 7.

Davis, M. 1999. In R.W. Smith. "Local Government Ethics Boards: A Panel Discussion on the New York Experience." *Public Integrity* 1 (Fall): 397–416.

deLeon, L. 1996. "Ethics and Entrepreneurship." *Policy Studies Journal* 24 (Autumn): 496–514.

Denhardt, R.B. 1981. *In the Shadow of Organization.* Lawrence: The Regents Press of Kansas.

Denhardt, K.G. 1988. *The Ethics of Public Administration: Resolving Moral Dilemmas in Public Organizations.* New York: Greenwood.

————. 1989. "The Management of Ideals: A Political Perspective on Ethics." *Public Administration Review* 49 (March/April): 187–192.

Dobel, J.P. 1993. "The Realpolitik of Ethics Codes: An Implementation Approach to Public Ethics." In *Ethics and Public Administration,* ed. H.G. Frederickson. Armonk, NY: M.E. Sharpe.

Editorial. 2005. *St. Petersburg Times,* March 21.

Ellsberg, D. 2004. "Truths Worth Telling." *New York Times,* September 28.

Fawcett, G. and M. Wardman. 2005. "Ethical Governance in Local Government in England: A Regulator's View." Paper presented at the Ethics and Integrity of Governance: The First Transatlantic Dialogue, Leuven, Belgium, June 2–5.

Ferrieux-Patterson, M.N. 2003. "Conflict of Interest—Vanuatu's Experience." Paper presented at the 4th Regional Anti-Corruption Conference of the ADB/OECD Anti-Corruption Initiative for Asia and the Pacific, Kuala Lumpur, Malaysia, December 3–5.

Finn, R. 2005. "Albany's Ethics Policeman Would Like More Muscle." *New York Times,* March 25.

Florida, Commission on Ethics. 2004. *Annual Report to the Florida Legislature for Calendar Year 2004.*

Florida Office of Inspector General. 2005. *Contract Management of Private Correctional Facilities.* Internal Audit Report Number 2005–61, June 30.

Folks, S.R. 2000. "A Potential Whistle-blower." *Public Integrity* 2 (Winter): 61–74.

Follet, M.P. 1924. *Creative Experience.* New York: Longmans, Green.

Frederickson, H.G. 1997. *The Spirit of Public Administration.* San Francisco: Jossey-Bass Publishers.

————. 2003. Ed., *Ethics and Public Administration.* Armonk, NY: M.E. Sharpe.

Frederickson, H.G. and D.K. Hart. 1985. "The Public Service and the Patriotism of Benevolence." *Public Administration Review* 45 (): 547–553.

Frederickson, H.G. and M. A. Newman. 2001. "The Patriotism of Exit and Voice: The Case of Gloria Flora." *Public Integrity* 3 (Fall): 347–362.

Fry, B.R. 1989. *Mastering Public Administration: From Max Weber to Dwight Waldo.* Chatham, NJ: Chatham House Publishers, Inc.

Garvey, G. 1992. *Facing the Bureaucracy: Living and Dying in a Public Agency.* San Francisco: Jossey-Bass.

Gawthrop, L.C. 1984. *Public Sector Management, Systems, and Ethics.* Bloomington: Indiana University Press.

———. 1998. *Public Service and Democracy: Ethical Imperatives for the 21st Century.* Chappaqua, NY: Chatham House Publishers.

———. 1999. "Public Entrepreneurship in the Lands of Oz and Uz." *Public Integrity* 1 (Winter): 75–86.

Georgia Municipal Association. 2005. *Ethics in Government: Charting the Right Course.*

Gerth, H.H. and C. W. Mills. 1946. Editors and Translators. *From Max Weber: Essays in Sociology.* Oxford: Oxford University Press.

Ghere, R.K. 1996. "Aligning the Ethics of Public-Private Partnership: The Issue of Local Economic Development." *Journal of Public Administration Research and Theory* 6 (October): 599–621.

Gilman, S.C. 1995a. www.oecd.org/dataoecd/30/22/2731902.htm. Accessed January 2, 2006.

———. 1995b. "Presidential Ethics and the Ethics of the Presidency." *Ethics in American Public Service: The Annals of the American Academy of Political and Social Science* 537: 58–75.

_____. 2005. "Ethics Codes and Codes of Conduct as Tools for Promoting an Ethical and Professional Public Service: Comparative Successes and Lessons." Paper prepared for the PREM, the World Bank, Washington, DC.

_____. 2006. Personal e-mail message. July 6.

Gilman, S.C. and C.W. Lewis. 1996. "Public Service Ethics: A Global Dialogue." *Public Administration Review* 56 (November/December): 517–524.

Glazer, M.P. and P.M. Glazer. 1989. *The Whistleblowers: Exposing Corruption in Government and Industry.* New York: Basic Books.

Goldsmith, S. and W.D. Eggers. 2004. *Governing by Network: The New Shape of the Public Sector.* Washington, DC: Brookings Institution Press.

Gong, T. 2000. "Whistleblowing: What Does It Mean in China?" *International Journal of Public Administration* 23 (11): 1899–1923.

Graham, K. 2005. "Parks Worker Accused of Taking Bribe." *St. Petersburg Times,* February 24.

Groeneweg, S. 2001. *Three Whistleblower Protection Models: A Comparative Analysis of Whistleblower Legislation in Australia, the United States and the United Kingdom.* Public Service Commission of Canada. www.psc-cfp.gc.ca/research/merit/whistleblowing_e.htm. Accessed January 3, 2006.

Grosenick, L. 1995. "Federal Training Programs: Help or Hindrance?" *The Public Manager* 24 (4): 43.

Gustafson, C. 2006. "City Ethics Groups Get Looked at by Council." *San Diego Union-Tribune.* May 6.

Harris, G. 2005. "Report Details F.D.A. Rejection of Next-Day Pill." *New York Times,* November 15.

Hart, D.K. 1984. "The Virtuous Citizen, the Honorable Bureaucrat, and 'Public' Administration." *Public Administration Review* 44: 111–120.

He, Z. 2004. "Improving Responsiveness in Government." In *Windows on China,* ed. M.T. Gordon, M.C. Meininger, and W. Chen. Amsterdam: IOS Press, 143–150.

Hejka-Ekins, A. 2001. "Ethics in In-Service Training." In *Handbook of Administrative Ethics*, ed. T.L. Cooper, 2nd ed. New York: Marcel Dekker, 79–103.

Henry, N. 1995. *Public Administration and Public Affairs*. 6th ed. Englewood Cliffs, NJ: Prentice Hall.

Herrmann, F.M. 1997. "Bricks Without Straw: The Plight of Government Ethics Agencies in the United States." *Public Integrity Annual*, 13–22.

Hess, A. 2003. "Assessing the Ethical Judgment of a Potential Employee-II." *Public Administration Times*, September.

Hirt, M.J. 2003. "Assessing the Ethical Judgment of a Potential Employee." *Public Administration Times*, July.

Hoekstra, A., A. Belling, and E. Van Der Heide. 2005. "Beyond Compliance—A Practitioners' View." Paper presented at the Ethics and Integrity of Governance: The First Transatlantic Dialogue, Leuven, Belgium, June 2–5.

Hoge, W. 2005. "Citing Abuse of Authority, U.N. Dismisses Elections Chief." *New York Times*, December 7.

Hunt, M. 2005. "Ethics and British Local Government: The Relevance of Compliance Strategies." Paper presented at the Ethics and Integrity of Governance: The First Transatlantic Dialogue, Leuven, Belgium, June 2–5.

Jenkins, C. 2005. "Penalty for Judge Is Seen Two Ways." *St. Petersburg Times*, November 19.

Jennings, Bruce, James Lindemann Nelson, and Erik Parens. 1994. *Values on Campus: A Report*. Briarcliff, NY: Hastings Center.

Jensen, D.P. 2004. "County Ethics Reform Stalled." *Salt Lake Tribune*, December 6.

Johnson, R. 2005. "Comparative Whistleblowing: Administrative, Cultural, and Ethical Issues." *Proceedings of 2005 International Conference on Public Administration*, October 21–22, Chengdu, China.

———. 2003. *Whistleblowing: When It Works—and Why*. Boulder: Lynne Rienner Publishers.

Jos, P.H. 1989. "In Praise of Difficult People: A Portrait of the Committed Whistleblower." *Public Administration Review* 49: 552–561.

Keller, E.K. Ed. 1988. *Ethical Insight, Ethical Action: Perspectives for the Local Government Manager*. Washington, DC: International City/County Management Association.

Kernaghan, K. 2003. "Integrating Values into Public Service: The Values Statement as Centerpiece." *Public Administration Review* 63 (November/December): 711–719.

Kudo, H. and J. Maesschalck. 2005. "The , June 2–5. Ethics Law and Ethics Code in Japanese Public Administration: Background, Contents and Impact." Paper presented at the Ethics and Integrity of Governance: The First Transatlantic Dialogue, Leuven, Belgium, June 2–5.

Lambert, B. 2005. "Audit Describes 8 Years of Looting by School Officials." *New York Times*, March 3.

Lewis, C.W. 1991. *The Ethics Challenge in Public Service: A Problem Solving Guide*. San Francisco: Jossey-Bass.

Lewis, C.W. and S.C. Gilman. 2005. *The Ethics Challenge in Public Service: A Problem Solving Guide*. 2nd ed. San Francisco: Jossey-Bass.

Light, P.C. 1999. *The New Public Service*. Washington, DC: Brookings Institution Press.

Lovell, Alan. 2003. "The Enduring Phenomenon of Moral Muteness: Suppressed Whistleblowing." *Public Integrity* vol. 5 (Summer): 187–204.

Lui, T.T. 1988. "Changing Civil Servants' Values." In *The Hong Kong Civil Service and Its Future,* ed. I. Scott and J.P. Burns. Hong Kong: Oxford University Press.

Lui, T.T. and I. Scott. 2001. "Administrative Ethics in a Chinese Society: The Case of Hong Kong." In T.L. Cooper, ed., *Handbook of Administrative Ethics.* New York: Marcel Dekker.

Mackenzie, G.C. 2002. *Scandal Proof: Do Ethics Laws Make Government Ethical?* Washington, DC: Brookings Institution Press.

Manske, M.W. and H.G. Frederickson. 2004. "Building a Strong Local Government Ethics Program." *Public Management* 86 (June): 18–22.

Markus, M.L. 1994. "Finding a Happy Medium: Explaining the Negative Effects of Electronic Communication on Social Life at Work." *ACM Transactions on Information Systems* 12 (April): 119–149.

Martirossian, J. 2004. "Russia and Her Ghosts of the Past." In *The Struggle Against Corruption: A Comparative Study,* ed. Roberta Ann Johnson. New York: Palgrave Macmillan.

Mayer, J.P. Ed. 1969. *Democracy in America.* New York: Harper & Row.

McAllister, K. 2005. E-mail message to author. May 5.

McAuliffe, D. 2002. "Social Work Ethics Audits: A New Tool for Ethical Practice." Paper presented at the IIPE/AAPAE Conference, Brisbane.

McFadden, R.D. 2005. "Stanley Kreutzer, 98, Author of New York City Ethics Code." *New York Times,* February 22.

Menzel, D.C. 1992. "Ethics Attitudes and Behaviors in Local Governments: An Empirical Analysis." *State and Local Government Review* 24 (Fall): 94–102.

———. 1993. "The Ethics Factor in Local Government: An Empirical Analysis." In *Ethics and Public Administration,* ed. H. George Frederickson. Armonk, NY: M.E. Sharpe, 191–204.

———. 1995. "The Ethical Environment of Local Government Managers." *American Review of Public Administration* 25 (September): 247–262.

———. 1996a. "Ethics Complaint Making and Trustworthy Government." *Public Integrity Annual,* 73–82.

———. 1996b. "Ethics Stress in Public Organizations." *Public Productivity & Management Review* 20: 70–83.

———. 1997. "Teaching Ethics and Values in Public Administration: Are We Making a Difference?" *Public Administration Review* 57 (May/June): 224–230.

———. 2001a. "Ethics and Public Management." In *Handbook of Public Management and Practice,* ed. K.T. Liou. New York: Marcel Dekker.

———. 2001b. "Ethics Management in Public Organizations." In *Handbook of Administrative Ethics,* ed. Terry L. Cooper. 2nd ed. New York: Marcel Dekker.

———. 2005a. "Research on Ethics and Integrity in Governance: A Review and Assessment." *Public Integrity* 7 (Spring): 147–168.

———. 2005b. "Building Public Organizations of Integrity." *Proceedings of 2005 International Conference on Public Administration,* Chengdu, China, October 21–22.

———. 2006. "Ethics Management in Cities and Counties." *Public Management* 88 (January/February): 20–25.

Menzel, D.C. and K. Carson. 1999. "A Review and Assessment of Empirical Research on Public Administration Ethics: Implications for Scholars and Managers." *Public Integrity* 1 (Summer): 239–264.

Miceli, M. and J.P. Near. 1985. "Characteristics of Organizational Climate and Perceived Wrongdoing Associated with Whistle-Blowing Decisions." *Personnel Psychology* 38: 525–544.

Miller, C. 2005. E-mail message to the author. April 25.

Morin, R. and D. Balz. 2005. "Bush's Popularity Reaches New Low." *Washingtonpost.com.* November 4.

Nelson, M. 1999. www.transparency.org/iacc/9th_iacc/papers/day4/ws3/d4ws3_mnelson.html.

New York State Ethics Commission. 2004. *The Ethics Report.* September.

O'Donnel, G. 2006. "Our 21st Century Civil Service—Creating a Culture of Excellence." Speech, June 6. www.civilservice.gov.uk/news/060606_speech.asp. Accessed July 6, 2006.

O'Leary, R. 2006. *The Ethics of Dissent: Managing Guerrilla Government.* Washington, DC: CQ Press.

Osborne, D. and T. Gaebler. 1992. *Reinventing Government: How the Entrepreneurial Spirit Is Transforming the Public Sector.* Reading, MA: Addison-Wesley.

Ouchi, W.G. 1981. *Theory Z: How American Business Can Meet the Japanese Challenge.* Reading, MA: Addison-Wesley.

Palidauskaite, J. 2006. "Codes of Ethics in Transitional Democracies: A Comparative Perspective." *Public Integrity* 8: 35–48.

Perry, J.L. 1993. "Whistleblowing, Organizational Performance, and Organizational Control." In *Ethics and Public Administration,* ed. H. George Frederickson. Armonk, NY: M.E. Sharpe, 79–99.

Peters, T.J. and R.H. Waterman. 1982. *In Search of Excellence.* New York: Harper & Row.

Pope, J. 2005. "Observations Concerning Comparative Administrative Ethics in Europe and the U.S." Paper presented at the Ethics and Integrity of Governance: The First Transatlantic Dialogue, Leuven, Belgium, June 2–5.

Reamer, F.G. 2000. "The Social Work Ethics Audit: A Risk-Management Strategy." *Social Work* 45 (July): 355–366.

Report of the National Performance Review. 1993. *Creating a Government That Works Better & Costs Less.* Washington, DC: U.S. Government Printing Office.

Roberts, R.N. 1988. *White House Ethics: The History of the Politics of Conflict of Interest Regulation.* New York: Greenwood Press.

Rohr, J.A. 1978. *Ethics for Bureaucrats: An Essay on Law and Values.* New York: Marcel Dekker.

———. 1986. To *Run a Constitution: The Legitimacy of the Administrative State.* Lawrence: University Press of Kansas.

———. 1989. *Ethics for Bureaucrats: An Essay on Law and Values.* 2nd ed. New York: Marcel Dekker.

———. 1998. *Public Service, Ethics & Constitutional Practice.* Lawrence: University Press of Kansas.

Rosen, B.A. 2005. *The Shadowlands of Conduct: Ethics and State Politics.* Washington, DC: Georgetown University Press.

Schneider, B. 1990. Ed. *Organizational Climate and Culture,* San Francisco: Jossey-Bass.

Scott, W.G. and D.K. Hart. 1979. *Organizational America.* Boston, MA: Houghton Mifflin Co.

———. 1989. *Organizational Values in America.* New Brunswick, NJ: Transaction Publishers.

Senge, P. 1990. *The Fifth Discipline: The Art and Practice of the Learning Organiza-tion*. New York: Currency Doubleday.

Simmons, C.W., H. Roland, and J. Kelly-DeWitt. 1998. *Local Government Ethics Ordinances in California*. California Research Bureau, California State Library.

Slackman, M. 2005. "Albany Ethics Case That Died Points to Loophole, Not a Crime." *New York Times*, February 25.

Smith, M.K. 2001. "Peter Senge and the Learning Organization." www. weleadinlearning.org/msapr003.htm. Accessed 12/6/05.

Smith, R.W. 2003. "Enforcement or Ethical Capacity: Considering the Role of State Ethics Commissions at the Millennium." *Public Administration Review* 63 (3): 283–295.

———. 2004. "A Comparison of the Ethics Infrastructure in China and the United States." *Public Integrity* 6 (Fall): 299–318.

Smothers, R. 2005. "11 New Jersey Officials, Including 3 Mayors, Face Charges of Corruption." *New York Times*, February 25.

Stahura, J. 2005. E-mail message to author. January 18.

Stilman, R. 1999. *Preface to Public Administration: A Search for Themes and Direc-tion*. 2nd ed. Burke, VA: Chatelaine Press.

St. Petersburg Times. 2005. Editorial. "Ethical Questions." March 20.

Tampa Tribune. 2005. Editorial. "Ignorant or Unethical." March 21.

Taylor, F.W. 1919. *Principles of Scientific Management*. New York: Harper & Brothers.

Tenenbaum, Jeffrey. 2002. "Lobbying Disclosure Act of 1995: A Summary and Over-view for Associations." www.centeronlilne.org/knowledge/whitepaper.cfm?ID =1796. Accessed January 2, 2006.

Terry, L. 1993. "Why We Should Abandon the Misconceived Quest to Reconcile Pub-lic Entrepreneurship with Democracy." *Public Administration Review* 53 (July/ August): 393–395.

———. 1995. *Leadership of Public Bureaucracies*. Thousand Oaks, CA: Sage Publications.

———. 1998. "Administrative Leadership, Neo-Managerialism, and the Public Man-agement Movement." *Public Administration Review* 58 (May/June): 194–200.

Testerman, J. 2005. "LaBrakes Get More Than 8 Years." *St. Petersburg Times*, Febru-ary 26.

Thompson, D.F. 1985. "The Possibility of Administrative Ethics." *Public Administra-tion Review* 45: 555–561.

———. 1992. "Paradoxes of Government Ethics." *Public Administration Review* 52 (May/June): 254–259.

Treaster, J.B. and J. Desantis. 2005. "Storm and Crisis: The Police." *New York Times*, September 6.

Troxler, H. 2005. "In Politics, What's Unethical Today Is Legal Tomorrow." *St. Pe-tersburg Times*, October 20.

Truelson, J.A. 1991. "New Strategies for Institutional Controls." In *Ethical Fron-tiers in Public Management*, ed. J.S. Bowman. San Francisco: Jossey-Bass, 225–242.

United Nations. 1999. *Public Service in Transition: Enhancing Its Role, Profession-alism Ethical Values and Standards*. Division for Public Economics and Public Administration. New York.

————. 2004. *Organizational Integrity Survey.* www.un.org/News/ossg/sg/ integritysurvey.pdf Accessed December 29, 2005.

_____. UN News www.un.org/apps/news/story.asp?NewsID=17185&Cr=UN&Cr1= staff Accessed June 26, 2006.

_____. General Assembly 2005, A/60/568. November 28.

U.S. Senate. 1987. Joint Hearings before the Senate Select Committee on Secret Military Assistance to Iran and the Nicaraguan Opposition and the House Select Committee to Investigate Covert Arms Transactions with Iran, One Hundredth Congress First Session 100–7 Part I, July 7, 8, 9, and 10.

U.S. Office of Government Ethics 2005. OGE, DT-05–003, February 23.

U.S. Office of Government Ethics. 2000. Executive Branch Employee Ethics Survey 2000: Final Report. Prepared by Arthur Andersen for the U.S. Office of Government Ethics.

Valentine, S. and G. Fleischman. 2004. "Ethics Training and Businesspersons' Perceptions of Organizational Ethics." *Journal of Business Ethics* 52: 381–390.

Valmores, D.J. 2005. Commissioner, Civil Service Commission. "Presentation on Fighting and Preventing Corruption." ASEAN+3 Senior Officials Consultative Meeting on Creative Management for Government, September 30–October 1, Bangkok, Thailand.

Van Blijswijk, J.A.M., R.C.J. van Breukelen, A.L Franklin, J.C.N. Raadschelders, and P. Slump. 2004. "Beyond Ethical Codes: The Management of Integrity in the Netherlands Tax and Customs Administration." *Public Administration Review* 64 (November/December): 718–727.

Varian, B. 2005. "E-mails Get Tampa Workers in Trouble." *St. Petersburg Times*, April 19.

Victor, B. and J.B. Cullen. 1988. "The Organizational Bases of Ethical Work Climates." *Administrative Science Quarterly* 33: 101–125.

Walker, D.M. 2005. "Ethics and Integrity in Government." *Public Integrity* 7 (Fall): 345–352.

Wang, D. 2004. "Striving for Excellence in Civil Service Training." In *Windows on China,* ed. M.T. Gordon. Amsterdam: IOS Press.

Waring, C.G. 2004. "Measuring Ethical Climate Risk." *Internal Auditor* 61 (December): 71–75.

West, J. 2005. E-mail message to author. August 23.

West, J.P. and E.M. Berman. 2004. "Ethics Training in U.S. Cities: Content, Pedagogy, and Impact." *Public Integrity* 6 (Summer): 189–206.

Wiley, C. 1995. "The ABC's of business ethics: Definitions, Philosophies and Implementation." *Industrial Management* 37 (1): 22–27.

Wilgoren, J. 2005. "Chicago Mayor Questioned in Federal Corruption Inquiry." *New York Times*, August 27.

Williams, R.L. 1996. "Controlling Ethical Practices Through Laws and Rules: Evaluating the Florida Commission on Ethics." *Public Integrity Annual*, 65–72.

Wilson, J.Q. 1993. *The Moral Sense.* New York: The Free Press.

Wilson, Woodrow. 1887. "The Study of Administration." Reprinted in *Political Science Quarterly* 56 (December 1941).

Witt, E. 1992. "Is Government Full of Crooks or Are We Just Better at Finding Them?" In *Essentials of Government Ethics,* ed. P. Madsen and J.M. Shafritz. New York: Meridian/Penguin.

Wye, C. 1994. "A Framework for Enlarging the Reform Agenda." *The Public Manager* 23: 43–46.

Xue, L. and Z. Peng. 2004. "China's Public Administration Education." In *Windows on China,* ed. M.T. Gordon. Amsterdam: IOS Press.

Zauderer, D.G. 1994. "Winning with Integrity." *The Public Manager* 23: 43–46.

Zajac, G. and L. K. Comfort. 1997. "The Spirit of Watchfulness: Public Ethics as Organizational Learning." *Journal of Public Administration Research and Theory* 7 (October): 541–569.

Zhu, Q. 2000. "The Process of Professionalization and the Rebuilding of Administrative Ethics in Post-Mao China." *International Journal of Public Administration* 23 (11): 1943–1965.

Index

About the Author

Donald C. Menzel is professor emeritus of public administration, Northern Illinois University and currently serves as Director of the Institute for Public Policy and Leadership at the University of South Florida Sarasota–Manatee. In 2005–2006, Dr. Menzel served as president of the American Society for Public Administration. He has conducted workshops on ethics and crisis management in the United States and abroad in China, Thailand, South Korea, Macau, England, France, Germany, Portugal, and Italy. He holds a Ph.D. from the Pennsylvania State University, a master's degree from Miami University (Ohio), and a bachelor's degree in mathematics from Southern Illinois University. He served in the U.S. Air Force from 1962 to 1967 and resides in Tampa, Florida.